ELIGIBLE FOR EXECUTION

ELIGIBLE FOR EXECUTION

70 ◀

The Story of the Daryl Atkins Case

Thomas G. Walker

Emory University

CQ PRESS

A Division of SAGE
Washington, D.C.

CQ Press
2300 N Street, NW, Suite 800
Washington, DC 20037

Phone: 202-729-1900; toll-free, 1-866-4CQ-PRESS (1-866-427-7737)

Web: www.cqpress.com

Photo and image credits:
AP Images: 3, 18, 21, 28, 63, 76, 95, 104, 109, 227, 233, 249, 253
Daily Press: 4, 6, 15, 133
James W. Ellis: 183
International Mapping Associates: 9
Landov: 191 (left, right), 231
North Carolina Department of Correction: 173
Thomas G. Walker: 7, 11, 102

Cover design: Matthew Simmons
Cover photo: AP Images

☉ The paper used in this publication exceeds the requirements of the American National Standard for Information Sciences—Permanence of Paper for Printed Library Materials, ANSI Z39.48-1992.

Printed and bound in the United States of America

12   11   2   3   4   5

Library of Congress Cataloging-in-Publication
Walker, Thomas G.
  Eligible for execution : the story of the Daryl Atkins case /
Thomas G. Walker. — 1st ed.
    p. cm.
  Includes index.
  ISBN 978-0-87289-418-1 (alk. paper)
  1. Atkins, Daryl, 1977—Trials, litigation, etc. 2. Trials (Murder)—Virginia. 3. Capital punishment—Virginia. 4. Insanity (Law)—Virginia. 5. Death row inmates—Mental health—Virginia. I. Title.

  KF224.A85W35 2008
  345.73'0773—dc22
                        2008027688

To S. Sidney Ulmer,
with deep respect and lasting gratitude

Contents

Preface

THERE IS NO MORE abhorrent and devastating crime than one human being taking the life of another. When government responds by seeking to execute an individual convicted of homicide, it is imposing the most grim and terrifying power a state can exercise over one of its own citizens. And when a juror casts a life or death vote in a capital case, he or she is engaging in perhaps the gravest and most disquieting act of civic responsibility.

This book examines the decision of the U.S. Supreme Court in the case of *Atkins v. Virginia.* It is the story of Daryl Atkins, who at the age of eighteen participated in a tragic and senseless murder. It is also the story of the victim of that crime, Eric Nesbitt, a young man serving in the U.S. Air Force. The book follows the *Atkins* case from commission of the crime through the Supreme Court's ruling and its aftermath. Along the way, the story involves law enforcement officers and prosecutors who apprehend and convict criminals as well as defense attorneys who ensure that those accused of crimes are fairly treated. It discusses the roles played by trial and appellate court judges applying criminal statutes and interpreting constitutional provisions. And it also examines the involvement of citizens as witnesses, jurors, or members of organizations with special interests in civil rights and criminal justice issues.

The purpose of this volume is fourfold. The first objective is to help the reader understand the Supreme Court's decision in the *Atkins* case—the issues that were contested, the reasons why the Court ruled as it did, and the implications of that ruling. The second aim is to inform the reader about the American judicial process and the criminal justice system. As the *Atkins* litigation evolves through its many stages it illustrates the roles of the institutions and officials who run our legal system. Third, the book examines the constitutional rights of the criminally accused, with special emphasis on the Eighth Amendment right against cruel and unusual punishment. This, of course, necessitates a discussion of capital punishment and the perennial controversies that surround it. And finally, the story of Daryl Atkins serves as a reminder that important Supreme Court rulings on constitutional issues are not just about legal theories, doctrines, and precedents. These decisions involve real people—often society's most vulnerable—who frequently have suffered catastrophic losses and have much at stake. Averting our eyes from the human element in legal disputes can distract our attention from the system's primary goal of securing justice.

The writing of any book inevitably requires decisions regarding what material to include and what to omit. *Eligible for Execution* is no exception. To assist those readers who desire additional information about the subjects discussed in this volume, a companion Web site can be found at http://walker.cqpress.com. The site contains extended documentation, including a lengthy bibliography of sources consulted during the writing of this book, citations to legal commentary about the Supreme Court's decision, and works that examine capital punishment and related matters. The reader will also find statistics about the death penalty, various documents and exhibits used by the prosecution and defense during Atkins's trial and sentencing, and information about any new developments in the case. Finally, for those who want to understand more thoroughly the Supreme Court's treatment of capital punishment issues, the Web site includes excerpts from the justices' most important death penalty rulings.

To enhance the readability of this book, standard footnote references have been omitted. At the end of each chapter, however, a bibliographic note has been added that outlines the basic sources that contributed to the writing. Readers who want more detailed references are urged to consult the book's Web site.

Although the idea of writing a detailed account of an important constitutional decision had always intrigued me, this book only came about because of two invitations I received. The first occurred in 2002, when my colleagues Gregg Ivers of American University and Kevin McGuire of the University of North Carolina asked me to contribute a chapter on the death penalty for their book, *Creating Constitutional Change: Clashes over Power and Liberty in the Supreme Court* (University of Virginia Press, 2004). My chapter focused on the recently issued *Atkins v. Virginia* decision. Examining the Atkins case for that project raised far more questions in my mind than could be answered in a single chapter. There was much more to be said.

Much later, Brenda Carter and Charisse Kiino of CQ Press invited me to consider writing a book devoted to a single Supreme Court decision. They were interested in a volume that would trace an important constitutional dispute from beginning to end and in the process inform readers about the way the American judicial system functions. Their vision and my interests matched perfectly, and we agreed that the Atkins case provided a fruitful subject.

While I bear full responsibility for what appears on the following pages, the book could not have been written without the contributions of a large number of other individuals. The professional staff at the Virginia State Law Library in Richmond were particularly helpful and gracious in making their holdings available to me. The archives contain a vast amount of documentary information related to the Atkins litigation. I am indebted to several individuals close to the case who were willing to answer questions that I could not resolve from the documentary materials. Because the case remained active during the time I was researching this book, I treated their comments in confidence. I also profited greatly from the work of journalists who covered the case at the various stages of the legal process. Especially helpful were reports filed by Patti Rosenberg, Keith Rushing, Donna St. George, and Danielle Zielinski. A full listing of journalistic accounts can be found on the book's companion Web site. I am also grateful to my friend Todd Peppers of Roanoke College, who provided insights and information gained from his own research on capital prosecutions in Virginia. And finally, I acknowledge the contributions of the scholars who reviewed an early draft of this manuscript, including Marc Gertz, Florida State University; Wendy Guastaferro, Georgia State

University; Ken Haas, University of Delaware; Valerie Hoekstra, Arizona State University; Drew Lanier, University of Central Florida; Christine Nemacheck, College of William and Mary; and Mark Richards, Grand Valley State University. Their comments and suggestions greatly influenced the book's contents, coverage, and accuracy.

As always, the support I received from CQ Press was phenomenal. Executive Director Brenda Carter and Chief Acquisitions Editor Charisse Kiino not only initially suggested this project, but also encouraged me throughout each stage of the process. Senior Development Editor Elise Frasier helped provide the book with needed direction and form. Anna Socrates skillfully edited the manuscript and oversaw the production. Her influence can be found on every page of the finished product. Allyson Rudolph doggedly hunted down photographs in order to provide visual images of the people and places discussed in the book. Dwain Smith and Jerry Orvedahl helped construct and design the Web site for the book. No editorial staff could be any more efficient and responsive and yet so patient with an author who often was neither.

Thomas G. Walker

ELIGIBLE FOR EXECUTION

The Murder of
Eric Michael Nesbitt

ON JUNE 20, 2002, the nine members of the U.S. Supreme Court assembled behind the raised mahogany bench in the Court's chamber. Chief Justice William Rehnquist announced that Associate Justice John Paul Stevens would deliver the decision in Case No. 00-8452, *Atkins v. the Commonwealth of Virginia.* As the eighty-two-year-old Stevens began reading the opinion of the Court's majority, Justice Antonin Scalia readied himself to express the views of the dissenting justices.

Hanging in the balance was the life of Daryl Renard Atkins, a convicted murderer sentenced to death by the state of Virginia. But the impact of the Court's decision would extend far beyond Daryl Atkins. It would also determine the fate of unknown numbers of other convicted murderers waiting on death row as well as those who might face capital charges in the future. To decide this case the justices needed to determine the meaning of the Cruel and Unusual Punishment provision of the Eighth Amendment to the U.S. Constitution. In the *Atkins* case, the Court addressed the specific question of whether the Constitution prohibits the imposition of the death penalty on convicted murderers suffering mental retardation or whether such offenders are eligible for execution.

The justices announce their decisions in the dignified atmosphere of the Supreme Court's majestic courtroom, long after the occurrence of the events that triggered the legal disputes brought before the Court. The *Atkins* case originated six years earlier when a series of actions resulted in the violent death of Eric Nesbitt, a young man who quite literally found himself in the wrong place at the wrong time.

THERE ARE STILL lingering questions about what happened on the night of August 16, 1996, especially in the two-hour period that began around 11:30 p.m. The evidence was not definitive. Testimony was in conflict. Forensic tests were not conclusive. Yet between 1998 and 2008 no less than three different juries and several judicial rulings reached similar factual conclusions about the events of that night and the men who participated in those events.

Daryl Atkins had spent all of his eighteen years in the Hampton Roads region of Virginia. This area, located in the far eastern, Tidewater section of the state, is composed of a diverse set of seven Virginia counties and ten independent cities ranging from Chesapeake and Virginia Beach in the south to colonial Williamsburg in the north. It has grown from the home of the nation's first English settlement at Jamestown in 1607 to a metropolitan population of 1.7 million today. Fed by the Elizabeth and James Rivers, the Chesapeake Bay is a natural harbor that has fueled the commerce and development of Hampton Roads. Today the region is home to U.S. naval and air force facilities in the Hampton/Portsmouth/ Norfolk area as well as the world's largest shipyards at Newport News.

August 16, 1996, was a warm and humid summer Friday in the city of Hampton. Daryl Renard Atkins spent that day inside an apartment at 1 Sacramento Drive where he lived with his father. The eighteen year old had dropped out of high school in the eleventh grade. He had no job and nowhere he needed to be. There was little reason to believe that this day would be any different than any other day. He would probably watch television, smoke marijuana, and drink.

Daryl was born in Hampton in 1977, the only child of an African American couple, Phillip Jr. and Elvira Atkins. He was slightly built, about 5'4" tall and 130–140 pounds. Although he had a mild asthmatic condition, Daryl enjoyed generally good health. He was born with one unusual physical characteristic—six fingers on each hand and six toes on each foot. This hereditary abnormality, known as polydactyly, was surgically corrected when Atkins was a young child. His father, employed almost thirty years as

a sheet metal worker in the Newport News shipyard, was also born
with an extra finger on each hand.
Atkins's mother was a long-term
telephone company employee.
Neither parent had any history of
crime or substance abuse, yet the
family was troubled. His parents
separated in 1985 and divorced a
year later. Daryl, close to both parents as a child, had difficulty
accepting the family's breakup.

Daryl Renard Atkins

Following the divorce, Daryl
lived with his mother, who remar-
ried in 1989. Daryl maintained a
good relationship with his natural father. As he entered his teenage years,
however, he began to transfer his loyalties away from his family and to a
group of friends whose influences were not always positive. Atkins had
always struggled with his schoolwork, resulting in a long history of
academic underachievement, but now he lost almost total interest in his
education. He also stopped participating in the programs at Hampton's
Morning Star Baptist Church. He lost two important male influences in
his life when his stepbrother Michael, one year his senior, suddenly died
during an asthma attack and his stepfather was incarcerated. These factors,
combined with some scrapes with the law and mounting substance abuse,
caused his relationship with his mother to deteriorate. As a result Daryl
moved in with his father in late spring 1996. He had never held a job, surviving on a $20 weekly allowance from his father and periodic handouts
from other relatives. He spent most of his money on alcohol and drugs.

Around 11:00 on that Friday morning, Atkins was joined by William
A. Jones, a twenty-six year old he had met at a bus stop about two months
earlier. Jones graduated from high school in 1989, but had accomplished
little since then. He was often unemployed, although at that time he
washed dishes at a local Golden Corral restaurant. Recently separated
from his wife and two sons, Jones had moved in with his father, an army

William A. Jones

veteran confined to a wheelchair. His father's apartment was located at 2 Sacramento Drive, a building adjacent to Atkins's residence. Atkins and Jones had become regular drinking buddies, especially on those weekend days when Jones was not visiting his children.

Throughout the day Atkins and Jones drank gin mixed with fruit juice and forty-ounce bottles of beer and malt liquor. They also smoked a large quantity of marijuana, some of it laced with cocaine. Periodically friends dropped by to share in the drinking and smoking. At various times everyone present pooled their money to buy more alcohol and smoking accessories. Atkins and Jones made periodic trips on foot to the 7-Eleven convenience store just around the corner on North Armistead Avenue to purchase more beer. At one point a friend drove them to a liquor store to replenish the supply of gin and juice.

One of the visitors that day was Mark Dallas, a friend of Atkins. Dallas partied with the others that evening but left relatively early because he had to work the next morning at Burger King. Before Dallas left, Atkins asked if he could borrow the .38-caliber, brown-handled, semi-automatic pistol that Dallas carried. He did not inform Dallas of any particular intended use, but he promised to return the gun the next morning.

After Dallas and the others left, Atkins and Jones continued drinking until about 11:30 p.m. when they realized that their once ample stockpile of alcohol had been consumed. The two decided to make one final beer run to the 7-Eleven. Before they left, Atkins tucked the borrowed handgun into the waistband of his pants where it was partially concealed by his belt buckle. When they arrived at the store, Atkins realized that he did not have enough money to make a purchase. Jones only had $1.50, just enough to buy one beer for himself.

Unwilling to go home without alcohol, Atkins began to panhandle from individuals driving up to the store. Jones waited off to the side in the parking area watching Atkins approach people as they arrived. These efforts were not particularly productive, however, yielding no more than some spare change. If Atkins and Jones were going to buy beer, more aggressive action would be necessary.

MEANWHILE, ONLY minutes away from the 7-Eleven Eric Michael Nesbitt and his coworker, Vivian Brown, were closing the Advance Auto Parts store for the night. It had been raining that evening, and Nesbitt offered to drive Brown's car closer to the store so she could avoid getting wet. Brown was grateful, but declined the suggestion, asking only that Nesbitt watch her to make sure she was able to leave the parking area safely. After wishing his coworker a good night, Nesbitt got into his purple 1995 Nissan pickup truck and drove away.

The twenty-one-year-old Nesbitt had been stationed at nearby Langley Air Force Base for over two years as a transportation specialist. Earlier that day he had worked a morning shift at the base and had enjoyed a squadron picnic in the afternoon. He had taken the part-time job at the auto parts store to earn enough money to repair his truck, which had been involved in a minor accident. Distinguished by his bright red hair and impish grin, he was well liked by his fellow airmen at the base and his coworkers at the auto parts store. Nesbitt was known as a hard worker who kept people's spirits up and made them laugh. He was only days away from being promoted to senior airman and was looking forward to a career in the Air Force.

Nesbitt grew up in Gilbertsville, a village of less than 500 people in upstate New York. He had three younger brothers and two younger sisters. Nesbitt spent his youth in a typical small-town fashion. He loved to camp, hike, and fish. He participated in basketball and track and was involved in church activities. He worked part-time for several years on a neighbor's dairy farm. Nesbitt was involved with the Boy Scouts for about eleven years, ultimately earning the rank of Eagle Scout. He also volunteered with the Gilbertsville fire department and rescue squad. He enlisted in the Air Force in August of 1993, only two months after his high-school

Eric Michael Nesbitt

graduation. Prior to his assignment at Langley, Nesbitt was stationed at Lackland Air Force Base in Texas where he took basic training and technical school instruction. He served short stints at Guantanamo Bay, Cuba, and Panama, and had already received medals for his military achievements.

After leaving the store at about 11:30 that night, Nesbitt first drove to the Coliseum Crossing branch of the Crestar Bank to get some weekend cash from the automated teller machine. He withdrew $60. He then headed toward the Air Force base where he had plans to meet a friend, but he was hungry and decided to stop for a quick snack. The 7-Eleven on North Armistead was right on his way, only a few blocks from the west gate of Langley.

ABOUT THE TIME Eric Nesbitt drove his truck into the 7-Eleven parking lot, Daryl Atkins had become frustrated with his unsuccessful panhandling efforts. Nesbitt got out of his truck and exchanged a few words with Atkins before he entered the store. After making a quick purchase, Nesbitt returned to his truck carrying a twenty-ounce bottle of Mountain Dew and a bag of Tostitos corn chips. As he began to back out of his parking space, Atkins whistled him down and walked over to the passenger-side window to talk to him. Jones, interested in what was happening, started walking toward the truck. To Nesbitt, the two must have appeared non-threatening. Jones, like Atkins, was 5'4", but at 120 pounds weighed even less than his younger friend. When Atkins pulled out the .38-caliber pistol and pointed it at Nesbitt, however, the situation immediately turned ominous.

Atkins entered the passenger-side door and ordered Nesbitt to "move over and let my friend drive." Nesbitt complied. Jones got behind the steering wheel and began driving away quickly. He maneuvered the pickup into

Daryl Atkins and William Jones abducted Eric Nesbitt and car-jacked his truck from this convenience store just before midnight on August 16, 1996.

a cluster of apartments behind the 7-Eleven. En route, the truck slid on the wet streets and collided with a parked vehicle, damaging the driver's-side door. All the while Atkins had the gun trained on the terrified Nesbitt.

Atkins ordered Nesbitt to surrender his wallet, and he removed what remained of the $60 Nesbitt had obtained earlier from the bank's cash machine. While doing so, Atkins noticed Nesbitt's Crestar Bank ATM card. Wanting more money, Atkins instructed Jones to drive to the bank. When they arrived, Nesbitt was forced to withdraw an additional $200 from his account.

Jones then drove the truck back to the neighborhood from which they had abducted Nesbitt. He stopped the truck in the parking lot of a school while Atkins and he discussed what they were going to do with Nesbitt now that they had taken his money. Jones suggested that they "just tie him up" and leave him somewhere "so we can get away." The frightened Nesbitt implored them, "Yes, yes, tie me up, as long as you just don't hurt me." When they could not think of a location in Hampton to leave him, Atkins volunteered that he knew of a good place just outside Yorktown, Virginia.

Atkins instructed Jones to drive the truck onto Interstate 64, heading northwest toward Williamsburg. During the drive, Nesbitt exchanged some nervous conversation with Jones about the Air Force and his job at the auto parts store. Atkins did not enter the conversation. He had become interested in the truck's stereo system and was attempting to remove the unit from the dash.

After about twenty minutes on the Interstate, Atkins instructed Jones to take the Lee Hall exit and head northeast on Highway 238. This was followed by a right turn onto Crafford Road, a curvy, two-lane stretch of asphalt. One half mile later, the truck crossed the Newport News city-limits boundary line and entered York County. At this point not only does the name of the road change (Crafford becomes Crawford), but the surroundings become radically different as well. Jones had driven Nesbitt's truck into an isolated, nature preserve section of the Colonial National Historical Park. This dark, desolate, and heavily wooded area is part of the Newport News watershed. There were no stores, houses, or streetlights. Some people used the road to cut across York County while driving between Newport News and Gloucester County; others visited the area to observe native wild turkeys and other animals. By and large, however, Crawford was infrequently used. Because of its isolation, some people were uncomfortable on that stretch of road even in broad daylight. The odds of any person witnessing what transpired were very low.

As the truck continued down Crawford Road, Nesbitt became increasingly fearful of what might happen. He pleaded with his abductors, "Please don't kill me."

Atkins directed Jones to come to a stop where Tower Lane joins Crawford Road. Tower Lane is a gravel road that allows maintenance access to a 320-foot telecommunications tower. It is gated to prevent traffic from entering. The site was well out of the way of normal traffic. The nearest house was just over a half mile away on the other side of the Newport News/York County line.

Jones claimed to have never previously been to this location, but Atkins likely knew the area well. His grandfather's house was not far from the other end of Crawford road, about three miles away.

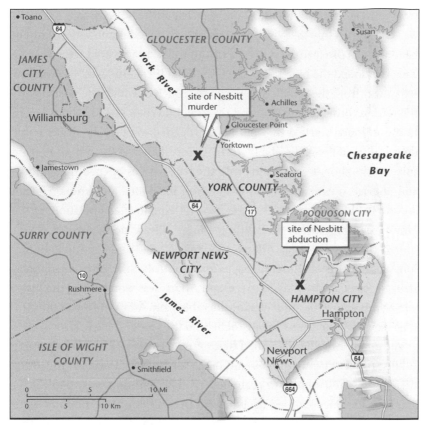

Hampton Roads region of Virginia

Unknowingly Atkins's decision to come to this location may have weakened his subsequent legal position significantly. In driving from the point of Nesbitt's abduction to the Crawford Road/Tower Lane intersection, Atkins and Jones left the city of Hampton and had gone just beyond the city limits of Newport News, as the map shows. They were now in York County, a more white and affluent area than neighboring jurisdictions. There was a high probability that any jury drawn from the communities of York County would be less sympathetic to Atkins and Jones than a jury selected from the general population of Hampton or Newport News.

IT WAS A WARM evening, about 72 degrees. The sky was cloudy and the night was very dark. Only the Nissan's headlights provided illumination. Gun in hand, Atkins directed Nesbitt to exit the truck. It appeared clear that he had abandoned the plan to tie up Nesbitt and leave him. Nesbitt took two steps away from the vehicle and began to crouch down in a defensive position. Atkins ordered him to stand up straight. When he did, Atkins began to shoot. Jones, startled by what he heard, tried to open the driver's-side door but the damage caused by the earlier collision stopped him. Fearing some of the shots were coming into the truck, Jones opened the window and crawled out of the truck, landing on his hands and knees. He ran around the back of the truck to see Nesbitt lying in a fetal position on the ground begging for his life and screaming, "Please don't shoot me anymore." Turning a deaf ear, Atkins stood over Nesbitt and continued to fire. Jones grabbed Atkins, attempting to seize control of the gun. During their struggle, the gun discharged twice, and Atkins was wounded in the lower left leg just above the ankle. In considerable pain, Atkins dropped the gun. Jones seized it and threw the pistol behind the seat of the truck.

Although Jones later testified that his efforts were directed at stopping Atkins from continuing his assault on Nesbitt, at no time after disarming Atkins did Jones attempt to evaluate Nesbitt's condition or stop to render aid. Instead, Jones jumped back behind the wheel of the truck and, with Atkins in the passenger seat, drove off. Jones claimed that he assumed that Nesbitt had already died from the gunshot wounds or from the tremendous loss of blood that resulted. The two sped away from the scene yelling and cursing at each other over what had just occurred.

The wound to Atkins's leg was sufficiently serious that medical treatment was necessary. Jones drove the truck to the emergency entrance at Riverside Hospital in Newport News, arriving at about 1:40 a.m. He took about $70 from the money they had robbed from Nesbitt, left Atkins at the emergency room door, and drove off in Nesbitt's truck.

Seeking help for the gunshot wound, Atkins hobbled into the emergency room with his ankle wrapped in a towel presumably taken from Nesbitt's truck. At this point he initiated what became a long series of misstatements and contradictions surrounding the events of that evening. Jacquelyn McIntyre, an emergency room nurse, was the first to

Eric Nesbitt was shot and killed at this remote location where Tower Lane meets Crawford Road in York County, Virginia.

see him. Atkins was calm and cooperative, explaining to her that he had been assaulted and shot right outside the hospital. He gave no explanation, however, for how he happened to have a towel with which to wrap his wound.

Later, while Atkins was lying on a hospital stretcher, he was interviewed by Newport News police officer Anthony Tutone who had responded to the reports of a gunshot wound. To the officer Atkins spun an even less believable story, explaining that he had been assaulted in an attempted robbery by a man wearing a dark ski mask near Deer Park, a thirteen-acre wooded recreation area in Newport News. Although shot in the leg, Atkins claimed to have escaped from his attacker, hopping on one foot the entire 1.8-mile distance from Deer Park to the hospital emergency room. Because no crime had been reported with facts consistent with Atkins's wound, he was not detained.

Emergency room physician Ozita Cooper treated Atkins. Two bullets had penetrated Atkins's lower left leg, and he had lost perhaps a half liter of blood. X-rays indicated that one bullet remained lodged in the ankle. It would have to be surgically removed at a later date, but Atkins faced no serious or immediate medical danger. The leg was iced and then placed in a temporary splint. After receiving antibiotics and pain medication, Atkins was discharged.

In the early morning hours of August 17 Daryl Atkins limped out of the hospital and headed for home while William Jones drove away seeking to evade the police investigation that would inevitably come. At that same time a heavy fog fell on the lifeless body of Eric Nesbitt left on the side of a remote country road. Eight bullets had penetrated his body. Only hours before, the enthusiastic, hardworking young airman looking forward to his promotion and military career had left his part-time job and stopped for a snack before meeting friends back at the base. In a few more hours his Air Force colleagues at Langley would learn that their coworker and friend had been killed, his mother would be informed of the loss of her son, and his brothers and sisters would be told that their big brother would not be returning home. Eric Nesbitt's life had been taken senselessly.

Daryl Atkins would later describe that the killing as unintended. "It just happened," he said. "It wasn't planned or anything. We just did something stupid.... We were just standing outside the 7-Eleven. That's when stuff started to occur; and we ended up robbing the guy.... When you're intoxicated like that you start thinking of all the stuff you want. But I wasn't down with hurting anybody."

BIBLIOGRAPHIC NOTE.

The account of Eric Nesbitt's murder provided here is reconstructed from testimony and other evidence introduced at Atkins's trials, investigations by police, psychiatric evaluations, and reports of probation and parole officers. In addition, the murder and subsequent investigation were covered during the summer and early fall of 1996 by a Newport News newspaper, the Hampton Roads *Daily Press,* in a series of articles by reporter Patti Rosenberg. Additional *Daily Press* reports were filed by Jennifer Andes and A. J. Plunkett. Details about the crime were later reported in the *Washington Post* and other major outlets. This chapter's portrayal of the homicide is informed in part by these journalistic accounts. There is no universal agreement regarding all of the events of August 16 and 17, 1996. Testimony provided by Daryl Atkins and William Jones, the only surviving witnesses to what occurred, agree in many respects, but deviate at key points. Where facts have been disputed, reliance here is placed on the findings of the jury at Daryl Atkins's trial and sentencing as well as the facts accepted as true by the appellate courts. These accounts largely accept the statements of William Jones as being more credible than the alternative versions provided by Atkins. Atkins and his lawyers to the very end claimed that it was Jones, and not Atkins, who fired the fatal shots that night.

Additional bibliographic information and supporting documentation for the subjects discussed in this and subsequent chapters can be found on this book's Web site: http://walker.cqpress.com.

Investigation and Prosecution

GARLAND CLAY ARRIVED at Petro's Tavern in Hampton at about nine o'clock on the evening of August 16. The thirty-year-old foreman for a local plumbing and mechanical contractor planned to spend a few hours that Friday with a group of coworkers eating dinner and playing pool. During the course of the night Clay consumed about six beers, but quit drinking at about midnight. When the bar shut down at around 2:00 a.m., Clay and some of his friends continued to socialize in the tavern's parking lot.

Clay headed for his home in Gloucester County at about 3:45 a.m. He took his usual route, which included using Crawford Road to cut across York County. Along the way he felt the need to relieve himself and decided to take advantage of the isolated, wooded surroundings. He pulled his vehicle over at the point that Tower Lane meets Crawford Road. As he turned off the road his headlights swept across the body of a man sprawled on the ground. Clay rolled down his window and yelled at the man twice. There was no response. He then honked his horn and yelled again. Still there was no movement, and it did not appear that there was going to be any. Clay turned his car around and sped back to the Newport News city line where he knocked on the door of the first house and asked the resident to call the police.

At approximately 4:45 a.m. the York County sheriff's department contacted Investigator F. Troy Lyons and directed him to go to the scene. Lyons, a member of the major crimes section of the York County Sheriff's Office, was an experienced law enforcement officer, having been a deputy sheriff for eight years and an investigator for five. He would lead the investigation of the Nesbitt murder case. At 5:15 a.m. when Lyons arrived at the intersection of Crawford Road and Tower Lane, three other members of the sheriff's department were already securing the crime scene and collecting evidence.

Investigator Troy Lyons

Nesbitt's corpse lay face down on the asphalt with his body extending onto the gravel, about thirty feet from the gate that blocked traffic from entering Tower Lane. He was wearing a white t-shirt with blue jeans. The front of the shirt was covered with blood. Multiple gunshot wounds were evident. Blood had soaked his clothes and was also spread on the ground around the body. From this investigators deduced that the victim was killed at the scene rather than shot elsewhere and later dumped on the side of Crawford Road. Although the humid early morning air was filled with a foggy mist and it had rained until about midnight, Nesbitt's clothes remained generally dry, indicating that the body had not been abandoned at the side of the road for very long. The investigators recovered six shell casings near the body. Because Nesbitt's wallet was missing and no vehicle was left at the scene, robbery appeared to be the most likely motive.

Fortunately the investigators were able to identify Nesbitt from an Advance Auto Parts pay stub found in his pants pocket. Now it was up to Investigator Lyons and the York County sheriff's department to determine how Eric Nesbitt arrived at such a secluded location and to identify the person who killed him. It was the county's first homicide of the year and only the second since 1992.

Investigators quickly learned that although Nesbitt worked part-time at the auto parts store, his primary employment was at the Air Force base.

His friends at Langley had become worried about him because he had not returned to the base that night. Normally when he worked the late shift at the store he arrived at Langley by 12:30 a.m. Air Force personnel and employees at the store were able to supply a good description of Nesbitt's vehicle. A bulletin was issued for local law enforcement agencies to look for a purple 1995 Nissan pickup truck, license number ZPD 1633, with black primer on the front. The public was also asked to report to the authorities if anyone should spot the vehicle. The sheriff's department hoped that a truck of such unusual color and markings would be quickly found.

Later that Saturday morning, with Lyons present, Dr. Leah Bush conducted an autopsy of Nesbitt's body. Dr. Bush, a forensic pathologist, had been an assistant medical examiner for the Commonwealth of Virginia in the Tidewater district for seven years. Bush found evidence of eight gunshot wounds, but several bullets had penetrated one part of the body and reentered another. Five of the gunshot wounds (to the left abdomen, left arm and hand, right arm, and right thigh) did not strike vital organs and would not have caused death if promptly treated. Three of the wounds, however, were lethal. The first entered the chest and caused damage to the lungs and heart, the second entered the chest wall and perforated the aorta, and the third struck the forearm and reentered the abdomen. The three lethal wounds caused profuse bleeding. None of the gunshot wounds caused immediate death. They were incapacitating and painful, but Nesbitt would have lived for several minutes before bleeding to death from internal injuries. He ultimately lost consciousness from extensive loss of blood.

After the autopsy, Lyons searched Nesbitt's barracks room at Langley Air Force Base. He was particularly interested in determining if Nesbitt had credit card accounts that might have experienced recent activity or bank accounts from which withdrawals might have been made. Lyons found no evidence that Nesbitt had any open credit card accounts, but he did establish that the murdered airman had a Langley Federal Credit Union account as well as an account at Crestar Bank into which his paycheck was automatically deposited. Lyons contacted these institutions and learned from Crestar that there had been some activity after 2:00

p.m., Friday, August 16, and on Saturday, August 17, but little additional information was available at that time. Crestar pledged to investigate and report back to Lyons.

THE NEWS of Eric Nesbitt's death was met with disbelief and sorrow by his friends and family. Vivian Brown, the woman who closed the auto parts store with Eric that Friday night and the last of his friends to see him alive, confessed that she was so upset that she cried the entire next day. His fellow airmen were deeply affected. Many of them had worked side-by-side with Nesbitt for many months. Several had eaten hamburgers with him at the squadron picnic just hours before he was killed. They remembered him as a reserved, but fun-loving New Yorker who was always willing to help other members of the squad. One colleague planned to help Nesbitt paint his truck that weekend. Another, who also worked part-time at the auto parts store, confessed to a reporter, "I keep thinking it could have been me. Or I wish I could have been there to do something. He was so quiet and sweet and easygoing. I don't know why anybody would do this to him."

Especially affected by Nesbitt's murder were his two best friends at the base, Mark and Sarah Armitage. Sarah met Eric when they were both in technical school at Lackland Air Force Base in Texas in 1993. They became like brother and sister, seeing each other almost every day. Following training they were both assigned to Langley where Sarah's husband Mark met Eric in 1994. Mark and Eric worked together, and the three of them spent considerable time together during their off hours. Sarah last saw Eric when Nesbitt visited the Armitage home on Thursday evening, the day before he was killed. She did not attend the squadron picnic the next day because she was nine months pregnant and under medical instructions to be on complete bed rest until the baby's arrival.

On Saturday, just hours after Nesbitt's body was found, Investigator Lyons and two other officers came to the Armitage home to ask some questions. That is when Mark and Sarah learned about the murder. Sarah became hysterical and couldn't stop crying. Her husband called the chaplain to help her cope with the loss. Three days later, on August 20, Sarah gave birth to her son.

Mary Sloan, mother of slain airman Eric Nesbitt, shown here at a 2005 court hearing related to the death of her son.

Meanwhile, an Air Force "death notification committee" drove up in a van to the Sloan home in Gilbertsville, New York. Mary Sloan, Eric's mother, was outside. Her husband Dan was not yet home. Eric's younger sisters and brothers were inside the house. Upon learning the news, the family was in shock, unable to comprehend how something so terrible could happen. Sloan later testified that the older children took their brother's death particularly hard. Eric's brother Marshall was seventeen years old when Eric died. Before joining the army, he spent a night sleeping on Eric's grave. Eric's sister Julie, age fifteen, took it the hardest because she and Eric were very close. Brenda, age ten, was always special to Eric because their birthdays were only a day apart. Timothy and Nathan, the two youngest children, ages six and four, had difficulty understanding that their big brother, who had visited them for a family reunion only two weeks earlier, would never come home again. At the breakfast table one morning several months after the murder, Nathan counted to eight and announced, "That's how many times Eric got shot."

While the whole family was deeply hurt by what had happened, Eric's mother undoubtedly suffered the most. She developed haunting fears that something terrible would happen to her other children. "I know it is unreasonable and I shouldn't think that way," she said, "but I can't help it. And I look at the other young children and think, Oh, my God, what's going to happen to them? Is something awful going to happen to them, too?"

The Air Force conducted a memorial service commemorating the life of Eric Nesbitt at Langley Chapel on Thursday, August 22, but the main funeral service took place in Gilbertsville. George Duncan, Eric's supervisor at Langley was responsible for assembling Eric's personal belongings and accompanying his body to New York. Years after Eric's funeral, Duncan still remembered that task as one of his most difficult. "Yes, I had to escort Eric home to his family. I had to go through his personal belongings. And he already ... had his uniforms lined up in the closet with his new rank already on his uniforms.... Even now with my 16 years in service, I know escorting Eric home was the hardest thing I've ever done. I was ashamed to take that little boy home in a pine box to his Mom. He was a good kid."

The church was packed for Eric's service. It seemed as if the whole town attended. The Air Force sent an honor guard, and about forty other people from Langley traveled to New York for the funeral. As Duncan described it, "I remember [several people who came from Langley for the funeral] walking into the funeral home, seeing Eric, and instantly walking back out because they couldn't handle seeing him like that. One of my peers, one of the supervisors from the shop, just broke down in tears, just seeing Eric in that state because ... the last time they saw him he was alive."

A number of Air Force personnel promised that as a symbol of support at least two or three of his Langley friends would attend every subsequent trial or hearing until justice was done.

WHILE THE initial stages of the investigation were under way, Daryl Atkins had returned to his father's apartment, but William Jones was in hiding. After leaving Atkins at the hospital emergency room early Saturday morning, Jones drove Nesbitt's truck to the King James Motel in Newport News. Jones parked the truck in the motel parking lot. He left the keys in the vehicle and walked away. Jones never returned to the truck, but began moving from motel to motel in the Newport News area in the hope of evading the police. Jones first checked into the King James and spent Saturday and Sunday there. He then checked in to the nearby Thrift Inn for one day, and then went back to the King James. Next was the Budget Inn and then back a final time to the King James. During this period he cut his hair in an attempt to disguise his appearance. Jones made one attempt to contact Atkins, calling his apartment from a pay phone, but Daryl was not home.

The most significant break in the case occurred on Tuesday, August 20, when Investigator Lyons received word that Crestar Bank's security personnel had studied the videotapes taken by cameras installed at the Coliseum Crossing ATM machine. They were able to extract useable images of the two transactions made by Eric Nesbitt on the night of his murder.

Lyons went to the Crestar corporate offices in Norfolk, Virginia, to pick up the evidence. He was given a copy of the tape along with some still pictures that Crestar investigators had made from the videotape. The videotape revealed Nesbitt's first transaction at just before midnight. He was alone and withdrew $60.

The recordings of the second transaction, however, provided the information necessary to solve the mystery of what happened to Eric Nesbitt. The tape showed three individuals driving up to the ATM in Nesbitt's truck at 12:16 on Saturday morning, no more than twenty minutes after the first withdrawal. The tape yielded an excellent image of a young African American man with short hair and a goatee sitting behind the wheel. The photographs of the person in the passenger seat were a bit more grainy, but he was another African American man who seemed to be pointing a handgun at the individual occupying the seat between the two others. The individual sitting in the middle was undoubtedly Eric Nesbitt. "I don't think those were acquaintances," Investigator Lyons was quoted in the Hampton Roads *Daily Press*. "It appears from the look on his face that he's rather scared." The videotape further showed Nesbitt withdrawing $200 from the automated teller. The images captured on tape constituted solid documentation of what had occurred at the ATM that night. One veteran of the York County sheriff's department called it the "clearest tape I've ever seen."

The task still remained to identify the men in the truck with Nesbitt. Lyons quickly took two actions to enlist the help of the public. First, information was provided to Crime Line, an independent, volunteer organization that solicits information from the public to solve crimes and offers rewards for information leading to the arrest of suspected offenders. Second, the sheriff's department sent still photographs made from the videotape to the local media. Those images first appeared on television news broadcasts on Tuesday evening, August 20, and in the newspapers

Bank surveillance cameras record William Jones driving Eric Nesbitt's truck while Daryl Atkins holds a gun on the abducted airman, forcing Nesbitt to make an ATM withdrawal.

the next morning. The public was asked to help identify the men sitting in the driver's and passenger's seats.

The compelling image of an obviously frightened Eric Nesbitt, taken only an hour before he was murdered, hit a responsive chord with the public. In less than twenty-four hours, ten individuals contacted authorities offering suggestions about the men in the ATM photographs. Five of those calls identified the driver as William Jones and provided information about his home address. One of those callers also implicated Daryl Atkins as being the individual in the passenger seat holding the gun, saying "a person Mr. Jones runs with was Daryl Atkins, who lives in the same apartment complex." Although individuals responding to the call for information could do so anonymously, it was later revealed that one of callers was Mary Rodgers, mother of William Jones. Rodgers later testified, "It was the right thing to do. If he was out hurting people, he needed to be caught."

Investigator Lyons was now confident he had sufficient grounds to take Jones into custody. Under the Constitution's Fourth Amendment, police cannot arrest a suspect without "probable cause." That is, police may make an arrest only if there is factual evidence sufficient to allow a prudent person reasonably to believe that a crime had been committed and that a particular individual committed it. The ATM photographs and responses of those individuals who identified Jones as the driver satisfied that standard. Based on these facts a judge issued a warrant authorizing the arrest of William Jones for participating in the abduction, robbery, and murder of Eric Nesbitt.

On Wednesday, August 21, Lyons and other deputies went to the apartment where Jones lived. Of course, Jones had gone into hiding in a series of Newport News motels and was not at home. Jones's father and the father's girlfriend were in the apartment. They verified that Jones had been spending time with Daryl Atkins and said that they had not seen William since Friday. Interviews with neighbors further verified the association between Jones and Atkins.

Lyons then proceeded to the Atkins apartment. When Lyons saw Daryl he immediately identified him as the man holding the pistol in the ATM photograph. This identification was sufficient to establish the probable cause necessary to place Atkins under arrest and transport him to the York County jail.

Atkins did not resist being taken into custody. In fact, he was fully cooperative. Lyons complied with rules established by the U.S. Supreme Court in *Miranda v. Arizona* (1966) by informing Atkins of his right to remain silent and that any statement he made could be used against him in court. Lyons also instructed Atkins that he could have a lawyer present during any questioning and that the state would pay for the attorney if Atkins did not have the funds to hire one. Atkins agreed to waive his right to remain silent and consented to be interviewed by Lyons. The interview lasted a little more than two hours. It produced a thirty-one-page statement of Atkins's account of the crime.

In his statement, Atkins fully admitted participating in the crime. He described how he had been a party to the abduction and robbery of Eric Nesbitt that ultimately ended in the killing of the young airman. Atkins, however, denied being the person who fired the shots. According to Atkins, William Jones orchestrated and directed everything that happened. It was Jones who borrowed the gun and Jones who initiated the abduction and robbery of Nesbitt. Furthermore, it was Jones who suggested the Crawford Road location as a place to take Nesbitt. And, most importantly, it was Jones, and not Atkins, who pulled the trigger over and over again as shots ripped through Nesbitt's body. Atkins claimed that he was sitting in the truck when the shooting began and that he did not handle the gun. "I didn't kill nobody," Atkins said. "I didn't take nobody's life."

Atkins's version seemed plausible. After all, Jones was the older, more experienced individual, and Atkins seemed to be a person more likely to follow than to lead. Although Atkins had two criminal violations on his juvenile record, one for breaking and entering when he was fourteen and a grand larceny at age seventeen, there was no history of violent crime that would predict an event like the savage murder of Eric Nesbitt. Atkins's confession, of course, placed even greater urgency on the need to apprehend William Jones as quickly as possible.

Having identified Jones as the driver of the Nissan truck and receiving Atkins's accusation that Jones was the triggerman in the murder, Investigator Lyons again turned to the public for help. He sent the following announcement to Crime Line for public distribution:

> The York County Sheriff's Office is looking for William A. Jones, who is black, 26, 5 feet, 4 inches, weighs 120 pounds, and has brown eyes, short black hair, a mustache and a goatee. Crime Line will pay up to $1,000 for information that leads to his arrest. Anyone with information can call 890-3630 anonymously.

The next major break in the case occurred later that Wednesday morning. Not more than twenty minutes after Atkins's arrest Troy Lyons received word that Nesbitt's pickup truck had been found. A Newport News police officer on routine patrol noticed the purple Nissan parked behind the King James Motel at 11:05 a.m.

Although Nesbitt's truck had been found in the motel parking lot, there was no sign of Jones. Guests and motel staff confirmed that the truck had been parked there for several days, but there was no factual basis to establish that Jones was hiding in any particular room, or that he had, in fact, ever rented any room at the motel. Once again, the protections of the Fourth Amendment applied. Just like its restrictions on arrests, this constitutional provision precludes unreasonable searches. There was no evidence that Jones had taken refuge in the King James. Finding the truck in the parking area was insufficient to justify a room-by-room search of the motel. Unless police obtained additional information about Jones's specific whereabouts, they could only conduct a continuous stakeout of the motel to determine if he was coming and going.

Fortunately for the police, the public again contributed to the investigation. The next day an informant called the Newport News police and provided information that linked Jones to room 578. With this additional supporting evidence, police readied to move on Jones. They first contacted the other occupants of the motel, instructing them to stay in their rooms until they completed the operation. The police then moved quickly, taking Jones into custody without incident.

By Thursday, August 22, the suspected murderers of Eric Nesbitt were behind bars. The investigation that began with a report of an unidentified body abandoned on the side of an isolated road less than six days earlier had culminated in two arrests. Daryl Atkins and William Jones were charged with murder, abduction, robbery, and the use of a firearm in the commission of a crime. The speed and success of the investigation was due to a number of factors. First, the perpetrators made several mistakes along the way, including the principle error of being photographed by the bank video recorder. Second, the public responded quickly to the request of the York County sheriff's department for information about the crime and the whereabouts of the suspects. And third, three law enforcement agencies, the police departments of the cities of Hampton and Newport News and the York County sheriff's department effectively cooperated in conducting the investigation.

But there remained much more to do. The evidence collected needed greater analysis to determine the individual roles played by Atkins and Jones on the night of the crime. And, of course, an effective investigation and the arrest of suspects does not necessarily mean that a conviction will result. As the investigation stage of the Nesbitt murder case was drawing to a close, it was time for the court system to begin carrying out its functions.

CRIMINAL LAW at its most basic level is little more than an authoritative declaration of those forms of behavior society considers unacceptable. The people's representatives in the legislature are entrusted to maintain the criminal code and determine a range of potential penalties that may be imposed on those who have violated society's expectations. When an individual commits a crime, the people's law is violated and the government must respond to address the infraction. The prosecutor is the public official who represents the people in the legal actions against the criminal offender. In carrying out this function, the prosecutor is ethically bound to pursue justice, not just seek convictions for their own sake.

The Virginia constitution created the office of Attorney for the Commonwealth as the state's primary prosecutorial officer. Unlike federal prosecutors who are appointed by and serve at the pleasure of the president, Commonwealth's Attorneys in Virginia are elected officials serving four-year terms. The office is the equivalent of a district attorney in other states. There is generally one Commonwealth's Attorney for each Virginia county and independent city.

As a criminal investigation progresses the prosecuting attorney begins to play an increasingly active role. For routine, minor crimes the prosecutor's office may not become involved until the investigation has been completed. For situations that present more serious or significant issues, however, the prosecutor may enter the process much earlier, working hand-in-hand with police to build a case against the accused.

Ultimately, the prosecutor is responsible for two actions. First, in every case the prosecutor must decide whether the facts are sufficient to justify formal criminal charges being brought against the accused. A number of legal, political, and institutional factors may influence the prosecutor's decision. For example, prosecutors may drop weak cases in order to focus their resources on those presenting higher probabilities of success. Or, a prosecutor might drop accusations of minor infractions in order to place a priority on more serious offenses. Additionally, pursuing cases where there is significant doubt concerning the guilt of the accused is considered by many to be an inappropriate use of prosecutorial power. If a conclusion is reached that prosecuting the case is not warranted, the charges are dismissed with little practical likelihood that the decision can be circumvented. As such, the prosecutor is a primary gatekeeper in the criminal justice system. When the decision is made to prosecute the case, the prosecuting attorney is faced with the second responsibility of the office—to represent the people in an effort to convict the accused.

The prosecutor's role in the criminal process cannot be overemphasized. The law gives prosecutors nearly unbridled discretion in determining who will be prosecuted and the specific charges against the accused. In addition, if the defendant is found guilty, the prosecutor's sentence recommendation may have considerable influence on a judge's determination of an appropriate punishment.

Prosecutors carry out their duties in the presence of cross-cutting pressures. Their primary responsibility is to make their communities safe by combating crime and putting offenders behind bars. But as government officials this power must be exercised as fairly as possible with a firm loyalty to the ends of justice. Further complicating matters, prosecutors are publicly elected officers, who must answer to the voters at reelection time. Retaining their positions often requires tending to the political demands placed upon them. When these competing interests point to different or conflicting actions, prosecutors may find themselves making very difficult choices.

To adjudicate criminal accusations as well as other legal disputes, the federal government and each of the states have developed a system of courts. In common with most states Virginia has a three-tiered judiciary. On top of the state's judicial hierarchy is the Supreme Court of Virginia, which traces its origins back to 1623 when the colonial House of Burgesses created a five-judge court to hear appeals from the decisions of local trial court judges. Today the supreme court is staffed by seven judges who serve for twelve-year terms. It regularly sits at the state capitol in Richmond. Loyal to the customs of its past, Virginia remains one of the few states that selects its judges at all court levels by majority vote of both houses of the state legislature. The primary function of Virginia's supreme court is to hear appeals from the lower courts that involve important constitutional questions or issues of significant precedential value. With few exceptions, the supreme court's jurisdiction is discretionary. The justices must agree to accept an appeal before it receives a full hearing. The standards and principles set by the supreme court are binding on the state's lower courts.

Below the Supreme Court of Virginia is the Court of Appeals. This intermediate appellate court began operation in 1985, created in response to the state's growing appellate caseload. The function of the court of appeals is to decide ordinary appeals from the state's trial courts, thus allowing the supreme court to allocate its resources to cases involving important legal questions of broad significance. The court of appeals has eleven judges who serve for eight-year terms. The court normally sits in panels of three judges. To make the court more accessible to Virginia's citizens, the panels hear cases in four different locations within the state. In most instances, the decision of the court of appeals is final, but some of its decisions are reviewed by the state supreme court.

The trial courts sit at the base of the judicial system. Virginia's trial court of general jurisdiction is the Circuit Court. Civil disputes involving claims of at least $4,500 as well as all felony and significant misdemeanor criminal cases are initially tried in one of the state's 120 circuit courts. Each circuit court has jurisdiction over a particular geographical area, normally a county or an independent city. The circuit court is staffed by at least one judge who serves for an eight-year term. Appeals from circuit court decisions normally go to the court of appeals, although cases in some special categories (such as death penalty appeals) are taken directly to the state supreme court.

In addition to the circuit courts, Virginia operates two other trial courts. The district courts handle minor criminal matters and civil disputes involving small claims. The Juvenile and Domestic Relations Courts hear cases involving juvenile delinquency, child welfare, spousal support, and related matters. Appeals from these two trial courts go to the circuit courts where the dispute is retried as if the case were newly filed.

Because the murder of Eric Nesbitt occurred within its boundaries the adjudication of the charges against Daryl Atkins and William Jones

Commonwealth's Attorney Eileen M. Addison in court pressing the prosecution's case against Daryl Atkins for the capital murder of Eric Nesbitt.

became the responsibility of the York County/Poquoson Circuit Court, a court having jurisdiction over the entire county of York and the neighboring city of Poquoson. Prosecuting cases in that circuit was the responsibility of Commonwealth's Attorney Eileen M. Addison.

With a 1975 psychology degree from the University of Michigan and a 1981 University of Denver law degree, Addison joined the York Commonwealth's Attorney's office as an assistant prosecutor in 1991. She brought with her ten years of general private practice experience, four in Colorado and six in Virginia. When the incumbent Commonwealth's Attorney accepted a judgeship in 1994, Addison was appointed as interim replacement.

In order to retain the position, Addison was required to run in a special election to serve the remaining year of her predecessor's unexpired term. She ran as a political independent, expressing the belief that the prosecutor's job had to be above partisan politics. Addison won handily by taking 55 percent of the vote against two opponents, one a Democrat and another also running as an independent. The next year Addison ran unopposed, winning a full four-year term. At the time of Eric Nesbitt's murder in 1996, the forty-two-year-old Addison was a seasoned lawyer with five years of experience in the York Commonwealth's Attorney's office.

In carrying out the prosecutions of Atkins and Jones, Addison was supported by a small staff of attorneys. Her first assistant was Benjamin Hahn, a College of William and Mary graduate, who had spent time in private practice in the Yorktown/Poquoson area before joining the prosecutor's office. Also assisting was Cathy Krinick, a part-time Assistant

Commonwealth's Attorney who brought with her capital murder experience from previous positions in the prosecutor's offices in Newport News and Hampton.

Daryl Atkins and William Jones also needed legal representation. Both were considered indigents, individuals lacking the financial ability to hire an attorney on their own. As early as 1932 in the case of *Powell v. Alabama,* the U.S. Supreme Court ruled that under certain circumstances poor defendants facing criminal charges that might result in the death penalty were entitled to effective counsel provided at state expense. This principle was significantly broadened in *Gideon v. Wainwright* (1963) when the justices expanded the Powell ruling to cover indigents accused of felonies. Later, in *Argersinger v. Hamlin* (1972) and *Scott v. Illinois* (1979) the principle was extended to cover poor defendants facing possible conviction for any crime that would result in incarceration. Under these rulings both Atkins and Jones were entitled to state-provided lawyers. In Virginia, as in most states, jurisdictions with heavy criminal caseloads usually employ a public defender system to meet the representation needs of poor defendants. These offices are staffed with government attorneys whose sole job it is to defend indigent clients. In smaller jurisdictions with less burdensome criminal dockets public defender offices are less common. These jurisdictions, like the York/Poquoson circuit, rely instead on court-appointed counsel. This procedure authorizes the trial court judge to assign a private attorney to represent a criminal defendant with the state paying a fee to the appointed lawyer. To assist the judge in selecting attorneys, the Virginia Defense Commission maintains a list of lawyers meeting state standards to represent defendants who face criminal charges but lack the means to hire an attorney.

Judge Prentis Smiley Jr., the presiding York circuit judge, appointed George M. Rogers III, a Hampton attorney with thirty years of criminal law experience, to represent Daryl Atkins. Because William Jones was facing charges of capital murder and a possible death sentence, he was entitled under Virginia law to have two attorneys appointed to prepare his defense. Timothy G. Clancy and Leslie Smith, also criminal lawyers from Hampton, were selected to represent him.

ONE CRITICAL question loomed over the Nesbitt murder investigation in the days immediately following the arrests of Atkins and Jones. Which of the two defendants committed the actual killing? The answer would likely determine the fate of the accused murderers. Under Virginia law "the willful, deliberate, and premeditated killing of any person" during the commission of a serious crime, such as robbery, abduction, or rape, constitutes "capital murder," carrying a penalty of either life in prison or death. Importantly, capital murder applies only to the individual who actually took the life of the victim. An individual who participates in a serious crime that results in the death of the victim, but who is not the actual killer, has committed "murder in the first degree," a crime punishable by twenty years to life in prison. Evidence pointed to the fact that both Atkins and Jones participated in a robbery that led to the murder of Eric Nesbitt, but only the actual killer would be eligible for execution.

The determination of formal charges to be filed against the defendants was the responsibility of Prosecutor Addison. Initially she thought Daryl Atkins's claim that Jones committed the murderous act was credible. The physical evidence as analyzed by that time appeared relatively consistent with Atkins's story, and he had voluntarily admitted his participation in the other facets of the crime. In addition, Jones did not attempt to counter Atkins's version of what had occurred at Crawford Road and Tower Lane. Instead, he exercised his right to remain silent, refusing to provide the police with any statement regarding the murder. Initially both defendants were tentatively charged with first-degree murder. Just a day after his arrest, however, the charges against Jones were upgraded to capital murder.

Individuals charged with crimes have a limited right to be released on bail and allowed to be free until their trial. Under this system the accused is required to put up cash or a bail bond in an amount determined by a judge. Under the Constitution's Eighth Amendment, the bail amount cannot be "excessive." The cash or bond provides a monetary guarantee that the accused will appear at the trial. If financially unable to meet the bail requirements, the defendant remains in jail until the trial.

Not every criminal defendant is eligible for bail. Those accused of the most serious crimes may be ineligible under state law as are those whose criminal histories would lead a judge to question the prudence of allowing the defendant to be released. Virginia's bail eligibility laws are similar to those of other states. They require a judge to consider a defendant's background and permit the judge to refuse bail if there is cause to believe (1) that the accused will not appear for the trial or (2) that the defendant's liberty will pose an unreasonable danger to himself or the public. In addition, there is the presumption that individuals charged with crimes punishable by life in prison or death are not eligible for bail.

On Thursday, August 22, Daryl Atkins had his bail set at $650,000. Because preliminary information indicated that he was not the actual killer and because he had no criminal history of violent acts, the judge concluded that Atkins was bail eligible. Yet the bail amount was set so high that there was no possibility that Atkins would be able to post bond. Consequently, Atkins remained in the York County jail. The following day William Jones, now charged with capital murder and facing a possible death sentence, was denied bail eligibility altogether. He, too, remained in jail. As events would unfold, neither Daryl Atkins nor William Jones would ever spend another day as a free man.

During the following weeks the analysis of the physical evidence continued. Significant ballistic evidence was recovered. Investigators at the murder scene found six shell casings. Three bullets were removed during the autopsy of Eric Nesbitt's body, two were found in Nesbitt's truck, and a final bullet was surgically removed from Daryl Atkins's ankle three weeks after his arrest. Tests on the bullets and shell casings indicated that they all came from the same handgun.

Considerable blood evidence also became available. Samples were removed from Nesbitt's shirt. The medical examiner also obtained blood directly from Nesbitt's body during the autopsy. A sample of blood was drawn from Daryl Atkins, and a pair of his shoes with apparent blood stains was seized during a search of his apartment. Blood was also found on the seat, backrest, doors, and door frame of the truck. All of the samples collected were consistent with the blood types of Eric Nesbitt and Daryl Atkins.

Mysteriously missing was the murder weapon. The gun was not found at the scene of the crime nor was it produced as a result of searches of Eric Nesbitt's truck, William Jones's motel room, or either of the defendants' residences. Potentially fingerprints taken from the handgun could have resolved the question of who the triggerman was. The pistol, however, was never recovered.

As more evidence became available the veracity of Atkins's version of the murder began to unravel. So did his credibility. Prosecutor Addison began to question seriously whether Atkins's story was an accurate account of the crime.

Perhaps the most important development was mounting evidence that Daryl Atkins was involved in significantly more criminal activity than was originally thought. Publicity over the investigation of the Nesbitt matter prompted a number of people to come forward and identify Atkins as a person who had committed crimes against them. These increasingly serious criminal offenses had occurred in the five months immediately preceding the Nesbitt murder. As it turned out, all of the incidents occurred in the city of Hampton in or near Atkins's neighborhood. The crimes had been reported earlier to the Hampton police, but they remained unsolved. As a consequence, the Hampton police intensified their investigations. While the investigations did not yield sufficient evidence to justify prosecution on some of the accusations, strong cases were built against Atkins on four.

First, on April 28, 1996, at about midnight, four men, Dennis Tuinei, Shane Stoops, John Hultquist, and Scott Thompson, drove up to a pay phone on West Mercury Boulevard in Hampton. They got out of the car and used the phone. As they returned to their vehicle they were confronted by three men, one of whom pointed a gun at them. The four men were ordered to lie down on the pavement, while their pockets were searched. Money and other valuables were taken. During the course of the robbery, one man hit Dennis Tuinei over the head with a gin bottle. From a photo lineup all four men picked Atkins as one of the participants in the crime, although he was not the one brandishing the firearm.

Second, at about 5:00 p.m. on June 4, 1996, Shavonda York returned to her home on Carmine Place in Hampton to discover the house had been broken into. The burglar entered through a kitchen window and took a television set, video recorder, leather coat, and jewelry. Later, Atkins claimed that he and William Jones had committed the break-in.

Third, on June 28, 1996, Kevin Phillips, a driver for Chanello's Pizza, was making his last delivery of the day to a residence on Sacramento Drive in Hampton. He had previously been warned about the neighborhood and told not to complete a delivery if anything seemed suspicious. When he drove up to the house there was a man standing near the front door. When he got within about thirty feet of the house, the man turned his back on Phillips. Then three men wearing black coats with hoods covering their faces approached him from behind. One of them put a gun to Phillips's head while the man who had been at the front door began searching Phillips's pockets. Twenty dollars was taken from him.

The men then made Phillips crawl to his car. Two of his assailants ran away, but two others got into the car with him. The men drove Phillips to a swampy area, while debating whether or not to shoot him. They made Phillips walk to the edge of the swamp with the gun at the back of his head. The men then told Phillips that he had five seconds to run. Phillips ran, then dove down and crawled through the swamp until he heard the car leave. Atkins later admitted to participating in the robbery.

Finally, on August 9, 1996, Amanda Hamlin was assaulted at her home on Aberdeen Road in Hampton. Hamlin had just finished mowing her lawn and was about to put her mower into a shed. Hamlin's daughter was inside the house. Suddenly she felt a gun at the side of her head. The man dragged her into the front yard and hit her on the head with the gun. She fell to the ground. The man started to walk away. Hamlin struggled to get up and began walking to her door. Then the man came at her again, put the gun to her stomach, and fired a shot. Hamlin survived, but was confined to the hospital for twenty-one days. Daryl Atkins was her assailant.

This record of criminal behavior was particularly damaging to the story of Nesbitt's murder that Daryl Atkins wanted the York authorities to believe. It demonstrated that he was in the midst of a major crime spree immediately before the killing of Eric Nesbitt. His recent history now included being involved with crimes such as robbery, abduction, car jacking, and use of a firearm. The last incident was perhaps the most relevant. The shooting of Amanda Hamlin demonstrated that Atkins was not just a follower, carrying out orders from people like William Jones.

Instead, Atkins was capable of executing a serious crime on his own. It also established that just one week before the Nesbitt murder Atkins shot a person at point-blank range. It looked increasingly possible that the killing of Eric Nesbitt was just one more escalated step in Daryl Atkins's pattern of criminal behavior.

With mounting evidence that Daryl Atkins was just as likely to have been the one who took Eric Nesbitt's life as Jones, Addison reconsidered her initial criminal complaints against him. On September 16, 1996, she formally upgraded the charges to capital murder. Now both Jones and Atkins faced identical accusations.

Although prosecutors are given primary authority to determine who to prosecute and the specific violations to be charged, they do not operate with complete independence. The Constitution requires that a check be built into the process to ensure that prosecutors do not abuse the broad powers they have been given. Virginia, in common with many other states, uses a grand jury for this purpose. In order to bind Atkins and Jones over for a trial on the capital murder charges, Addison would now have to convince the grand jury that sufficient evidence existed to justify those charges.

A grand jury is comprised of a group of citizens before whom the prosecutor presents the evidence collected and asks the grand jurors to issue an order compelling the accused to stand trial on specific charges. If the grand jurors conclude that there is sufficient evidence to justify a trial, they will issue a "true bill of indictment" which officially authorizes the trial of the accused. On the other hand, if the grand jury decides that the prosecutor's case is too weak to support the alleged criminal charges, the jurors can refuse to allow the case to go forward.

The grand jury is an ancient institution dating back to twelfth-century England and included in the Magna Carta of 1215. The English colonists brought the institution with them to America. The right of the criminally accused to a grand jury hearing is recognized in the Fifth Amendment to the United States Constitution. The purpose of the grand jury is to provide an opportunity for citizens to intervene if the government abuses its prosecutorial powers by pursuing criminal charges that lack sufficient supporting evidence.

The grand jury, however, is a controversial institution that adheres to procedures developed centuries ago. Grand juries, for example, hold their hearings in secret, with the jurors legally bound not to discuss what transpires during its meetings. While this cloak of silence may protect the reputations of those who are not indicted by the grand jury, it is inconsistent with today's prevailing interest in making government actions more open to the public. Perhaps more importantly, grand jury hearings are one-sided affairs. The prosecution presents its evidence to the jurors, but the defense is not allowed to attend the meetings or counter the information submitted by the prosecution. This, of course, is a significant advantage for the prosecution. A competent prosecutor with even a modest amount of supporting evidence can almost always persuade a group of laypeople that an accused person should be bound over for a trial.

Eileen Addison presented her case against Daryl Atkins to the grand jury for the York County/City of Poquoson circuit in November of 1996, requesting an indictment for capital murder and related charges. The grand jurors obliged, issuing the following murder indictment on November 19: "The Grand Jury charges that: on or about August 17, 1996, in the County of York, Virginia, Daryl Renard Atkins did feloniously, willfully, deliberately, and with premeditation kill and murder Eric Michael Nesbitt in the commission of a robbery while armed with a deadly weapon" in violation of "Section 18.2-31, subparagraph 4, Virginia Code (1950) as amended. Capital murder of the victim of a robbery." The grand jury authorized similar charges against William Jones.

Although Jones and Atkins had both been indicted, the question of who was the actual triggerman had yet to be answered. Jones remained the number one suspect, yet every new piece of evidence led Addison to move closer to concluding that the killer was Atkins and not Jones. Particularly important was a new witness, Stephen R. Burton.

Burton was an inmate with Atkins in the York County jail. He was facing grand theft charges for stealing a television and video recorder from a K-Mart store. In early 1997, Burton wrote a letter to the Commonwealth's Attorney describing conversations he had had with Atkins. According to Burton, Atkins admitted that he shot at Nesbitt, but that his memory of the events of that night was not very good because "he was too messed up" on drugs and alcohol. He expressed no fear of a conviction, because he had disposed of the murder weapon and the police would never find it. But Atkins added that if he was convicted, he was not going down alone.

Ultimately prosecutors reduced Burton's charges from grand theft to petit larceny in exchange for a guilty plea. Nothing in the negotiated arrangement required Burton to testify against Atkins, but there was every expectation that he would be willing to do so.

Burton's information provided yet another reason to doubt Atkins's account of the murder. Furthermore, if Burton proved credible, his testimony would suggest that Atkins's statements were motivated by his desire to shift criminal responsibility to his friend William Jones. Yet even with this new information there was still insufficient evidence to provide conclusive answers to the mysteries surrounding the killing of Eric Nesbitt.

Attorneys for both the prosecution and the two defendants hoped that some forensic evidence would emerge that would answer the triggerman question definitively. The blood samples were a potentially fruitful source. Determining whose blood was recovered at various locations at the crime scene might allow a more accurate reconstruction of the events surrounding the murder. Sophisticated DNA analysis would be required for the most effective use of this evidence. The results of such tests would not be available for twelve to fifteen weeks. As a consequence, on January 7, 1997, Judge Smiley granted a request to postpone the trial until a reasonable time after the DNA results became available. Smiley tentatively scheduled trials for Atkins and Jones to be held during the late summer of 1997.

To everyone's disappointment, the blood sample results did not resolve the question of the exact identity of the triggerman. The majority of the results ran contrary to Atkins's story, however. For example, Nesbitt's blood was found on the passenger seat and on the passenger-side backrest. This was hardly compatible with Atkins's account of Jones shooting Nesbitt outside the truck while Atkins moved from the center to the passenger-side seat. Yet while the evidence did nothing to support Atkins's account, it also did not provide a sound basis for any other theory of the crime.

Meanwhile, the criminal process continued to progress against Atkins. On March 7, 1997, he admitted to multiple felony counts stemming from the four previous incidents. They included aggravated maiming, robbery, attempted robbery, abduction, breaking and entering, grand larceny, and various counts of illegal use of firearms. On May 1, Hampton Circuit Judge Walter Ford sentenced Atkins to life in prison for the aggravated maiming charge and more than 100 years in prison for the other charges. Hampton Circuit Commonwealth's Attorney Linda Curtis reportedly reacted to the sentence by commenting, "It was very important to make sure Mr. Atkins would not be in our community again to terrorize these folks. I think this sentence will go a long way towards protecting this community."

As the summer trial dates approached, Addison found herself in a quandary. Only one of the two defendants committed the actual killing, and the physical evidence was insufficient to establish the identity of the triggerman. Getting a conviction against either defendant would require the other to provide testimony for the prosecution. On this score the case against Jones seemed exceedingly weak. Addison had not only grown increasingly skeptical about Atkins's claims, but she now thought his testimony would be ineffective.

Atkins's credibility had been seriously damaged by his recent felony convictions. In addition, his story was simply falling apart. Atkins's statements were filled with contradictions and mistruths. For example, he told two different stories to the hospital personnel about how he had been shot. In one version he claimed to have been shot right outside the hospital. In another version he described being shot almost two miles away and claimed to have hopped on one foot all the way to the hospital. At one point he gave a completely different account to Investigator Lyons, asserting that he was wounded when he jumped in front of Jones in order to save Nesbitt from the shots Jones was firing. He had also told Lyons that he never held the gun that night, a statement clearly rebutted by the photographs of the ATM cash withdrawal.

The Crestar Bank photographs had additional significance. They show Daryl Atkins holding the handgun on Eric Nesbitt. Except for Atkins's own statements, no evidence supported a conclusion that any person other than Atkins held the gun that night. Atkins's story, of course, was consistent with his own self-interest. If accepted as true, his account of what occurred that night would foreclose any possibility of his own execution.

Addison reached the conclusion that the physical evidence and the testimony of Atkins would not be enough to convict Jones of capital murder. Consequently, she notified Jones's court-appointed attorneys, Timothy Clancy and Leslie Smith, that she would no longer pursue capital murder charges against their client. She would proceed only on charges of first-degree murder, along with the related offenses of abduction, robbery, and use of a firearm.

Pursuing a capital murder charge against Jones also ran contrary to Addison's revised thinking about the case. She now had come to the conclusion that it was in fact Daryl Atkins who committed the actual homicide. But she faced the same obstacle in proceeding against Atkins as she had with Jones. Once again, the physical evidence was not conclusive. She would need the testimony of William Jones against his friend. What Jones would say, however, was unknown. He had steadfastly exercised his right to remain silent about the case, declining to answer questions from sheriff's deputies or prosecutors.

In order to evaluate her options, Addison opened negotiations with Clancy and Smith to determine if Jones would be willing to be interviewed by prosecutors and consider testifying against Atkins. Of course, there was no reason for Jones to cooperate with Addison. Clearly, he could not testify against Atkins without jeopardizing his own case by admitting that he had participated in abduction and robbery that led to the murder of the victim. And there was no way that Addison could force Jones to testify. The Fifth Amendment to the U.S. Constitution guarantees that "No person ... shall be compelled in any criminal case to be a witness against himself." This means that the government cannot force an individual to testify in any proceeding if the testimony would implicate that person in criminal activity.

Doing justice sometimes requires a prosecutor to proceed with leniency toward one defendant in order to place a priority on convicting a more culpable co-defendant. To secure Jones's cooperation, Addison was willing to cut a deal. As she would later describe it, "Sometimes you have to dance with sinners if you're going after Satan."

Plea bargains are common in the American criminal justice system. In fact, most prosecuted criminal cases are terminated not by trial, but by a negotiated agreement between the prosecution and the defense. Normally this entails an arrangement in which the defense agrees to forfeit the right to a jury trial and plead guilty in return for the prosecution making valuable concessions. Those concessions usually take the form of reducing the severity of the crime charged, the number of counts charged, or dismissing some of the charges. For example, a grand theft charge might be reduced to petit larceny, as occurred in the Stephen Burton case. Or six counts of passing bad checks might be reduced to two. Both sides benefit. The prosecutor does not have to spend the time and expense of a jury trial, and a guilty plea eliminates the uncertainty of a jury's verdict. The defendant profits because the ultimate sentence will almost always be less severe than being convicted on the original charges.

A preliminary deal was struck. The prosecution and defense reached a multi-step arrangement with which William Jones agreed. First, Jones initially would plead guilty to non-capital murder, abduction, robbery, and three firearms violations, with sentences to be imposed at a future date. Second, Jones would cooperate with the prosecution as a witness in the Atkins capital murder trial. Third, after Jones satisfied his obligation to cooperate fully and give complete, truthful testimony against Atkins, the prosecution would move to drop all the charges against him except for the reduced murder charge and one firearms violation.

Jones would be pleading guilty to participating in a crime that resulted in the murder of Nesbitt. Virginia law classified this crime as a Class 2 felony, punishable by twenty years to life in prison. The plea arrangement did not guarantee any particular sentence, but the prosecution did agree to ask the sentencing judge to give favorable consideration to Jones's willingness to cooperate with the state in its case against Daryl Atkins.

It was important to the prosecution to determine if Jones's version of the crime was credible and sufficiently consistent with the physical evidence to obtain a capital murder conviction against Atkins. Recognizing this, Clancy and Smith agreed to the prosecution's request to interview Jones. The interview took place on Wednesday, August 6, 1997, only five days before the scheduled start of Atkins's trial. The participants met in a conference room at the Virginia Peninsula Regional Jail where Jones was being held. Clancy and Smith were present at the meeting to advise their client, although Clancy left the meeting to attend to another obligation before the interview was completed. Commonwealth's Attorney Eileen Addison, Investigator Troy Lyons, and Assistant Commonwealth's Attorney Cathy Krinick attended the meeting for the prosecution.

The interview took two hours, with Krinick in charge of questioning Jones. Lyons taped the session and later made transcripts available to the attorneys. Jones was cooperative and forthcoming. His verbal responses were supplemented by the use of drawings and a role-playing exercise to demonstrate what had happened at the scene. Contrary to his co-defendant's account, Jones described Atkins as the one who initiated the abduction of Nesbitt and selected the location on Crawford Road. It was Atkins who demanded that Nesbitt get out of the Nissan pickup, and it was Atkins who opened fire on Nesbitt after he had walked only a few feet away from the truck. Jones described how he had crawled out of the driver's-side window when the door would not open, how he had wrestled the gun away from Atkins, and how Atkins had been wounded in the struggle. At the end of the session, prosecutors were satisfied that Jones would provide credible evidence against Atkins.

Addison had the option of pursuing a life sentence against Atkins or capital punishment. She decided that death was the more appropriate choice. Consequently, the day after the interview, she appeared before Judge Smiley and announced that the Commonwealth would seek the death penalty against Daryl Atkins.

The Atkins trial would be Addison's first death penalty case. Two factors played a significant role in her decision. First, Atkins had now been convicted of multiple felonies for his crime spree in Hampton. He had been sentenced to life in prison for shooting Amanda Hamlin plus over 100 years in the state penitentiary for the other offenses. Obtaining a life sentence as a penalty for the killing of Eric Nesbitt would add nothing to the sentence Atkins was already obliged to serve. The murder would "almost be a freebie," she would later say. Second, Mary Sloan and the other members of Eric Nesbitt's family supported the death penalty for Atkins.

Addison's announcement changed the nature of the legal proceedings that were to follow. Death is different than other criminal punishments. It is the ultimate penalty a government can impose on any of its citizens. And, importantly, it is a punishment that once carried out cannot be reversed. Because of these factors, the law imposes more rigorous safe-guards to protect the rights of the accused. The process moves with greater caution and levels of appellate review. The trials are more com-plex and demanding than normal criminal proceedings.

Addison's decision to seek the death penalty against Atkins surprised George Rogers, who had anticipated that his client would ultimately tes-tify to capital murder charges against William Jones. Because the decision to seek the death penalty came so close to the scheduled trial start date, Rogers asked for additional time to prepare. Judge Smiley granted the request, rescheduling the trial for February 9, 1998. Rogers also asked for the appointment of a second lawyer to assist in the defense as well as a mental health expert to evaluate Atkins. Judge Smiley agreed to both requests. As a result, Bryan Saunders, a Newport News criminal defense lawyer, joined the Atkins defense team.

AS THE FALL and early winter months passed, attorneys for both sides prepared their cases. The prosecution carried the obligation to prove guilt beyond a reasonable doubt. Addison was convinced that she had correctly determined who was immediately responsible for Eric Nesbitt's death, but meeting the high threshold of proof would be a difficult task. No one witnessed the murder except Daryl Atkins and William Jones. Not sur-prisingly, they were offering different accounts of what had happened. The murder weapon had never been found. Other forensic evidence was not conclusive.

Most disappointing were the results that came from the DNA tests of the blood samples. The tests were not completely consistent with either of the defendants' stories. Particularly puzzling was the blood found on the passenger seat and backrest of Nesbitt's truck. Tests showed that the blood came from Eric Nesbitt. Jones claimed that Atkins began firing at Nesbitt after the airman had taken a couple steps away from the truck. If that were the case, how did Nesbitt's blood get on the truck's seat? Nor did the evi-dence lend credibility to Atkins's version of the events. According to Atkins's statement, he was in the process of sliding from the middle to the passenger seat when the shooting began. If that were the case, how did Nesbitt's blood get on the truck seat where Atkins claimed to have been sitting?

This is not to say that Addison was without significant evidence supporting her theory of the case. She could easily show that Atkins was familiar with the place of the crime. She had jail-mate Stephen Burton's testimony that Atkins had admitted to him that he had shot at Nesbitt. Then, of course, there was the ATM photo with Atkins training the pistol on a terrified Eric Nesbitt. The visual impact that the image would have on a jury would be very difficult for the defense to counter. Still, would this be enough?

Similarly, George Rogers and Bryan Saunders now faced a difficult task in preparing a defense for Daryl Atkins. In constructing their case, the defense was aided by Virginia statutes and the decisions of the U.S. Supreme Court that permitted them to have access to the evidence collected by the prosecution. This procedure, known as "discovery," allows the defense to respond more fully and effectively to what the prosecutor intends to present at trial. The defense made a formal request for this privilege, and Judge Smiley granted "full and unfettered access to the Commonwealth's file."

Rogers and Saunders could certainly challenge the sufficiency of the prosecution's case. There was no direct evidence that Akins had fired the fatal shots. Although the agreement between Jones and the prosecution was a blow, they could easily attack William Jones's credibility and argue that his testimony was motivated by a desire to reduce his prison term. Similarly, the defense could portray Stephen Burton's offer to testify as nothing more than an attempt to make it worthwhile for the prosecution to substitute a petit larceny charge for the original grand theft accusation. Still, there was little the defense could offer in direct support of Daryl Atkins's version of the crime.

The more Rogers and Saunders dealt with their client the more they realized that there was much more to Daryl Atkins than a hardened, violent criminal. Although only eighteen years old when the murder of Eric Nesbitt occurred, Atkins had already led an unusually difficult life.

His family had experienced a painful divorce. A stepbrother, with whom Daryl was close, died in an asthma attack. He was born with physically deformed hands and feet.

Perhaps most important of all, Daryl Atkins seemed mentally slow. Many of the conditions of his life were consistent with the consequences of very low intellectual ability. From his very first years in school his academic performance was inadequate. He consistently earned below-average, frequently failing marks. He had to repeat the second and tenth grades. His classmates teased him for his low mental capacity. When he dropped out of high school, he carried a 1.26 grade-point average and ranked 347 out of 371 students. Daryl never held a job, could not pass a driver's license test, and never lived outside his parents' homes. The clinical psychologist retained by the defense administered standard intelligence tests and reported shockingly low scores.

As a possible consequence of repeatedly failing to meet conventional expectations, Daryl found acceptance with friends who consistently got into trouble, abused drugs and alcohol, and had little ambition. He increasingly spent time on the streets and away from his family. He began drinking in the ninth grade and soon graduated to marijuana with acid and cocaine to follow. These outside influences, coupled with his limited natural abilities, led him down a troubled path that ended with the death of Eric Nesbitt.

If the prosecution successfully obtained a conviction, Rogers and Saunders hoped that Atkins's background and mental deficiencies would be seen as sufficient mitigation to convince the jury that a long prison term would be a sufficient punishment. There was, in their view, no sound reason to take Daryl Atkins's life.

The trial of Daryl Atkins was quickly approaching. If convicted, the issue of capital punishment would be raised on sentencing. The trial and the sentencing phase that would follow would take place in accordance with Virginia law and a long line of U.S. Supreme Court decisions dealing with the death penalty.

BIBLIOGRAPHIC NOTE.

The story of the investigation of the Eric Nesbitt murder and the prosecution of Daryl Atkins and William Jones presented here is based on accounts provided from a number of sources. Among these are the transcripts from the pretrial motions, the trials and sentencing hearings for Atkins and Jones, as well as police, probation, and medical examiner reports and appellate court opinions. In addition, the Hampton Roads *Daily Press* covered the unfolding investigation quite well in both news reports and expressions of editorial opinion. The work of reporter Patti Rosenberg was particularly helpful, along with reports filed by Deborah Straszheim, Mark Di Vincenzo, Jennifer Andes, Beverly Williams, and Amy Gardner.

For those desiring to read more generally on the topics raised in this chapter, the following works may be of interest:

On the nature and function of criminal law: John M. Scheb and John M. Scheb, Jr., *Criminal Law,* 4th ed. (Belmont, Calif: Thomson/ Wadsworth, 2006); Joel Samaha, *Criminal Law,* 9th ed. (Belmont, Calif.: Thomson/ West, 2008).

On constitutional criminal procedure: Phillip Johnson and A. Morgan Cloud, *Constitutional Criminal Procedure: Investigation to Trial,* 4th ed. (St. Paul, Minn.: West, 2007); Jerrold H. Israel, Yale Kamisar, Wayne R. LaFave, and Nancy J. King, *Criminal Procedure and the Constitution* (St. Paul, Minn.: West, 2007); Marvin Zalman and Larry J. Siegel, *Criminal Procedure: Constitution and Society,* 2d ed. (Belmont, Calif.: West/ Wadsworth, 1997); John M. Scheb and John M. Scheb Jr., *Criminal Procedure,* 4th ed. (Belmont, Calif.: Thomson/Wadsworth, 2006).

On the law pertaining to criminal investigations: Frank W. Miller, Robert O. Dawson, George E. Dix, and Raymond I. Parnas, *The Police Function,* 6th ed. (New York: Foundation Press, 2000); Lloyd L. Weinreb, *Criminal Process: Investigation,* 3d ed. (New York: Foundation Press, 2004); Joshua Dressler and George C. Thomas III, *Criminal Procedure: Investigating Crime,* 3d ed. (St. Paul, Minn.: West, 2006); Samuel Dash, *The Intruders: Unreasonable Searches and Seizures from King John to John Ashcroft* (New Brunswick, N.J.: Rutgers University Press, 2004).

On the legal aspects of the prosecutorial stages: Frank W. Miller, Robert O. Dawson, George E. Dix, and Raymond L. Parnas, *Prosecution and Adjudication,* 5th ed. (New York: Foundation Press, 2000); Lloyd L. Weinreb, *Criminal Process: Prosecution,* 3d ed. (New York: Foundation Press, 2004); Joshua Dressler and George C. Thomas III, *Criminal Procedure: Prosecuting Crime,* 3d ed. (St. Paul, Minn.: West, 2007).

On the court system and judicial process of the United States: Lawrence Baum, *American Courts,* 6th ed. (Boston: Houghton Mifflin, 2008); Robert A. Carp, Ronald Stidham, and Kenneth L. Manning, *Judicial Process in the United States,* 7th ed. (Washington D.C.: CQ Press, 2007); David W. Neubauer and Stephen S. Meinhold, *Judicial Process: Law, Courts, and Politics in the United States,* 4th ed. (Belmont, Calif.: Thomson/Wadsworth, 2007).

On the *Powell* and *Gideon* decisions extending the right of government provided attorneys for indigent criminal defendants: Dan T. Carter, *Scottsboro: A Tragedy of the American South* (New York: Oxford University Press, 1969); Anthony Lewis, *Gideon's Trumpet* (New York: Vintage Books, 1964).

On the role of a criminal defense attorney in capital cases: Welsh S. White, *Litigating in the Shadow of Death: Defense Attorneys in Capital Cases* (Ann Arbor: University of Michigan Press, 2006).

On plea bargaining: Mary E. Vogel, *Coercion to Compromise* (New York: Oxford University Press, 2007); Richard P. Adelstein, *The Negotiated Plea* (New York: Garland, 1984); Milton Heumann, *Plea Bargaining* (Chicago: University of Chicago Press, 1978); George Fisher, *Plea Bargaining's Triumph* (Stanford, Calif.: Stanford University Press, 2003); Michael McConville and Chester Mirsky, *Jury Trials and Plea Bargaining* (Portland, Ore.: Hart Publications, 2005); James Edward Bond, *Plea Bargaining and Guilty Pleas* (New York: Boardman, 1982).

Capital Punishment from Jamestown to *Furman*

THE USE OF EXECUTION as a penalty for criminal violations can be traced back to the very first chapters of recorded history. As early as the eighteenth century BC, Babylon's King Hammurabi promulgated a legal code that included the death penalty. The Greek and Roman civilizations that followed also practiced capital punishment. And the death penalty was regularly used in England. It is not surprising, then, that the English settlers who first came to the colonies along the Atlantic Seaboard brought capital punishment with them. The first execution by English colonists took place in Virginia in 1608, 168 years before the colonies declared their independence from Britain. Captain George Kendall, one of the original settlers and a leader in Jamestown Colony, was convicted by a jury of spying for Spain and shot to death.

Throughout U.S. history, the death penalty has been a constitutionally permissible sentence for those who have committed society's most serious crimes. Executions in the modern era reached a peak in the 1930s when between 140 and 199 felons were put to death each year. As the nation entered the twenty-first century, thirty-eight states, the federal government, and the U.S. military had laws permitting the use of capital punishment, although lawsuits and executive orders at times have required temporary suspension of the punishment in some states.

The method of execution has evolved over time as more humane methods of inflicting death have been developed. At the time the Constitution was ratified, hanging was the primary means of execution. Firing

46

squads were also employed, but most commonly for crimes related to military conduct. In the late nineteenth century, electrocution was touted as a more certain and humane method of execution. In 1890 New York became the first state to use the electric chair, an execution method that quickly spread to other states. In the 1920s cyanide gas was suggested as an even more humane way to implement a death sentence. Nevada led the way, putting convicted murderer Gee Jong to death by lethal gas in 1924. California used its gas chamber more frequently than other states, executing almost 200 convicts at San Quentin prison over a six-decade period. In the more contemporary era, electrocution and gas have given way to lethal injection as the primary method of carrying out a death sentence. Once again, the movement toward this alternative was motivated by the goal of adopting a method more humane and less prone to malfunction than other means. In 1977 Oklahoma became the first state to write lethal injection into its criminal code, and five years later Texas first executed a man using this procedure.

By 2007, all of the death penalty states except Nebraska had adopted lethal injection. In most of those states it has become the only authorized method for those sentenced after its implementation. A handful of states prefer lethal injection, but give those convicted the choice of selecting another authorized option. And a few other states have approved an alternative method should lethal injection not be available for any reason.

American citizens have long supported capital punishment. Polling data, extending as far back as the 1930s, have consistently revealed that between 60 and 80 percent of the public favors permitting the death penalty for those convicted of murder. For only a brief period during the 1960s did the rate of support dip below 50 percent. This is not to say that a majority of Americans believe that all murderers should be executed. In fact, many capital punishment supporters would advocate the application of lesser penalties, such as life in prison without parole, for most defendants convicted of homicidal acts. It does mean, however, that the general reservoir of support for the death penalty is sufficiently strong and widespread that it would be politically difficult to eliminate it as an available sentencing option.

In spite of this general support, there have always been active groups of individuals who have objected to the death penalty and campaigned for its abolition. The first major success occurred in 1846 when Michigan abolished the death penalty for all crimes except treason. This was soon followed by legal reforms in Rhode Island and Wisconsin that totally rejected the penalty. Most abolitionist victories, however, were more limited. Some states significantly reduced the number of crimes for which execution was a possible penalty or limited mandatory death sentences. In the long run, however, supporters of the death penalty have held the upper hand. By 2008 only fourteen states and the District of Columbia did not permit capital punishment, although some death penalty states (for example, Kansas and New Hampshire) almost never use it.

UNDER THE AMERICAN system of justice, criminal punishments cannot be handed down in an arbitrary or capricious manner. Rather, sentences must be rationally related to valid government interests. Criminal justice theorists traditionally cite four legitimate objectives that are advanced by imposing punishments on those who violate the law: retribution, deterrence, incapacitation, and rehabilitation. Supporters and opponents of capital punishment often argue their positions based on the relationship of the death penalty to one or more of these four goals.

Retribution is based on elementary concepts of justice. If a criminal law is broken, the perpetrator must pay a penalty for the transgression. In addition, the penalty or sentence should be comparable in harshness to the severity of the offense and the culpability of the accused. Retribution, therefore, resembles the biblical prescription: "But if there is serious injury, you are to take life for life, eye for eye, tooth for tooth."(Exodus, 21:23–24). Offenders must pay their debts to society by enduring a punishment proportionate to their crime. Only then are the scales of justice brought into proper balance. Sentences that are unreasonably harsh or excessively lenient are not considered just.

Capital punishment supporters argue that for society's most serious crimes, especially premeditated murder, only the death penalty can bring about justice. If society values life above all else, then the injustice resulting from a deliberate homicide can only be redeemed by the forfeiture of the murderer's life. No lesser penalty is just, and no lesser penalty adequately expresses society's reprehension over taking innocent life.

Death penalty opponents reject this reasoning as a contradiction. The state cannot proclaim the value of human life and at the same time execute those found in violation of the law. If killing is an immoral act that merits condemnation, then a state that sponsors executions also engages in an immoral act. Capital punishment for retribution purposes provides no tangible benefits to society, opponents say. At best the death penalty appeals to rudimentary notions of justice, but civilization has advanced to the point that such primitive emotions should be replaced by more important values.

Deterrence, a second objective of punishment, offers the promise of a more tangible benefit, a reduction in the incidence of crime. When punishment is imposed with deterrence objectives in mind, society uses the offender as an example for others. The sentence should teach that committing a crime does not pay. Consequently, when others contemplate an illegal act they may decide not to carry out their planned crime because of the potential penalty. For deterrence to work effectively the punishment must be sufficiently severe to outweigh the potential payoff flowing from the criminal act.

Capital punishment advocates argue that the death penalty has a deterrent effect. Persons contemplating homicide will be more reluctant to proceed if it is likely that they will have to sacrifice their own lives as a consequence, especially if the sentence is swift and certain.

Death penalty opponents respond that there is no convincing evidence that capital punishment has any deterrent effect above and beyond that of life imprisonment without parole. The fact that those states with the highest murder rates also tend to be the states that impose capital punishment undermines the validity of deterrence claims. Murders occur at an alarming pace; murderers are not deterred. Many do not consider the possible consequences before they act. In addition, death sentences are meted out in a small proportion of all capital cases, and appeals from death sentences may take decades. Thus, justice is neither swift nor certain, blunting any possible deterrent effect capital punishment may have.

In the end, of course, the effectiveness of deterrence is exceptionally hard to evaluate. We know that each time a crime is committed deterrence has not worked. Yet we have little way of identifying the number of times criminal activity is contemplated, but fear of punishment persuades the would-be offender not to carry out the illegal act.

Incapacitation, a third objective of punishment, recognizes that criminal behavior is frequently not an isolated event. Rather, those who engage in crimes may do so repeatedly. When such recidivism is likely, society may need to impose penalties to protect the law-abiding public. In the most common situation persons convicted of crimes are incarcerated in order to isolate them from society, thus removing their capacity to violate the law. If an individual is sentenced to ten years in prison for robbery, for example, society is protected against being victimized by that person for the length of the incarceration. Like deterrence, the objective of incapacitation is to reduce future infractions.

Capital punishment supporters claim that the death penalty is the ultimate method of incapacitation. Once the sentence is carried out, there is no danger that a murderer will ever kill again. Society may be generally protected by long prison terms, but without capital punishment imprisoned convicts may engage in homicidal acts against fellow inmates without fear of significant, additional punishment. And, of course, early release programs, such as parole, and possible prison escapes reintroduce a danger to the public.

Death penalty opponents reject this reasoning. They argue that long prison terms, especially those without the possibility of parole, impose sufficient protections, virtually removing the possibility of innocent people becoming victims. In addition, there are relatively few instances of escapes from penal institutions or homicides taking place in the structured environment of a prison. In short, incarceration is sufficient; there is no need to execute.

A fourth objective of criminal punishment is rehabilitation. This theory basically holds that many convicts, with appropriate support, can turn their lives around and lead a productive existence. When capital punishment is imposed, of course, rehabilitation goals are sacrificed for other objectives. Death penalty supporters argue that this sacrifice is appropriate, because many murderers are beyond the point where rehabilitation is likely. Some death penalty opponents, however, emphasize the value of rehabilitation, claiming there is always the possibility of redemption. Even if never released back into society, a person may be able to lead a life of some merit in the confines of a correctional facility.

In addition to these traditional arguments for and against capital punishment, other objections to the death penalty are frequently raised. One of the most important is that "death is different." Unlike a prison sentence from which a person may be released if sufficient evidence emerges that the conviction was unjust, the death penalty, once administered, is irrevocable. There are no methods of reversal. In spite of the many procedural safeguards that are in place in capital cases, errors do occur. These may be due to any number of factors including over-zealous prosecutors, ineffective defense attorneys, evidence of questionable validity, and honest misjudgments by jurors. There is also evidence that racial and ethnic bias make it more likely that minority defendants, especially those who murder white victims, will be sentenced to death. According to the Death Penalty Information Center, between 1973 and 2005 more than 120 people were released from death row because of evidence of their innocence. For death penalty opponents, such statistics are a staggering indictment of America's capital punishment system and reason alone to abolish the death penalty.

Supporters of the death penalty counter that the number of individuals who are released from death row are actually examples of the system working correctly. In each case the procedural safeguards firmly in place have identified and corrected errors that may have occurred at the trial court level. There is no significant evidence, they argue, of innocent individuals being executed, a claim denied by those favoring abolition.

Another factor, more practical than legal or moral, is the financial cost of capital punishment. Contrary to the belief of many, it is much more expensive for a state to impose the death penalty than to condemn a convict to life in prison. Capital trials are more expensive than trials for which the death penalty is not sought. Every death sentence is appealed, most of them multiple times. For appeals of capital cases the legal fees for both the prosecution and, in most cases, for the defense as well, are borne by the state. The appellate process and subsequent procedural maneuverings literally may take well over a decade to complete, a time during which the state is supporting the convicted murderer in prison. And, of course, it is not unusual for the final court ruling to commute the defendant's sentence to life in prison. One report published in the *Dallas Morning News* found that in Texas, the state that leads by far all others in the number of executions, the average death penalty case costs the state $2.3 million, more than three times the expense of maintaining a convict in a high security prison for a forty-year term.

Capital punishment supporters often challenge the validity of such financial comparisons, but also contend that imposing just punishments and deterring future crimes make the added expense worthwhile. Many argue that the system can be improved by restricting the seemingly endless appellate process in order to limit the extended delays in applying the penalty, reduce the overall costs, and make the penalty more effective in discouraging future crimes.

Debates over the death penalty involve complex issues of morality, law, and fact. They have been ongoing since the days the English colonists first brought capital punishment to the newly established American settlements. Although the penalty itself was generally accepted, influential early Americans such as Benjamin Franklin, William Bradford, and Thomas Jefferson advocated significantly reducing the range of crimes for which death could be imposed.

Today the debate is largely fueled by organizations made up of members who are passionately committed to their beliefs. Abolitionist groups exist in large numbers. Some, such as the National Coalition to Abolish the Death Penalty, have a national orientation while others, like Amnesty International, have operations in many nations. Many more anti-death penalty groups are organized at the state and local level, focusing their efforts on conditions existing in their own communities. Additional organizations opposing capital punishment are based on professional positions (e.g., criminal defense attorneys) or religious beliefs. Still others, such as various civil rights groups, oppose capital punishment in part because of its disproportionate impact on minorities and the poor. The abolitionist organizations engage in a wide variety of activities, including litigation, education, publicity campaigns, and lobbying governments to restrict the use of the death penalty.

Given that public opinion generally supports the death penalty, some anti-capital punishment groups focus on legal strategies such as sponsoring lawsuits and funding appeals. Bringing legal arguments to the federal courts where public opinion has a minimal effect on the non-elected, life-tenured judges is viewed as a particularly effective way to oppose capital punishment. Two of the most influential groups that have waged long-standing legal campaigns against the death penalty are the American Civil Liberties Union (ACLU) and the National Association for the Advancement of Colored People (NAACP). Both groups, of course, have areas of interest that extended far beyond capital punishment. The ACLU is involved in a wide array of civil liberties issues, such as speech, religion, discrimination, and criminal due process more generally. The NAACP, through its Legal Defense Fund affiliate, has been the leading litigator against discrimination based on race.

Pro-death penalty groups are less numerous, with most representing law enforcement interests or those advocating for victims' rights. Among the most prominent of the national organizations is the Criminal Justice Legal Foundation, a public interest organization devoted to supporting strong enforcement of criminal laws and maintaining what it believes to be the proper balance between the rights of the accused and the importance of prosecuting and punishing criminals. It mainly focuses on bringing legal arguments to the courts that promote a swift and decisive criminal justice system. Many of the other pro-death penalty groups are dedicated to advancing the rights of crime victims. They oppose the portrayal of capital offenders as sympathetic figures and the martyrs of injustice. Too often forgotten, they argue, are the brutality and senselessness of the crimes and suffering of the victims and their families.

IN THE EIGHTEENTH CENTURY the Framers of the U.S. Constitution instituted legal assurances that criminal procedures would be fair and proper. In drafting the Bill of Rights, members of the first Congress sought to guarantee more than just the freedoms of speech, press, and religion. They also limited the government's ability to abuse individual rights during the criminal process. The investigation and prosecution of Daryl Atkins and William Jones for the murder of Eric Nesbitt highlight some of these safeguards. In their attempt to apprehend Jones, for example, police initially could not search the King James Motel because they lacked the necessary probable cause required by the Fourth Amendment. When taken into custody, the two suspects were informed of their Fifth Amendment right to remain silent. And Atkins and Jones, both indigent, were supplied defense attorneys at state expense consistent with the Sixth Amendment's guarantee of the right to counsel.

As part of their concern for a fair criminal justice system, the Framers addressed the issue of unjust punishments. Having witnessed the imposition of unacceptably barbaric criminal penalties in early modern Europe, they desired a constitutional barrier against such sentences in the United States. For this reason the Eighth Amendment was adopted. After prohibiting excessive fines and bail, this amendment includes the following language prohibiting barbaric penalties: "nor cruel and unusual punishments inflicted."

The Eighth Amendment, like the other provisions of the Bill of Rights, was originally intended to apply to the federal government only, not the states. But through a long historical process that started in the late nineteenth century the U.S. Supreme Court extended portions of the Bill of Rights to the states. Invoking a doctrine called "selective incorporation," the justices on a case-by-case basis considered the degree to which each of the various provisions of the Bill of Rights protected a "fundamental freedom." Those rights that were considered fundamental could not be violated by the states. For a state to do so would be to deny a person "life, liberty or property without due process of law," a deprivation prohibited by the Fourteenth Amendment. By the end of the twentieth century, the Court had extended all but a few Bill of Rights provisions to the states.

The application of the Cruel and Unusual Punishment Clause to the states occurred relatively late in the selective incorporation process. In *Louisiana ex rel. Francis v. Resweber* (1947), the Supreme Court expressed an assumption that the states were constitutionally obliged to abide by the Eighth Amendment, but the justices waited until *Robinson v. California* (1962) to mandate state compliance officially. Prior to the incorporation of the Eighth Amendment the Supreme Court heard few cases challenging the constitutionality of state-imposed punishments, but when it did the justices evaluated the penalty against a general due process of law standard that prohibits arbitrary and capricious government actions.

The phrase "cruel and unusual punishment" has a long history in English common law. The term is included explicitly in the 1689 English Declaration of Rights and its roots can be traced back to the Magna Carta of 1215. Although the phrase lacks specificity, Chief Justice Earl Warren's opinion in *Trop v. Dulles* (1958) summed up its general meaning: "The basic concept underlying the Eighth Amendment is nothing less than the dignity of man. While the State has the power to punish, the Amendment stands to assure that this power be exercised within the limits of civilized standards."

The general intent of the provision is obvious, but its specific meaning defies precise interpretation. What kinds of punishments fall into the "cruel and unusual" category? The wording is vague, and the debates over the adoption of the Bill of Rights are not enlightening. Legal provisions that lack clarity in wording or intended purpose often lead to legal disputes that the courts are obliged to settle. Ultimately, the U.S. Supreme Court in the course of deciding an appeal may be called upon to provide an authoritative interpretation of a contested constitutional provision. When the Supreme Court does so, its interpretation becomes binding precedent. Under a principle known as *stare decisis,* the Supreme Court is expected to adhere to its interpretation in deciding future cases until such time as the justices find sufficient cause to alter the precedent or the Constitution is amended. In addition, all state and federal lower courts are bound to apply the Supreme Court's interpretation when hearing similar cases. *Stare decisis* brings a degree of stability and predictability to the law.

The Supreme Court periodically has been called upon to interpret the Cruel and Unusual Punishment Clause. The Court's decisions have yielded some basic principles that help us understand what the Eighth Amendment means.

First, there is universal agreement that the cruel and unusual punishment provision was designed to bar sentences that inflict great pain or torture. Justice Nathan Clifford, speaking for a unanimous Court in *Wilk-erson v. Utah* (1878), acknowledged the problems inherent in providing a precise meaning of the Eighth Amendment, but did offer some sugges-tions concerning constitutionally unacceptable punishments. "Difficulty would attend the effort to define with exactness the extent of the consti-tutional provision which provides that cruel and unusual punishments shall not be inflicted; but it is safe to affirm that punishments of torture, such as [drawing and quartering, disemboweling, beheading, burning alive], and all others of the same unnecessary cruelty, are forbidden by that amendment to the Constitution." This emphasizes the importance not only of the punishment, but also of the manner by which the punish-ment is carried out. Imprisonment, for example, may be a perfectly acceptable penalty, yet the conditions of the prison could be such that the Eighth Amendment is violated.

Second, the Supreme Court has emphasized that the Eighth Amend-ment is not static. Its reach is not confined to those punishments that were considered cruel and unusual when the Eighth Amendment was ratified in 1791. Instead, the amendment's prohibitions change as society's view of which punishments are cruel and unusual changes. This principle was most clearly articulated in *Trop v. Dulles* (1958).

U.S. Army private Albert Trop, serving in French Morocco in 1944, was placed in the stockade at Casablanca for breach of discipline. On May 22 he escaped. The next day, having a change of heart, Trop started walking back toward Casablanca to turn himself in. Along the way he was picked up by an army truck and turned over to the military police. Although he had been gone less than a day and had willingly surrendered, Trop was charged with desertion during wartime. Convicted by a general court martial, he was sentenced to three years at hard labor, loss of all pay and allowances, and a dishonorable discharge. In 1952, long after World War II had ended and his sentenced served, Trop applied for a passport and was denied. He was informed that under federal law any person dishon-orably discharged for wartime desertion suffered an automatic loss of U.S. citizenship. As a stateless person, he was not entitled to travel abroad under the authority or protection of the United States. Trop later sued to have his citizenship restored.

A five-justice majority of the Supreme Court ruled in favor of Trop, vacating the government's action against him. Four members of that majority reached this conclusion based on the Eighth Amendment. Speaking for them, Chief Justice Warren stated, "[T]he words of the [cruel and unusual punishment provision] are not precise and their scope is not static. The Amendment must draw its meaning from the evolving standards of decency that mark the progress of a maturing society." Warren concluded that the stripping of citizenship as a criminal penalty now violated America's standards of decency. He explained, "We believe ... that use of denationalization as a punishment is barred by the Eighth Amendment. There may be involved no physical mistreatment, no primitive torture. There is instead the total destruction of the individual's status in organized society. It is a form of punishment more primitive than torture, for it destroys for the individual the political existence that was centuries in the development."

The "evolving standards of decency" principle makes the interpretation of the Cruel and Unusual Punishment Clause unusual compared to other sections of the Constitution. The provision does not impose firmly established standards, but allows the identification of prohibited punishments to adjust over time as society's values mature and change. How does a court determine the status of society's evolving standards? What criteria would a judge use in determining whether society now considers a particular penalty to be unacceptable? The Supreme Court often looks to the actions of the various state legislatures for guidance. If the states in significant numbers begin to modify or repeal certain punishments, the justices are more likely to conclude that the nation's standards of decency have changed. The justices might also look to the decisions of juries and even public opinion as guides to such standards. Some members of the Court have advocated looking to the international community to define what punishments are acceptable to civilized mankind. There are, however, often deep divisions inside the Court concerning what sources should be given credence in the process of determining society's standards.

A third basic principle is that criminal punishments cannot be imposed because of a person's status or condition. Rather, such penalties can only be meted out when an individual commits an illegal act or fails to carry out a legally required one. This principle was set in *Robinson v. California* (1962). At issue was the constitutionality of a state law making it a crime "to be addicted to the use of narcotics." The state, according to the Court, is free to punish the acts of purchasing, possessing, or selling illegal drugs, but addiction to them is a condition. "It is unlikely that any State at this moment in history would attempt to make it a criminal offense for a person to be mentally ill, or a leper, or to be afflicted with a venereal disease," Justice Potter Stewart wrote for the Court. "But, in the light of contemporary human knowledge, a law which made a criminal offense of such a disease would doubtless be universally thought to be an infliction of cruel and unusual punishment in violation of the Eighth and Fourteenth Amendments."

A fourth basic principle, and one over which there is significant controversy, is proportionality. This standard simply means that the severity of the sentence should be roughly equivalent to the seriousness of the crime. The Court's first significant pronouncement of this principle came in *Weems v. United States* (1910). The case involved Paul Weems, a Coast Guard dispersing officer serving in the Philippines when it was a territory of the United States. Weems was convicted under Philippine law of falsifying documents in order to defraud the United States. His sentence was fifteen years at hard and painful labor (during which time he was to be chained from the wrist to the ankle), a fine, and the loss of various parental, marital, and property rights. Even after his release from prison he was subject to government surveillance, loss of retirement pay, and forfeiture of various rights of political participation. The majority cited several crimes of greater seriousness that carried maximum penalties much less severe and concluded that Weems's sentence was unconstitutionally excessive and disproportionate to the seriousness of the crime.

In the more contemporary period, the Court has experienced a great deal of fragmentation over the proportionality principle. While more liberal justices tend to adhere to the traditional approach, some members of the Court, such as Antonin Scalia, reject the notion that the Eighth Amendment requires proportionality at all. These debates have been played out in decisions such as *Harmelin v. Michigan* (1991), which upheld a Michigan statute imposing life in prison for those convicted of possessing large quantities of cocaine, and *Ewing v. California* (2003), holding constitutionally valid so called "three strikes" laws that allow long prison sentences for those convicted of a third serious felony. The proportionality principle remains viable, but the contemporary Court is not likely to vacate a sentence unless it is "grossly disproportionate" to the seriousness of the crime. Commonly the justices have given considerable deference to the legislatures in determining what range of penalties is needed and appropriate for various crimes.

THE RELEVANCE OF the cruel and unusual punishment provision to capital punishment has a long and continuing legal history. The Supreme Court has been called upon many times to consider challenges to the death penalty. In a number of cases the justices found constitutional defects with the way in which capital punishment decisions were reached or how death penalty laws were applied. Some of these cases involved constitutional provisions other than just the Eighth Amendment. Criminal sentencing, for example, must also be consistent with concepts of essential fairness as required by due process guarantees of the Fifth and Fourteenth Amendments. And the Equal Protection Clause of the Fourteenth Amendment prohibits discrimination based on race or other illegitimate characteristics in determining guilt and appropriate penalties. In spite of these guarantees the Court has never ruled that the death penalty *per se* violates the Eighth Amendment or any other constitutional provision.

There is no evidence to support an argument that the Framers intended the Eighth Amendment to prohibit the death penalty. Capital punishment was not only quite common in England and other European nations in the eighteenth century, but was also standard for serious offenses in the American colonies. After ratification of the Bill of Rights, the death penalty remained a customary punishment with no significant vocal protest that it violated the new amendments. In addition, the text of the Bill of Rights allows an inference that capital punishment was viewed as an acceptable penalty. The Fifth Amendment declares that "No person shall ... be deprived of life, liberty or property, without due process of law." This implies, of course, that the government may take a person's life as long as it does so consistent with due process principles. The same language was repeated with specific reference to state governments when the Fourteenth Amendment was ratified in 1868.

With capital punishment commonly accepted, nineteenth century legal arguments against death sentences focused more on the method of execution. Whatever mode is used, death should be relatively painless and instant. Torturous, long, and lingering deaths were constitutionally suspect.

The first challenge to a method of execution reached the Supreme Court in *Wilkerson v. Utah* in 1878. Wallace Wilkerson was charged in the Utah Territory with the "willful, malicious, and premeditated murder" of William Baxter in a saloon brawl over a card game. A jury found him guilty of first-degree murder, a crime punishable by death under the laws of the Utah territory. The law, however, did not prescribe the mode of execution, presumably leaving this decision to the trial court judge. For Wilkerson, the judge commanded that he "be publicly shot until . . . dead." Wilkerson challenged the sentence, in part because hanging was the more commonly used method of execution, making public shooting "cruel and unusual." The Supreme Court did not agree, however. Unanimously the justices ruled that "Cruel and unusual punishments are forbidden by the Constitution, but the authorities . . . are quite sufficient to show that the punishment of shooting as a mode of executing the death penalty for the crime of murder in the first degree is not included in that category, within the meaning of the eighth amendment."

A decade later, the Supreme Court faced a similar issue, only this time the target was a new and not yet widely applied execution method—electrocution. William Kemmler, convicted of killing his mistress Tillie Ziegler with a hatchet during a drunken quarrel, was sentenced to death under a new law in New York establishing the electric chair as the state's method of taking a convict's life. Because the Eighth Amendment had not yet been made applicable to the states, Kemmler challenged the sentence claiming that electrocution was not consistent with Fourteenth Amendment due process standards. In *In re Kemmler* (1890) the Supreme Court denied his petition. The justices upheld the conclusions of the lower New York courts, saying "Punishments are cruel when they involve torture or a lingering death; but the punishment of death is not cruel, within the meaning of that word as used in the Constitution. It implies ... something inhuman and barbarous, and something more than the mere extinguishment of life." Electrocution was unusual only in the sense that it was new. The intent of the legislature was to employ a method of death that was purportedly less cruel and barbarous than those previously used. No federal constitutional right was violated. On August 6, 1890, less than three months after the Supreme Court's ruling, William Kemmler became the first person in the United States executed by electrocution.

In the first half of the twentieth century public support for the death penalty was quite high as was the number of executions that took place. For most of that period the Supreme Court did not face any serious Eighth Amendment challenges to capital punishment. An exception came in 1947 when the justices were presented with a rather unusual set of facts in the case of *Louisiana ex rel. Francis v. Resweber*.

In November 1944, a white pharmacist in St. Martinville, Louisiana, was found murdered. His wallet and other valuables had been taken. The crime remained unsolved for some time until Willie Francis, an African American teenager who had previously lived in St. Martinville, was detained in Texas during a routine investigation of another crime. Texas authorities found the wallet of the murdered druggist in Francis's pocket. He was returned to Louisiana where he confessed to the murder. He was quickly tried in September 1945, found guilty, and sentenced to death.

On May 3, 1946, the portable electric chair used for Louisiana executions was set up and wired. At noon Francis was strapped into the chair. At the given command, the executioner pulled the switch. After a momentary delay, a jolt of electricity surged through Francis's body. As witnesses of the execution later described, Francis's lips puffed up, his body tensed, shook, and jumped. He groaned and pleaded for air. But he did not die. It was obvious to those present that the chair was malfunctioning. After unsuccessful attempts to increase the voltage, the machine was shut off. Francis, stunned but in otherwise good health, was led back to a cell. The governor scheduled another execution date for one week later.

Before the second execution date, however, lawyers took legal action on Francis's behalf. Their attack rested on a number of grounds, one of which was an argument that a second execution attempt would violate due process of law because it would be a cruel and unusual punishment. Specifically they claimed that the second attempt would cause Francis once again to undergo the psychological stress and torment of having to prepare mentally for another electrocution. This would constitute a long, lingering application of the death penalty, much more severe than that suffered by others who are sentenced to be executed for similar crimes. Certainly, they argued, this constitutes a punishment that is cruel and unusual.

The Court's majority, however, rejected this and other arguments. "[T]he fact that petitioner has already been subjected to a current of electricity does not make his subsequent execution any more cruel in the constitutional sense than any other execution," wrote Justice Stanley Reed. "The cruelty against which the Constitution protects a convicted man is cruelty inherent in the method of punishment, not the necessary suffering involved in any method employed to extinguish life humanely. The fact that an unforeseeable accident prevented the prompt consummation of the sentence cannot, it seems to us, add an element of cruelty to a subsequent execution. There is no purpose to inflict unnecessary pain nor any unnecessary pain involved in the proposed execution."

On May 9, 1947, four months after the Supreme Court ruled, Willie Francis was again strapped into the electric chair and the switch was thrown. This time the process and the equipment worked as intended, and Willie Francis died.

If the Supreme Court was not willing to find a constitutional violation under such extreme circumstances, it was not likely that the justices would declare standard executions to be prohibited by the Constitution. Given the Court's hard-line position in the *Francis* case, it was almost two decades before another significant attempt was made to persuade the justices to eliminate or limit the death penalty.

By the mid-1960s, however, things started to change. The political winds began shifting to a more liberal position. In 1966 public support for capital punishment declined to 42 percent, according to the Gallup Poll, the lowest recorded level of support in U.S. history. The 1960s had witnessed a Supreme Court whose members were much more sensitive to the rights of the criminally accused than at any previous time in the institution's history. Such trends gave anti-death penalty forces renewed motivation to attack capital punishment. Given the Supreme Court's history, however, a direct frontal attack on the constitutionality of the death penalty appeared hopeless. Instead, abolitionist lawyers decided a better strategy was to chip away at the application of capital punishment by convincing the Court to remove certain classes of people from death penalty eligibility or to tighten procedures to make it less likely that capital trials would end in a death penalty sentence.

Like Daryl Atkins, Willie Francis was a teenager charged with murder who challenged the constitutionality of his death sentence. He is shown here with the date of his second scheduled execution, May 9, 1947, circled on his calendar.

Initial appeals to the justices were encouraging. In *United States v. Jackson* (1968), for example, the justices struck down a provision of the Federal Kidnapping Act that allowed the death penalty to be imposed only if it were recommended by a jury. The Court found this statute unconstitutional because it encouraged kidnapping defendants to waive their right to a jury trial as a means of avoiding the death penalty. This, the justices found, was an impermissible burden on the exercise of the constitutional right to a jury trial.

That same year the Court in *Witherspoon v. Illinois* (1968) struck down a state statute that allowed the dismissal of potential jurors who expressed "conscientious scruples" against the death penalty. State prosecutors used this law to challenge prospective jurors who had any death penalty reservations. The justices found that eliminating potential jurors who expressed even modest objections to capital punishment produced unrepresentative juries biased in favor of the death penalty. As Justice Potter Stewart said for the Court, "Whatever else might be said of capital punishment, it is at least clear that its imposition by a hanging jury cannot be squared with the Constitution. The State of Illinois has stacked the deck against the petitioner."

In subsequent decisions, the Court made clear that jurors, whatever their views on the death penalty, must be capable of applying the law. Prospective jurors whose capital punishment views are so strong that they are unable to recommend the death penalty under any circumstances can be rejected. So too, jurors who steadfastly hold to the position that all capital offenders must be executed can also be excused. In both cases, such prospective jurors are incapable of carrying out their responsibilities to apply the law based on the evidence presented at trial.

Cases such as *Jackson* and *Witherspoon* were only the first of many appeals working their way through the judicial system advancing constitutional attacks on significant aspects of the capital punishment system. With so many capital punishment issues pending the states imposed an unofficial moratorium on executions while they awaited definitive rulings by the U.S. Supreme Court. In 1968, for the first time there were no executions in the United States.

The long awaited response of the Supreme Court came like a thunderbolt in 1972 when the justices handed down *Furman v. Georgia.* The decision was a stunning victory for death penalty opponents. The case originated in August 1967. Twenty-nine year old William Micke Jr. and his wife were asleep in their Savannah home when they heard unusual noises from the kitchen. Thinking one of their five children had gotten up from bed, Micke went to investigate. Rather than a child, Micke found William Furman, a black man in his twenties, who had broken into the house. Furman, armed with a gun, reacted by attempting to run from the house. In the commotion that ensued a shot was fired, hitting Micke in the chest and killing him. Furman claimed the shooting was unintentional, that he had tripped in his attempt to escape and the gun accidentally discharged. Whether Furman was telling the truth will never be known, but legally it made little difference. Under Georgia law at that time, the killing of another person, intentional or not, during the commission of a burglary was potentially punishable by execution. After finding Furman guilty, the jury recommended a death sentence. The Georgia Supreme Court later upheld the jury's decision.

With *Furman* as the lead case, the Court consolidated for review two other appeals presenting similar issues. *Jackson v. Georgia* focused on the fate of Lucious Jackson, an escapee from a prison work gang, who broke into a home and raped a woman while holding scissors to her throat. And *Branch v. Texas* presented the appeal of Elmer Branch, who had been found guilty of using physical force to rape a sixty-five-year-old widow in her home. Jackson and Branch, like Furman, were African American and their victims were white. Each was sentenced to death. The Court asked the parties to focus their arguments on a single question: does the imposition and carrying out of the death penalty in these cases constitute cruel and unusual punishment?

Furman's case attracted the participation of anti-death penalty and civil rights groups such as the ACLU and NAACP. The civil rights position was strongly asserted by the NAACP Legal Defense Fund, which contended that capital punishment violated the Eighth Amendment in part because juries disproportionately applied the death penalty to African Americans. Black defendants whose crimes and criminal backgrounds were similar to white defendants were much more likely to receive the ultimate penalty. The racial disparities, the organization's attorneys argued, could not be explained away by legally relevant factors.

Many Court observers thought William Furman and his supporters had little chance of winning the case. One of their main points of argument was that the states gave excessive discretion to juries during the process of arriving at sentencing recommendations. The lack of clear sentencing guidelines enhanced the probability of extra-legal factors influencing sentencing decisions and increased the likelihood of arbitrary and discriminatory outcomes. Just one year before in *McGautha v. California* (1971), the justices, by a 6–3 vote, rejected the argument of a condemned murderer that state laws giving unbridled discretion to juries violated the Due Process Clause of the Fourteenth Amendment. Even though Furman's lawyers were resting their arguments on the Cruel and Unusual Punishment Clause rather than the Due Process Clause, most anti-death penalty advocates were not overly optimistic. That is why it was so shocking when the Court announced on June 29, 1972, that the death penalty in all three cases violated the Eighth Amendment. Furthermore, the decision was not confined to any specific case facts that occurred in the three appeals. Rather, the Court found systemic constitutional defects in the application of the death penalty common in all capital punishment statutes.

Understanding the Court's conclusions is more difficult in *Furman* than is normally the case. The justices found it impossible to coalesce around a single rationale. Instead the Court issued a single, terse statement of about 200 words overturning the sentences. This was followed by 230 pages devoted to nine separate opinions in which each of the justices expressed his own views. Five justices voted to strike the death penalty and four to uphold its application.

The five members who voted against the application of the death penalty had their individual reasons for doing so, yet a consistent theme ran through their opinions. For all those persons convicted of capital offenses, such as murder or rape, relatively few were sentenced to death. Credible nationwide statistics were not available, but some authorities at that time estimated that less than 10 percent of individuals convicted of death-eligible crimes actually received a capital punishment sentence. Perhaps more importantly, the seriousness of the crime and other legally relevant factors did not distinguish those who received the death penalty from those who escaped it. There was evidence, although not completely convincing to some members of the majority, that racial factors influenced the decision to execute. These facts led the majority to conclude that the death penalty at best was applied randomly and at worst was imposed in a racially discriminatory manner. In either case, its application was unconstitutionally arbitrary. Justice Potter Stewart, a 1958 Eisenhower appointee from Ohio, likened the application of the death penalty to "being struck by lightning," and as such, was "freakishly and wantonly imposed."

Capital punishment was being applied in an arbitrary and capricious manner because juries were generally given open-ended discretion to choose between long prison sentences or the death penalty, with little or no guidance on proper criteria to use in making the choice. This permitted each jury to proceed in its own way and led to unexplained differences from case to case. Furthermore, jurors, consciously or unconsciously, were more susceptible to being influenced by racial prejudice when their attention was not focused on legally relevant factors and the individualized blameworthiness of the defendant.

Two members of the majority, William Brennan and Thurgood Marshall, condemned America's capital punishment system as being so inhumane and arbitrary as to cause them to conclude that the death penalty was unconstitutional under any and all circumstances. They preferred to ban executions altogether. Justice William O. Douglas stopped just short of reaching the same conclusion. For Brennan, the death penalty was cruel and unusual punishment because it was degrading to the dignity of human beings, arbitrary, unacceptable to contemporary society, and unnecessarily excessive. Marshall, a former head of the NAACP Legal Defense Fund, emphasized racial and class biases in the application of the death penalty. He also argued that the infrequency of its application had effectively removed any deterrent effect the death penalty may have had, a point cited by other members of the majority as well. The remaining two members of the majority, Justices Potter Stewart and Byron White, had markedly changed their positions. Both voted with the majority in *McGautha,* rejecting the previous due process attack on jury discretion.

The four members of the Court appointed by Richard Nixon (Chief Justice Warren Burger and Associate Justices Harry Blackmun, Lewis Powell, and William Rehnquist) dissented. Their arguments centered on traditional interpretations of the cruel and unusual punishment provision, emphasizing original intent and precedent. With respect to intent, the cruel and unusual punishment prohibition was designed to bar torture and other inhumane punishments. Nothing in the wording or history of the provision implies that penalties failing to advance additional legislative purposes violate the Constitution. Consequently, just because the deterrent effect of capital punishment compared to that of lengthy prison terms was called into question does not make the penalty cruel and unusual.

The dissenters noted that during the course of history the Supreme Court repeatedly rejected claims that the death penalty *per se* violates the Eighth Amendment. Because the definition of cruel and unusual will necessarily evolve over time, the Court may periodically revisit the acceptability of certain penalties. In doing so, the Court looks to the state legislatures for guidance, but the continued support of capital punishment by those institutions indicates that American society has not rejected the death penalty.

The dissenters additionally criticized the majority for deserting *McGautha v. California* (1971) so soon after it had been decided. Chief Justice Burger wrote in dissent, "it would be disingenuous to suggest that today's ruling has done anything less than overrule *McGautha* in the guise of an Eighth Amendment adjudication." But Justice Marshall countered that rejecting *McGautha* was appropriate because that decision "was an open invitation to discrimination," which allowed race, sex, and class characteristics to enter sentencing decisions impermissibly.

Furman wrote a new chapter in Eighth Amendment jurisprudence. Prior to this ruling, a penalty would violate the Cruel and Unusual Punishment Clause if it inflicted unnecessary pain, imposed suffering that served no valid purpose, or was disproportionate to the seriousness of the offense. But the majority concluded in *Furman* that even if these traditional boundaries were not transgressed, a violation of the Eighth Amendment could still occur if the sentencing process was arbitrary and discriminatory. The challenged laws were struck down by the majority because they did not provide jurors with reasonable criteria to guide their decision making; rather, they permitted juries to exercise untrammeled discretion that created an unacceptable risk of arbitrary and discriminatory outcomes.

The defects found in the Georgia and Texas death penalty statutes were common to other jurisdictions as well. No state imposed the limitations on jury discretion that the Court was now demanding. The decision in *Furman* effectively nullified the capital punishment laws of all death penalty states, the District of Columbia, and the federal government. It also vacated the sentences of more than 600 inmates serving time on death row when *Furman* was decided. Each had been sentenced to death under a system now found constitutionally defective. Many observers, especially those aligned with anti-capital punishment organizations, thought that *Furman* spelled the end of the death penalty in America.

Even Chief Justice Burger, who dissented from *Furman*, believed that the Court's decision effectively ended the death penalty. He reportedly predicted that there "will never be another execution in this country."

BIBLIOGRAPHIC NOTE.

Statistics on capital punishment cited in this chapter and general reviews of the history of capital punishment are available from the Bureau of Justice Statistics of the U.S. Department of Justice and the Death Penalty Information Center. The results of public opinion polls on the death penalty, crime, and the courts can be found in chapter 8 of Lee Epstein, Jeffrey A. Segal, Harold J. Spaeth, and Thomas G. Walker, *The Supreme Court Compendium: Data, Decisions and Developments*, 4th ed., (Washington, D.C.: CQ Press, 2007).

A number of good treatments of the Supreme Court and capital punishment from various perspectives have informed the discussion in this chapter. These include: Nina Rivkind and Steven F. Shatz, *Cases and Materials on the Death Penalty*, 2d ed. (St. Paul, Minn.: West, 2006); Randall Coyne and Lyn Entzeroth, *Capital Punishment and the Judicial Process*, 3d ed. (Durham, N.C.: Carolina Academic Press, 2006); Lee Epstein and Joseph F. Kobylka, *The Supreme Court and Legal Change* (Chapel Hill: University of North Carolina Press, 1992); Craig Brandon, *The Electric Chair: An Unnatural American History* (Jefferson, N.C.: McFarland, 1999); Richard Moran, *Executioner's Current: Thomas Edison, George Westinghouse, and the Invention of the Electric Chair* (New York: Random House, 2002); Stuart Banner, *The Death Penalty: An American History* (Cambridge: Harvard University Press, 2002); Austin Sarat, *When the State Kills* (Princeton, N.J.: Princeton University Press, 2001); Franklin E. Zimring, *The Contradictions of American Capital Punishment* (New York: Oxford University Press, 2003); Laura E. Randa (ed.), *Society's Final Solution: A History and Discussion of the Death Penalty* (Lanham, Md.:

University Press of America, 1997); Eric W. Rise, *The Martinsville Seven: Race, Rape, and Capital Punishment* (Charlottesville: University of Virginia Press, 1995).

For a controversial look behind the scenes of the Supreme Court during the time of the *Furman* case, see Bob Woodward and Scott Armstrong, *The Brethren* (New York: Simon and Schuster, 1979). The story of Willie Francis is chronicled in Arthur S. Miller and Jeffrey H. Bowman, *Death by Installments: The Ordeal of Willie Francis* (Westport, Conn.: Greenwood Press, 1988); Gilbert King, *The Execution of Willie Francis: Race, Murder, and the Search for Justice in the American South* (New York: Basic Civitas, 2008), and in the first chapter of Rocco J. Tresolini, *These Liberties: Case Studies in Civil Rights* (Philadelphia: J. B. Lippincott, 1968).

Capital Punishment Reinstated

THOSE WHO PREDICTED the end of the death penalty in the aftermath of *Furman v. Georgia* (1972) seriously underestimated the public's support for capital punishment and the political effectiveness of those who wanted to reinstate it. In spite of the Court's failure to reach a consensus opinion, the statements of the individual justices were sufficiently clear to highlight their objections to the existing death penalty laws. Indeed, in his dissenting opinion Chief Justice Warren Burger undoubtedly encouraged capital punishment supporters when he suggested how lawmakers might proceed when enacting new laws:

> [I]t is clear that if state legislatures and the Congress wish to maintain the availability of capital punishment, significant statutory changes will have to be made. Since the two pivotal concurring opinions turn on the assumption that the punishment of death is now meted out in a random and unpredictable manner, legislative bodies may seek to bring their laws into compliance with the Court's ruling by providing standards for juries and judges to follow in determining the sentence in capital cases or by more narrowly defining the crimes for which the penalty is to be imposed.

A number of states moved immediately to revise their laws in an attempt to bring their capital punishment procedures in line with what the Court ordered in *Furman*. Florida was the first, reinstating the death penalty just five months after *Furman* was announced. Florida was followed quickly by Arkansas, Georgia, Nebraska, and Indiana.

The new laws in Georgia perhaps best illustrate the trend and were the first to undergo a constitutional test. Georgia's new law was enacted in March 1973. The revised law incorporated four new features.

First, the new statute allowed capital punishment to be imposed for six crimes: murder, armed robbery, rape, treason, aircraft hijacking, and kidnapping for ransom or where the victim is harmed. This was a modest reduction in the range of infractions for which capital punishment could be imposed.

Second, bifurcated trials were required in all capital cases where the prosecution seeks the death penalty. This procedure divided the trial into a guilt phase and a penalty phase. The guilt phase is conducted in the standard manner. If the jury finds the defendant guilty, the trial then moves to the penalty phase. During this stage, the prosecution and defense present evidence and arguments supporting their respective views of the most appropriate sentence to impose. Evidence previously admitted in the guilt phase may be considered in the sentencing phase as well.

Third, the law reduced the discretion of the jury by requiring it to consider the presence of aggravating circumstances (factors that made the crime more serious or the accused more culpable) and mitigating circumstances (factors that made the crime less serious or the accused less culpable). The existence of an aggravating circumstance would not require the death penalty, but juries could not return a capital punishment recommendation unless they identified beyond a reasonable doubt the presence of at least one aggravating circumstance authorized by law. The statute explicitly stated ten possible aggravating circumstances:

1. The capital crime was committed by a person with a prior capital offense conviction or a substantial history of serious assaultive criminal convictions.

2. The capital offense was committed while the person was engaged in another capital offense.

3. The capital offense took place in a public place and endangered the lives of more than one person.

4. A murder was committed for the purpose of receiving money or any other thing of monetary value.

5. The murder victim was a judicial or prosecutorial officer and murder was committed because of the victim's exercise of official duties.

6. The accused hired another person or was hired by another person to commit murder.

7. The capital offense was outrageously or wantonly vile, horrible, or inhuman in that it involved torture, depravity of mind, or aggravated battery to the victim.

8. The victim of a murder was a law enforcement officer, corrections official, or fire fighter engaged in the performance of official duties.

9. The murder was committed by a person in lawful custody or escaping from lawful custody.

10. The murder was committed to avoid or interfere with a lawful arrest.

In addition, under the revised law, juries were to be instructed by the judge to consider the presence of any mitigating circumstances. Unlike aggravating circumstances that are specified in the statute, mitigating circumstances are not enumerated or limited, but left to the jury's discretion. The law, therefore, does not preclude consideration of any circumstance that might prompt the jury to have mercy on the defendant. The use of mitigating factors in the sentencing phase allows defense attorneys to argue for leniency based on any factor that might lessen the culpability of the accused or make the crime appear less serious. The defendant's youth, disadvantaged background, history of suffering from irresponsible parenting, physical and sexual abuse, or limited mental capacity are examples of common mitigating factors. Evidence in mitigation can prompt a jury to reject the death penalty even if aggravating circumstances are found.

Finally, the new law mandated that all capital sentences be appealed to the state supreme court for review to ensure that the correct procedures were followed, that the sentence was not the product of prejudice, and that the death penalty was not excessive compared to previous cases involving similar crimes. In conducting its review, the state supreme court would receive a complete transcript of the trial as well as a report from the trial court judge. The law required the judge to characterize the trial on several dimensions, including the quality of the defense attorney, any role race may have played, and any doubts the judge may have had about the guilt of the accused. This information would assist the appellate court in assessing if there was any arbitrariness in the process or if the sentence was disproportionate to the crime.

By making these four changes in the state's capital punishment law, Georgia legislators hoped to reestablish the death penalty and avoid the constitutional problems cited by the justices in *Furman*. It did not take long for the new law to be challenged.

On November 21, 1973, Fred Simmons and Bob Moore were driving north from Florida. Along the way they picked up two hitchhikers, Troy Gregg and Floyd Allen. Later the four men stopped at a rest area north of Atlanta, Georgia. Gregg decided to rob Simmons and Moore. Armed with a .25-caliber pistol, Gregg shot each of them as they returned to the car. When Simmons and Moore fell to the ground, Gregg fired another shot into each of their heads. He then stripped them of their valuables and with Allen drove off in their car. The two subsequently were apprehended in Asheville, North Carolina, and returned to Georgia.

Gregg claimed he shot Simmons and Moore in self-defense when they attacked Allen and him with a knife and a piece of pipe, but the jurors did not believe the story. They found Gregg guilty of two counts of murder and two counts of armed robbery. At the penalty stage, the judge instructed the jury that they could recommend either life in prison or the death penalty on each count. The judge further instructed the jury that in determining the recommended sentence they were required to take into account any aggravating and mitigating circumstances. Upon deliberation the jury identified beyond a reasonable doubt the presence of two aggravating circumstances: that the murders occurred during the commission of another capital offense (armed robbery) and that the murders were committed for the purpose of receiving money and the automobile. The jury recommended death on each count, and the judge imposed the recommended sentence. The sentence was later affirmed by the Georgia Supreme Court, which found no evidence of any prejudice or other arbitrary factor affecting the jury's decision. The court also determined that the sentence was not disproportionate to penalties imposed in similar crimes.

Gregg's sentence was appealed to the U.S. Court. The justices granted review and used *Gregg v. Georgia* (1976) as a vehicle for evaluating the constitutionality of the new generation of capital punishment statutes enacted in response to *Furman.* Along with *Gregg,* the Court accepted cases from Louisiana, Texas, North Carolina, and Florida.

On July 2, 1976, by a 7–2 vote, the justices upheld Troy Gregg's death sentence and approved the new Georgia capital punishment scheme. The majority held that the revised statute sufficiently limited and guided jury discretion. It provided the necessary conditions for the jury to make its sentencing decision based on the specific offense and the individual culpability of the accused. The revised law also required sufficient appellate review to combat prejudicial and arbitrary decision making and sentences that were disproportionately severe. Only Justices Marshall and Brennan dissented, holding, as they did in *Furman,* that the death penalty was cruel and unusual punishment under any and all circumstances.

At the same time, the justices approved similarly retooled death penalty statutes in Texas (*Jurek v. Texas*) and Florida (*Proffitt v. Florida*). But the revised laws in North Carolina (*Woodson v. North Carolina*) and Louisiana (*Roberts v. Louisiana*) were not as warmly received. These two states took a different approach to reducing jury discretion in that they eliminated jury discretion altogether. The death penalty was made mandatory for first-degree murder convictions. The Supreme Court found the mandatory death sentence unacceptable. The sentencing process must include some discretion, sufficient to make an individualized determination of an appropriate sentence. The total elimination of factors that might move a jury to a more lenient outcome is inconsistent with the fundamental respect for humanity that underlies the Eighth Amendment. Thus, states can neither permit complete discretion to juries nor remove all discretion. Instead, individualized consideration of both aggravating and mitigating circumstances is required.

CAPITAL PUNISHMENT trends quickly reversed themselves. Even before *Gregg* was handed down, twenty-nine states had enacted new death penalty laws in attempts to comply with the standards established by the Court in *Furman.* Polls showed that support for capital punishment had risen to levels exceeding two-thirds of Americans. With *Gregg* conferring Supreme Court approval of a revised capital punishment structure, states

Gary Gilmore, the first convicted murderer to be executed following the Supreme Court's reinstatement of the death penalty, enters the courtroom on December 1, 1976.

were free once again to execute those convicted of capital offenses. The moratorium against the death penalty ended after nine years without an execution.

Gary Gilmore was the first person to be put to death in the post–*Gregg* era. A career criminal, Gilmore killed Max Jensen, a gas station attendant on July 19, 1976, in Orem, Utah. The next day he murdered motel manager Ben Bushnell in Provo and was quickly arrested. In October of that year, after a two-day trial, a jury convicted Gilmore and he was sentenced to death. Under Utah law at that time, individuals receiving the death penalty had the right to select either hanging or a firing squad as the method of execution. Gilmore opted to be shot. Because he put up no significant defense at his trial and rebuffed all attempts by his attorneys to appeal, the case ended quickly. Gilmore was executed by a five-person firing squad on January 17, 1977, only six months after his crime.

The dramatic change in the national capital punishment environment caught the anti-death penalty groups off guard. Predictions that *Furman* would mark the end of the death penalty in the United States could not have been more inaccurate. The abolitionist movement badly miscalculated the underlying support for capital punishment and did not anticipate the rush of so many state legislatures to reenact their death penalty statutes. They also misinterpreted the position of the Supreme Court. Rather than signaling that the justices were on the verge of rejecting capital punishment altogether, *Furman* proved to mean exactly what the justices said in their opinions: the death penalty was unconstitutional as applied because juries were given unguided discretion that inevitably resulted in inconsistent, arbitrary, and discriminatory sentences. Remove this constitutional infirmity and the Court would likely approve the reintroduction of executions.

As the nation entered the 1970s there was also a significant change in the public mood. Voters shifted toward the right, reacting generally against the more permissive atmosphere of the 1960s. Republicans dominated the White House, and more conservative justices received appointments to the Supreme Court. In the four decades beginning with Richard Nixon's election in 1968 only two Democrats were selected to be president—Jimmy Carter, who had no opportunities to appoint a member of the Court, and Bill Clinton, who generally supported the death penalty. From 1973 to the turn of the twentieth century, opinion polls consistently revealed that more than 80 percent of the public thought that the courts were not harsh enough in dealing with criminals. Legislatures in many states responded by enacting tougher general sentencing laws. So, too, did Congress, which, among other measures, reinstituted the death penalty in 1988 and reduced post–conviction relief alternatives with the Antiterrorism and Effective Death Penalty Act of 1996.

These conditions created a difficult environment for death penalty foes. The political atmosphere was not at all conducive to convincing state legislatures to outlaw capital punishment. And having just approved the reinstatement of the death penalty, it was highly unlikely that the Supreme Court would change directions and ban its use altogether. But the abolitionist movement was not about to concede defeat. Instead death penalty opponents prepared for a long, relentless battle against state-sponsored executions. They reverted to the strategy of attempting to limit the use of capital punishment wherever they could, hoping that over time the cumulative effect of small legal victories would result in near abolition. Generally, they pursued five legal strategies, each with mixed results.

The first objective was to reduce the range of crimes for which the death penalty could be imposed. In *Coker v. Georgia* (1977), attorneys challenged the death sentence given to Erlich Coker, a prison escapee who had been serving time for murder, rape, kidnapping, and assault. Coker broke into a home, raped the woman living there, and stole the family car. He was convicted of rape and sentenced to death. The Supreme Court,

7–2, ruled that the punishment was unconstitutionally excessive by contemporary standards. No state other than Georgia at that time permitted execution for the rape of an adult woman that did not result in a loss of life. Thus, the sentence was considered cruel and unusual under contemporary societal standards.

Five years later, in *Enmund v. Florida* (1982), the Court ruled against the use of the death penalty for certain felony murder convictions. Earl Enmund and two codefendants were convicted of robbing and killing an elderly couple in their central Florida farmhouse. All three received the death penalty. Enmund, however, was the getaway driver, who waited in the car while the other two committed the actual crime. As a participant in a serious crime that resulted in murder, however, Enmund was as guilty under Florida law as the others.

The Supreme Court held that Enmund's role in the offense was not "so grievous an affront to humanity that the only adequate response may be the penalty of death." After reviewing the decision-making records of legislatures, juries, and prosecutors, a five-person majority concluded that death sentences in such cases were rare. As a consequence the Court held that the Eighth Amendment prohibits the execution of a person who participates with others in a felony that results in a murder, but who did not kill, intend to kill, or attempt to kill the victim. The culpability of such persons is considerably less than that of the actual triggerman. However, in *Tison v. Arizona* (1987), the justices permitted an exception to the *Enmund* rule, holding that a non-triggerman can be sentenced to death if he played a major role in the underlying felony and did so with a mental state of "reckless indifference or disregard" for human life.

In each of these cases the justices, consistent with *Trop v. Dulles* (1958), evaluated the crime and the death penalty in light of society's "evolving standards of decency." The end result was that the death penalty may only be administered for the most serious crimes. Although federal laws and those of some states still allow the death penalty for some offenses other than homicide, since *Gregg* no person has been executed for a crime other than murder.

A second line of attack on the death penalty was to challenge its application as racially discriminatory. This argument, perhaps the broadest challenge to capital punishment, took the position that race remained a factor in capital sentencing even under the revised statutes approved in *Gregg*. Abolitionists hoped the discrimination argument would persuade the justices as it had in *Furman*.

The discrimination challenge was presented to the Supreme Court in *McCleskey v. Kemp* (1987). Warren McCleskey and three accomplices, all armed, attempted to rob a furniture store in Atlanta, Georgia. Before they could subdue all of the customers and employees, one worker set off a silent alarm. A thirty-one-year-old white police officer answered the call. He was shot twice, once in the face, and died. Based on ballistics tests and other evidence, a jury convicted McCleskey, an African American, of the murder. Finding evidence of aggravating circumstances beyond a reasonable doubt, the jury imposed the death penalty.

NAACP Legal Defense Fund lawyers took over McCleskey's case on appeal. Their argument rested primarily on the results of a large statistical study of 2,484 murder cases tried in Georgia from 1973 to 1979. The research demonstrated the importance of the defendant's race and the race of the victim in sentencing. The results showed that a defendant was more than four times more likely to be sentenced to death if the victim was white rather than black, with the highest rates of capital punishment occurring when the murderer was black and the victim was white. This demonstrated, the NAACP-LDF attorneys argued, that despite the new procedures designed to eliminate racial bias, discrimination still played a major role in capital sentencing.

This argument and the supporting evidence was designed to convince the justices that discrimination was so pervasive that death sentences were still arbitrarily and capriciously applied in violation of both the Eighth Amendment and the Equal Protection Clause of the Fourteenth Amendment. But a five-justice majority rejected McCleskey's position and upheld the sentence. Speaking for the Court, Justice Lewis Powell concluded that McCleskey failed to show the discriminatory intent required in constitutional discrimination claims. Further, although the statistical evidence might have revealed general patterns, McCleskey was unable to prove that racial discrimination accounted for his individual sentence. The loss was a devastating blow to the anti-capital punishment forces because the racial discrimination argument was thought to be the most powerful in the abolitionist arsenal.

A third strategy—and one of the most successful lines of attack on the death penalty—was to oppose any state limitations on the right of the defendant to introduce mitigating factors. In *Lockett v. Ohio* (1978), the justices ruled that state laws restricting the number of mitigating circumstances that could be considered in sentencing violated the Eighth Amendment. Individualized sentencing requires that capital defendants be permitted to introduce any factor relating to their character, record, or circumstances that might provide reason for imposing a sentence less than death. And in *Eddings v. Oklahoma* (1982), the Supreme Court reversed a death sentence given to a sixteen-year-old murderer on the grounds that the sentencing judge refused to take into account as mitigation the defendant's turbulent upbringing, emotional disturbances, and severe beatings by his father.

A fourth approach was to attack procedures used in capital cases that provided an advantage to the prosecution. *Payne v. Tennessee* (1991), a challenge to the use of victim impact statements, is an example. Pervis Payne was charged with the murder of Charisse Christopher and her two-year-old daughter and the assault with intent to murder her three-year-old son. The killings were the result of a savage attack with a butcher knife that occurred when Christopher rejected Payne's sexual advances. Presented with overwhelming evidence, the jury found Payne guilty. At the sentencing phase of the trial, the prosecutor introduced evidence of the negative impact the murders had on Christopher's extended family, and especially on her son who survived the attack. The jury sentenced Payne to death on each of the murder counts.

Payne challenged the sentence on the grounds that the trial court should not have allowed the prosecutor to introduce evidence of the impact of the murders on Christopher's family. The objection to such victim impact evidence is that it moves the jury to focus on the qualities of the victim rather than the culpability and blameworthiness of the defendant. In addition, victim impact inevitably treats the murder of some individuals as more serious than others. For example, the murder of a mother with several young children is often seen as more grievous than a person with no dependents or significant responsibilities. Two equally blameworthy defendants may not receive similar sentences because of the differing ramifications of their offenses.

Payne's appeal seemed to be on firm legal ground. The Supreme Court in Booth v. Maryland (1987) and South Carolina v. Gathers (1989) held that victim impact statements relating to the personal characteristics of the victim or the effect of the crime on the victim's family were not admissible under the Eighth Amendment. Victim impact information permitted an unacceptable risk that the jury might impose the death penalty in an arbitrary and capricious manner.

In Payne, however, the Supreme Court changed course. It ruled that states are free to permit victim impact statements during the sentencing phase of capital trials. In doing so the justices overruled the precedents set in Booth and Gathers. They concluded that the effects of a crime are relevant. The Eighth Amendment erects no bar to the use of victim impact statements in a jury's individualized consideration of an appropriate punishment. The majority noted that the Court had protected and expanded the rights of a defendant to present a wide range of mitigating evidence, and it likewise was reasonable to allow the prosecutor to introduce evidence of the human costs of the crime.

A final line of argument was to attempt to remove certain classes of people from death penalty eligibility. In Ford v. Wainwright (1986), for example, the Court confronted the issue of executing individuals who are insane. Alvin Ford had been convicted of the murder of a police officer during an attempted robbery and was sentenced to death. There was no suggestion of any mental incompetence at his trial or sentencing. While on death row, however, he developed increasingly delusional behavior, demonstrating a clear lack of being in touch with reality. The justices held that the Eighth Amendment is violated when a state executes persons who are incapable of understanding the punishment about to be administered and the reasons why they are being punished. Applying the death penalty to such persons amounts to "mindless vengeance" and serves no legitimate penal purpose. Further, such defendants are entitled to a full and fair hearing regarding their mental competency.

Juveniles constituted another category of persons that capital punishment foes sought to protect from the death penalty. The first attempt came in *Thompson v. Oklahoma* (1988). William Thompson, then fifteen, along with three adults, brutally killed his brother-in-law. The victim, who had been mistreating Thompson's sister, was shot twice, stabbed, and had several bones broken. His body was chained to a concrete block and thrown into a river where it was found weeks later. The four defendants were tried separately. The prosecutor received special authority to try Thompson as an adult on the grounds that the juvenile justice system offered no reasonable prospects for rehabilitating him. All four were convicted and sentenced to death.

Death penalty opponents argued that the Supreme Court should shield from the death penalty all those under eighteen years at the time of their offense. The Supreme Court, however, lacked a majority willing to go that far. With only eight justices sitting (Justice Anthony Kennedy had just been confirmed and did not participate) the Court voted 5–3 to reverse the imposed death sentence. A plurality of four held that societal standards had evolved to the point that executing individuals under sixteen at the time of their offense is unacceptable, and therefore Thompson's death penalty violated the Eighth Amendment. But Sandra Day O'Connor, the fifth member of the majority, was not prepared to declare such a prohibition. Instead, she found a more narrow ground to support the reversal of Thompson's sentence, preferring to wait for a future case to explore a more general ban against the execution of minors.

The very next year, however, in *Stanford v. Kentucky* (1989) and *Wilkins v. Missouri* (1989), the issue of juvenile executions returned to the Court. The cases involved Kevin Stanford who repeatedly raped and sodomized the attendant of a Kentucky gas station following a robbery and Heath Wilkins who robbed a Missouri convenience store and a woman working there. In both cases the defendants then proceeded to murder their victims for the expressed purpose of removing a potential witness against them. Stanford was seventeen years old and Wilkins sixteen.

The Court refused to extend blanket protection against the death penalty to all juveniles under eighteen. Because the execution of individuals as young as sixteen or seventeen was not considered cruel or unusual punishment at the time of the ratification of the Constitution, the key issue before the Court was whether the nation's standards had evolved to the point that such death sentences had become unacceptable. In surveying the states, the Court found that of the thirty-seven capital punishment states at that time, fifteen did not allow the execution of sixteen year olds and twelve shielded seventeen year olds. A five-justice majority, including the swing votes of Justices Kennedy and O'Connor, supported the position that these data did not establish that a national consensus against such executions had emerged. Instead, the majority took the position that the age of the defendant should continue to be used as a potential mitigating factor. Juries should consider the accused's maturity on an individualized basis to determine the extent to which it affects culpability and, thus, the appropriateness of the death penalty. The question of capital punishment for sixteen and seventeen year olds, however, was so important that the issue would reappear on the Court's docket years later.

BETWEEN THE COURT'S MORATORIUM on the death penalty following *Furman* in 1972 and 1998 when Daryl Atkins stood before a jury charged with capital murder, the Supreme Court's capital punishment jurisprudence had changed significantly. *Gregg* allowed for the reestablishment of the death penalty in states that wanted to impose it. The Court required that death penalty procedures reduce jury discretion and focus the jurors' attention on an individualized consideration of legally relevant factors. A bifurcated trial separating the decision of guilt from the determination of an appropriate sentence and automatic appellate court review introduced new safeguards intended to eliminate arbitrary and excessive punishments. Capital punishment became reserved only for the most serious crimes, procedures were tightened, the proper use of aggravating and mitigating factors was better defined, and individuals with certain characteristics were exempt from death penalty consideration. Ultimately thirty-eight states and the federal government responded by revamping their capital punishment procedures to bring them into line with the Court's decrees. Twelve states elected not to incorporate the death penalty into their criminal justice systems. In each of those twelve states the death penalty had already been eliminated or had fallen into disuse prior to the *Furman* ruling.

Death penalty opponents have fought an uphill battle since *Furman.* They were unable to persuade a majority of the Court in *Gregg* to eliminate the death penalty altogether and were politically unable to stop the stampede of states to reintroduce capital punishment. Attorneys representing condemned criminals have achieved only modest success before the post–*Furman* Supreme Court. Certainly, they have won some rounds of litigation, but their victories have not affected large numbers of executions. Obtaining constitutional protection for the lives juveniles under sixteen years, the insane, and those convicted of rape or felony murder have been important symbolically, but few such death sentences were ever handed down. The losses were more significant, especially the failure to convince the Court that racial discrimination significantly affected capital sentencing, that victim impact statements should be prohibited, and that all juveniles should be shielded from death sentences. On balance, the Supreme Court has leaned decidedly in the direction of supporting the states' use of capital punishment.

Death penalty foes, however, have not conceded. There has always been hope that increased public awareness would move individual states, or perhaps the nation as a whole, to reject the death penalty. This belief was expressed by Justice Thurgood Marshall's opinions in both *Furman* and *Gregg,* where he stated: "the American people are largely unaware of the information critical to a judgment on the morality of the death penalty, and . . . if they were better informed they would consider it shocking, unjust, and unacceptable."

The Supreme Court's decisions have often been the product of deep divisions among the justices, allowing capital punishment opponents hope that modest changes in the Court's membership would help the anti-death penalty cause. In addition, the sentence in every capital case, no matter how overwhelming the evidence of guilt, has been vigorously contested at both the trial level and on appeal. An ever growing anti-capital punishment bar has emerged, consisting of zealous attorneys dedicated to keeping their clients alive, often for decades, while they used every possible procedural means to challenge the sentences. Of course, individuals and organizations sympathetic toward law enforcement and supportive of victims' rights actively have opposed the death penalty foes every step of the way.

When the trial of Daryl Atkins began it was little noticed outside the Hampton Roads area of coastal Virginia. Yet the controversy emerging from that trial would prove to have a significant impact on death penalty law in the United States. At issue was the question of mental retardation. Do low levels of intellectual ability reduce the culpability of an accused murderer to the point that the death penalty should not be a sentencing option? Daryl Atkins was certainly not the first capital defendant to raise this question. Issues concerning mental retardation and the criminal process have long been a concern in the development of American criminal law. Relevant Supreme Court precedents on this question would surely structure the way George Rogers and Bryan Saunders would attack Eileen Addison's goal of making Daryl Atkins pay the ultimate price for the murder of Eric Nesbitt.

BIBLIOGRAPHIC NOTE.

In addition to the sources included in the bibliographic note at the end of Chapter 3, the following readings provide information and analysis of particular relevance to the topics discussed in this chapter: David C. Baldus, George Woodworth, and Charles A. Pulaski, *Equal Justice and the Death Penalty* (Boston: Northeastern University Press, 1989); Barry Nakell and Kenneth A. Hardy, *The Arbitrariness of the Death Penalty* (Philadelphia: Temple University Press, 1987); Michael A. Foley, *Arbitrary and Capricious: The Supreme Court, the Constitution, and the Death Penalty* (Westport, Conn.: Praeger, 2003); Scott Turow, *Ultimate Punishment* (New York: Farrar, Straus, and Giroux, 2003); Mary W. Atwell, *Evolving Standards of Decency* (New York: Peter Lang, 2004); Welsh S. White, *Litigating in the Shadow of Death* (Ann Arbor: University of Michigan Press, 2006); James R. Acker and David Reed Karp (eds.), *Wounds That Do Not Bind: Victim-Based Perspectives on the Death Penalty* (Durham, N.C.: Carolina Academic Press, 2006); Mary W. Atwell, *Wretched Sisters: Examining Gender and Capital Punishment* (New York: Peter Lang, 2007); Kent S. Miller and Michael L. Radelet, *Executing the Mentally Ill: The Criminal Justice System and the Case of Alvin Ford* (Newbury Park, Calif.: Sage Publications, 1993); L. Kay Gillespie, *Inside the*

Death Chamber: Exploring Executions (Boston: Allyn and Bacon, 2003); Evan J. Mandery, *Capital Punishment: A Balanced Examination* (Boston: Jones and Bartlett Publishers, 2005); Norman Mailer, *The Executioner's Song* (New York: Random House, 1979); Mikal Gilmore, *Shot in the Heart* (New York: Doubleday, 1994).

Retardation, the Death Penalty, and Johnny Paul Penry

DEFENSE ATTORNEYS George Rogers and Bryan Saunders continually pressed the position that Eric Nesbitt died at the hands of William Jones and not their client, Daryl Atkins. Commonwealth's Attorney Eileen Addison saw the crime differently. She was determined to obtain a conviction against Atkins and a death penalty sentence. As the evidence mounted, Addison appeared to hold the stronger hand. Rogers and Saunders knew it was quite possible that a jury would convict Atkins. Consequently, the defense team needed not only to prepare for the guilt phase of the trial, but also to make ready a case against a possible death sentence. As they learned more about their client, it became increasingly clear that Atkins's sub-average intellectual ability might be their best hope to save him from death row.

An important initial step in analyzing the significance of retardation in criminal law is to distinguish it from other mental disorders. Importantly, mental retardation is not insanity. According to standard definitions, insane persons, because of serious diseases or defects of the mind, lack the capacity to appreciate the criminality of their actions. They have an inability to distinguish right from wrong and to conform their behavior to what is required by the law. They often fail to notice the difference between fantasy and reality. Since 1843, when an English jury found Scottish assassin Daniel M'Naghten not guilty, British and American laws have conceded that those who suffer from insanity are not legally responsible for their acts. The minds of such individuals are incapable of reaching the required level of criminal intent. Thus, insanity is a traditionally recognized defense against criminal charges.

Retardation is also not mental illness. Depression, psychoses, schizophrenia, or other mental and emotional illnesses may contribute to criminal actions and may also reduce criminal culpability. These disorders, however, are generally independent of mental ability. They affect sufferers at all intellectual levels and, unlike retardation, mental illnesses can frequently be treated by therapy or medication.

Retardation is characterized by significantly sub-average intelligence. It is a condition that normally begins at birth or shortly thereafter and is manifest in early childhood. While retarded people often are capable of limited learning and coping, they exhibit difficulty adapting to the world around them. Retardation is not a disease that can be reversed. It is a permanent condition. Retarded persons fall into a wide range of intellectual deficits. Depending on the extent of the retardation, an individual, while mentally slow, may retain the ability to distinguish right from wrong and the capacity to control personal behavior. Because of this, those with less severe forms of retardation may be morally and legally responsible for their actions.

For centuries the law has acknowledged that retardation, if sufficiently severe, may render an individual blameless for criminal acts. Early English common law recognized different categories of reduced mental capacity. The most profoundly retarded were classified as idiots. Such persons lacked normal reasoning abilities. Idiocy was considered a permanent condition that began at birth and affected every aspect of an individual's life. Because of seriously low intelligence levels idiots did not have the capacity to form criminal intent or even to understand legal right from wrong.

Imbeciles were those who suffered from less severe intellectual impairments. Like idiots, imbeciles were plagued with permanent mental limitations. They possessed some reasoning powers and a basic understanding of the world around them, but far less than the general population. Adults with imbecility commonly were unable to mature intellectually beyond a level normally associated with children. Depending on the level of intellectual impairment and the circumstances surrounding an illegal act, however, imbeciles could be held criminally accountable for their behavior.

Common law also recognized lunacy as a mental condition. Lunatics did not suffer from congenital defects or intellectual deficits from birth. Rather lunacy referred to a lack of mental capacity and understanding usually brought about because of an illness or traumatic event. Those born with perfectly normal levels of intelligence could fall into such a state. Unlike idiocy and imbecility, lunacy was neither a necessarily permanent or continuous condition. Lunatics were capable of temporary periods of lucidity when their intellectual powers returned to normal.

Such categories seem archaic, even offensive, today. Nevertheless, we still categorize individuals with seriously substandard intelligence levels. Today, however, we employ more scientific criteria for our classifications, drawing from decades of research on human intelligence. Contemporary approaches commonly define retardation according to three criteria.

The first criterion is intellectual ability as measured by standardized intelligence quotient (IQ) testing. The instrument most commonly used to identify intelligence levels is the Wechsler Adult Intelligence Scale, the origins of which can be traced back to the research of clinical psychologist David Wechsler in the 1930s. The goal of the test, according to Wechsler, is to measure the capacity of an individual "to act purposefully, to think rationally, and to deal effectively with his environment." As contemporary knowledge of human intelligence has grown, the test has been updated. Revisions are also needed in order to keep pace with the general upward drift in human intelligence. The third version of the scale, known as WAIS-III, was released in 1997 and was the test used to evaluate the intelligence levels of Daryl Atkins. An updated edition (WAIS-IV) was issued in 2008. Although sometimes controversial, the Wechsler test has been shown to be generally valid and reliable, and its results correlate well with those of other standard measures of intelligence such as the Stanford-Binet test.

The Wechsler test evaluates a number of complex components of intelligence, ultimately summarizing them into scores for verbal intelligence, performance intelligence, and a full-scale intelligence quotient.

The results are normed with a full-scale IQ of 100 representing a person of average intelligence. Indices are also constructed for verbal comprehension, perceptual organization, working memory, and processing speed. Those individuals with significantly sub-average intelligence levels are generally grouped into four categories.

The largest group consists of those with mild mental retardation. Measured statistically, mild retardation begins with intelligence levels two standard deviations below the average IQ score of 100 for the general population. In more concrete terms, intelligence experts classify persons falling into an IQ score range of 50 to 70 as mildly retarded. However, the administration of intelligence tests carries a degree of measurement error, estimated to be as much as five points. Therefore, some individuals may score as high as 75 on standardized IQ examinations and still suffer from mild retardation. The mildly retarded comprise approximately 85 percent of all mentally challenged persons. These individuals often are able to live on their own with support from their family or community.

About 10 percent of retarded individuals have IQs of between 35 and 50. They are classified as having moderate mental retardation. Such individuals are able to function in a relatively normal way if they have appropriate supervision. Many cope best if they reside in group homes with other retarded persons.

The lowest levels of intelligence are the severely retarded (IQs of 20–35) and the profoundly retarded (scores under 20). Together they comprise only about 5 percent of the total population of mentally disabled people. They require significant supervision because they can master few of the most basic skills used in daily life.

The second criterion for identifying retardation focuses on adaptive behavior. Adaptive behavior involves the traits necessary to interact successfully with one's environment on a daily basis. A retarded individual will have significantly below-average abilities in this regard. This condition might manifest itself in restricted conceptual skills, such as expressing oneself verbally, reading, writing, and dealing with basic monetary exchanges. The retarded also exhibit limited social skills. They may be less adept at interpersonal interaction, suffer from gullibility and naiveté, and be much more likely to follow than to lead. Handling practical matters may also be difficult. Cooking meals, using the telephone, managing finances, maintaining personal hygiene, and keeping house may be beyond their individual capabilities.

The third and final element of retardation is that the condition makes its presence known at an early age. Although the exact cause of an individual's mental retardation is not always discoverable, intelligence deficits are commonly inherited, caused by prenatal conditions, or triggered by trauma or illness early in life. Retardation is not an adult-onset condition.

Debates over the most appropriate way to deal with retarded individuals in the criminal justice system focus almost exclusively on the mildly mentally retarded. This is for good reason. The incidence of criminal behavior among the more seriously challenged is quite rare. Because of their intellectual deficits they often do not possess the capacity to contemplate, plan, and execute a crime. They have a tendency to please people rather than to rebel against rules and expectations. When they do engage in wrongful behavior it is often spontaneous and without the required level of criminal intent.

The mildly retarded, however, may well possess the ability to act with deliberation and be capable of distinguishing right from wrong. Thus, many in this category of mental development are personally culpable for their actions, including being responsible for violations of criminal law. As such they may be legally guilty of crimes and be required to suffer legally imposed punishments.

Proponents of the interests of the retarded have long argued that their reduced intellectual capacity makes them less responsible when they do violate the law. Although they may not be blameless, their personal culpability is less than that of a person of normal intelligence who commits the same act. As a consequence, their punishments should be less severe. With respect to capital punishment, advocates of the mentally retarded hold that the death penalty is unreasonable and a violation of the Cruel and Unusual Punishment Clause of the Eighth Amendment. A number of factors are offered to support their position.

First, those with intellectual deficiencies have a limited ability to understand the consequences of their actions. For example, they may not comprehend the finality that results from murder. And unlike those with normal intelligence levels they may be unable to understand the possible consequences they may personally suffer for their criminal acts. In addition, a lack of impulse control, common among the retarded, exacerbates the problem. Thus, the threat of punishment that might deter others from engaging in crime is less effective on the retarded.

Second, as people who are eager to please, the retarded are more susceptible to the influence of others; and their characteristic gullibility and naiveté makes them doubly so. They have little ability to think independently and to stand up against anti-social pressures. As a result, when a retarded person comes under the influence of those who have little respect for the law, they may easily be led into criminal conduct.

Third, if accused of illegal acts, the retarded are especially vulnerable during the prosecution and trial stages of the criminal process. Because the mildly retarded generally display no observable physical traits associated with their disability, they may be treated and evaluated in ways inappropriate for their intelligence levels. When approached by police they may waive their *Miranda* rights without understanding the consequences of their decision to do so. Their eagerness to please may cause them to make statements that put them in legal jeopardy. They may even admit to crimes they have not committed. Their limited intelligence diminishes their capability to assist their attorneys in constructing a defense. During trials, their demeanor may falsely signal to juries that they are disinterested, not remorseful for their acts, or disrespectful to the court. Further, if defendants do not display outwards signs of conditions such as Down Syndrome, jurors may be reluctant to believe claims of mental retardation. All of these factors may increase the probability of being convicted and receiving a harsh sentence.

Finally, those supporting special protections for the mentally retarded compare the legal status of the retarded to that of children. We do not execute young children even if they commit acts that lead to the death of their victims. We do not do so because of the diminished capacities of children to understand the nature of the crime or the consequences that will result. Why, then, should we allow the execution of a mentally retarded adult who possesses intelligence and reasoning levels no more advanced than the young children we shelter from the death penalty?

Those who oppose a blanket exemption for the retarded place their primary emphasis on one important factor. The mildly retarded are a heterogeneous group. They are not all the same. They have different levels of intelligence, with varying abilities to reason and interact with the world around them. Some have greater abilities than others to control their impulses, resist negative social pressures, understand consequences, and distinguish right from wrong. In short, all retarded people should not be treated the same. For some retarded persons the death penalty may be totally inappropriate given their limited criminal culpability. For others, however, a severe sentence may well be the most just course. Individualized consideration by a jury, taking into account the specific retardation level of the accused as a mitigating factor, is seen as preferable to exempting all those with intelligence deficiencies.

The debate over capital punishment and the mentally retarded ultimately led the U.S. Supreme Court in 1989 to review a death sentence handed down by a Texas jury against convicted murderer and rapist Johnny Paul Penry. The questions confronting the justices were straightforward ones: does the Eighth Amendment's ban against cruel and unusual punishment require that all mentally retarded people be exempt from the death penalty? Or, does the Eighth Amendment require only that mental retardation be considered as a mitigating circumstance to be evaluated on an individualized, case-by-case basis?

ON THE MORNING of October 25, 1979, Johnny Paul Penry, then age twenty-two, forced himself into the Livingston, Texas, home of Pamela Moseley Carpenter, sister of former Washington Redskins place-kicker Mark Moseley. Three months earlier Penry had been paroled from prison after serving about half of a five-year sentence for rape. He supported himself with odd jobs. Weeks earlier he had delivered appliances to Carpenter's home. Carpenter was alone that morning, working on a Halloween costume for her nine-year-old niece.

In a subsequent confession Penry admitted that he broke into the house intending to rape and rob the twenty-two-year-old East Texas homemaker. Confronting Carpenter in the kitchen, he grabbed her around the neck, holding an open pocketknife to her throat. The young woman fought back, but Penry was too strong. He knocked her to the floor and pushed her face against the stove. During the skirmish, Carpenter was able to grab a pair of scissors she had been using on her niece's costume and lashed out at Penry in an attempt to ward off the attack. Penry dislodged the scissors from the woman's hands and dragged her into the bedroom. After he kicked and hit Carpenter several times, Penry forced himself on her sexually. He then used the scissors to stab her.

After Penry left the house Carpenter, still alive, was able to telephone a friend for help and described her assailant as a thin, white man with curly hair. Despite receiving emergency treatment, Carpenter died in the hospital hours later. The description she provided prompted sheriff's deputies immediately to suspect Penry. He was apprehended later that day.

Penry confessed to the crime twice. In his first statement, he described his actions this way: "I went on and [raped] her on the bedroom floor and then after I got through I got up and walked over to the kitchen floor where the scissors had landed and picked them up. I walked back to her and got down on her. I sat down on her stomach and told her that I loved her and hated to kill her but I had to so she wouldn't squeal on me."

In the second confession, Penry explained the motives prompting the crime: "I got up and went to town somewhere around 8 or 9 a.m. I saw a girl in City Hall who reminded me of the Chick. I decided I would go over to the Chick's house and get me a piece. I also wanted to get the money that she had in her purse. I knew that if I went over to the Chick's house and raped her that I would have to kill her because she would tell who I was to the police and I didn't want to go back to the pen."

There was no doubt that Penry had committed the crime. In 1980 a jury promptly convicted him of capital murder, rejecting a defense argument that Penry did not understand the wrongfulness of his act. But the question of sentencing was an entirely different matter. An examination of Penry's background and mental abilities raised serious questions about the appropriateness of executing him no matter how brutal his crime.

Penry was diagnosed early in life with organic brain damage, probably due to trauma to the head during birth. Tests estimated his intelligence level in the 50 to 63 IQ range. This placed his intellectual development at the level of a normal six-and-one-half-year-old child. Experts evaluated

his social maturity as that of a
nine- or ten-year-old boy. Additionally, Penry's mother subjected
him to significant abuse, caused
perhaps by her own psychological
problems or her frustration over
her inability to handle a special-
needs child. His mother reportedly
beat young Penry's head with a
belt, burned him with boiling
water and cigarettes, forced him to
eat his own feces and drink his
own urine, and locked him in a
room for long periods without
access to a toilet. He had impulse-
control deficits and an inability to
learn from experience. Although
Penry was legally sane and could
distinguish right from wrong, he
had severely limited abilities to

*Johnny Paul Penry sits in the courtroom
during a 2002 sentencing hearing. In
1989 the Supreme Court rejected Penry's
petition to ban all executions of the
mentally retarded.*

understand the consequences associated with his actions. Never finishing
the first grade, he exhibited virtually no ability to read or write and had
difficulty with everyday matters such as understanding the days of the
week. During his years in prison, Penry displayed many childlike traits.
He believed in Santa Claus. He spent his days looking at comic books and
drawing stick figures with crayons.

Did these factors constitute sufficient mitigation to save Penry from
being executed by the state of Texas? Not according to the jurors who
convicted him in 1980. Following the judge's instructions, the jury considered three "special issues," the aggravating circumstances that under
Texas law would determine the sentence. First, was the conduct of the
defendant committed deliberately with the reasonable expectation that
the death of the victim would be the result? Second, was there a probability that the defendant would commit violent crimes that would constitute
a continuing threat to society? And third, was the killing an unreasonable

response to provocation, if any, from the victim? The jury unanimously affirmed the presence of all three aggravating circumstances and recommend death.

Penry's lawyers immediately appealed the decision on several grounds. This touched off a legal battle over Penry's sentence that was fought in state and federal courts over the next quarter-century. The most important of these court decisions occurred in 1989 when the U.S. Supreme Court accepted the case of *Johnny Paul Penry v. James A. Lynaugh, Director of the Texas Department of Corrections.*

Penry's attorneys brought two major issues to the Court. Their first argument attacked the judge's instructions to the jury for failure to give sufficient attention to the consideration of Penry's mental retardation and childhood abuse as mitigating circumstances. The second argument, a more general and significant one, asked the justices to remove categorically mentally retarded people from death penalty eligibility. The state of Texas argued against both positions taken by Penry's attorneys.

The Court's response to these issues reflected the deep ideological divisions that characterized the sitting justices. Four liberal members of the Court generally sided with Penry on both issues, and the four conservatives leaned toward the state. In the center was Justice Sandra Day O'Connor who often found herself casting the Court's swing vote. O'Connor, an Arizona Republican, was appointed as the Court's first female member by President Ronald Reagan in 1981. O'Connor's record in criminal cases was decidedly conservative, generally favoring law enforcement interests over those of criminal defendants. But in previous cases she had expressed sympathetic attitudes toward juveniles and other more vulnerable individuals charged with serious crimes. It was Justice O'Connor who announced the Court's decision and authored the majority opinion.

On the issue of the judge's instructions, O'Connor ruled in favor of Penry. Predictably she was joined in this portion of the opinion by members of the Court's more liberal wing. This included the Court's two most liberal members, William J. Brennan and Thurgood Marshall, whose long services extended back into the Court's activist era under the leadership of Chief Justice Earl Warren. Also joining the majority were two moderate Republicans, Harry Blackmun, a Minnesota appointee of President Richard Nixon, and John Paul Stevens, a President Gerald Ford appointee from Illinois.

This first issue asked the Court to decide whether the judge's instructions to the jury violated the Cruel and Unusual Punishment Clause of the Eighth Amendment because the jury was not adequately instructed by the judge to consider all of the mitigating evidence. The Court previously established a standard that punishment should be directly related to the personal culpability of the defendant. Individualized assessments were needed to determine, as in Penry's case, if the defendant should be executed or committed to prison for life. Although Penry's attorneys had presented mitigating evidence of retardation and abuse, the judge's instructions focused the jury's attention only on the three aggravating circumstances issues: deliberation, probability of future dangerous acts, and unreasonable response to provocation. The jurors were not explicitly told that upon full consideration of mitigating circumstances they could show leniency and not impose the death penalty. Thus, directing the jury to focus on the aggravating factors had the effect of steering its members away from considering evidence of mitigation. As a result the majority reversed the lower court's ruling and called for a new, properly conducted penalty phase.

The Court's answer to this first question at a minimum gave Penry a new opportunity to avoid the death penalty, but Penry's second line of argument, if accepted by the justices, could save him from capital punishment altogether. Specifically, Penry asked the justices if it is cruel and unusual punishment under the Eighth Amendment to execute a mentally retarded person.

On this issue O'Connor rejected Penry's plea. Her views received the supporting votes of her three fellow Ronald Reagan appointees, Chief Justice William Rehnquist and Associate Justices Antonin Scalia, and Anthony Kennedy, as well as the more moderate Byron White, an appointee of President John F. Kennedy.

This coalition of more conservative justices rested its decision on the precedent set in Trop v. Dulles (1958). Trop held that the Eighth Amendment bars penalties that were considered cruel and unusual when the Bill of Rights was adopted, as well as those sentences that the "evolving standards of decency that mark the progress of a maturing society" would consider unacceptable. And to O'Connor, "[t]he clearest and most objective evidence of contemporary values is the legislation enacted by the country's legislatures."

In casting her eye to the states, O'Connor found only two instances of state lawmaking bodies categorically removing the retarded from those eligible for execution. Georgia passed legislation protecting the retarded from the death penalty in 1988, prompted by an uproar over the 1986 execution of Jerome Bowden, a mentally retarded man many thought to be innocent of the murder charges brought against him. The Maryland legislature recently had passed a similar prohibition that was about to go into effect. Opinion polls showing increased public sentiment against such executions and the existence of several activist groups working to protect the retarded might well predict future change. "But," according to O'Connor's opinion, "at present, there is insufficient evidence of a national consensus against executing mentally retarded people convicted of capital offenses for us to conclude that it is categorically prohibited by the Eighth Amendment."

Instead, O'Connor supported the status quo. Mental retardation should be considered a mitigating circumstance that is considered by juries on a case-by-case basis. Persons classified as mentally retarded constitute a heterogeneous group. Although they have common intellectual deficits, they have diverse capacities in terms of learning and adaptive functioning. They also are capable of different levels of culpability for their actions. Not all those with mild mental retardation are unable to achieve a level of culpability that is required for the imposition of the death penalty. Absent a national consensus to the contrary, the Cruel and Unusual Punishment Clause of the Eighth Amendment is not violated by a capital punishment sentence that results from a jury's full and individualized consideration of mitigating evidence of mental retardation.

In a separate opinion joined by Marshall, Justice Brennan took a strong stance against the majority's failure to grant blanket protection to the mentally retarded. He argued that capital punishment made little sense for either retribution or deterrence purposes. Although retarded individuals are not a homogeneous population, by definition they share the common trait of limited intelligence. This condition restricts the degree to which the retarded are able to appreciate the consequences of their actions. It renders them less culpable for their offenses. The principle of retribution requires sentences proportionate to the culpability of the individual offender. Thus, execution becomes an inappropriate penalty when applied to the mentally retarded. Furthermore, because those with normal intelligence levels would still be subject to capital punishment penalties, removing the retarded from execution eligibility would not reduce whatever general deterrent effect the death penalty might have.

The Supreme Court handed down the *Penry* decision on June 26, 1989. This was the same date that the justices announced their decisions in *Stanford v. Kentucky* and *Wilkins v. Missouri,* finding that there was insufficient evidence of a national consensus to provide blanket constitutional protection from the death penalty for sixteen and seventeen year olds. The justices divided along the same 5–4 split in these cases as they did in *Penry.*

Johnny Penry's fight to avoid execution continued long after the U.S. Supreme Court's 1989 ruling. State prosecutors remained convinced that Penry was much smarter than he let on, suggesting that he feigned retardation to escape execution. He was certainly smart enough to plan his crime, and he killed Pamela Carpenter appreciating the consequences of her testifying against him if he allowed her to live. Prosecutors continued to believe that justice had not been done for Pamela Carpenter and her family. Penry's sentencing was taken to Texas juries three times, and each one ended in a jury's recommendation of death. And the appellate courts found reason to reverse each of the death sentences. These appellate reviews included a second trip to the U.S. Supreme Court where, in *Penry v. Johnson* (2001), the justices found that the state again had failed to provide adequate instructions on mitigating circumstances to the jury.

Johnny Penry remains incarcerated in the Texas correctional system three decades after the murder of Pamela Carpenter. In 2005 the Texas Court of Criminal Appeals found defects in the most recent sentencing hearing. The state's attempt to appeal that decision to the U.S. Supreme Court in 2006 failed when the justices refused to consider the case. Still, neither the prosecution nor the defense was willing to back down from their positions, setting the stage for additional legal battles over Penry's fate.

The Supreme Court's 1989 *Penry* ruling had a significant bearing on the trial of Daryl Atkins. If Atkins was found guilty of killing Eric Nesbitt, would the jury spare his life? There was a mounting body of evidence that Atkins suffered significant cognitive deficits. But was the evidence sufficiently strong to establish enough mitigation for the jury to exercise leniency? This question loomed large as defense lawyers George Rogers and Bryan Saunders prepared to counter prosecutor Eileen Addison's attempts to convict Atkins and have him put to death.

BIBLIOGRAPHIC NOTE.

Information on mental retardation is readily available in the scientific literature as well as in more popular outlets. Groups such as the American Association on Intellectual and Developmental Disabilities (formerly known as the American Association on Mental Retardation) also distribute large amounts of information on retardation.

For a discussion of the Penry Case, see Emily F. Reed, *The Penry Penalty: Capital Punishment and Offenders with Mental Retardation* (Lanham, Md.: University Press of America, 1993).

For additional views and analyses of retardation and the criminal process, see Jamie Fellner, Rosa Ehrenreich, and Michelle Caldera, *Beyond Reason: The Death Penalty and Offenders with Mental Retardation* (Washington, D.C.: Human Rights Watch, 2001); Ronald W. Conley, Ruth Luckasson, and George N. Bouthilet (eds.), *The Criminal Justice System and Mental Retardation* (Baltimore, Md.: P. H. Brookes, 1992); Margaret Edds, *An Expendable Man: The Near Execution of Earl Washington, Jr.* (New York: New York University Press, 2003); Miles B. Santamour and Patricia S. Watson (eds.), *The Retarded Offender* (New York: Praeger, 1982).

The Trial

MONDAY, FEBRUARY 9, 1998, was a chilly, mostly cloudy day in Yorktown. Early that morning the participants in Daryl Atkins's murder trial assembled at the York County/Poquoson Courthouse. The newly constructed brick building, located on Ballard Street in the city's historical district, had been dedicated only five months earlier. The courthouse was surrounded by green lawns, trees, and other government offices. Compared to many American courthouses located in busy urban centers, the physical setting appeared more peaceful and less hectic. The Yorktown courthouse was only about twenty-five miles from the site of the first recorded imposition of the death penalty in the American colonies, the 1608 execution of convicted spy George Kendall in Jamestown Colony.

A more contemporary and ominous event for Daryl Atkins took place on the second day of his trial. On February 10, Virginia authorities executed Tony Mackall, a thirty-three-year-old black man convicted of the 1986 killing of Mary Elizabeth Dahn. Dahn, working in the cashier's booth at a Prince William County Shell gas station she owned, was shot in front of her five-year-old daughter. Like Atkins, Mackall suffered from low intelligence levels. In spite of an IQ estimated to be as low as 64 by one psychiatrist, a jury recommended death.

The prosecution was convinced that Daryl Atkins was the triggerman in the slaying of Eric Nesbitt. Eileen Addison, the Commonwealth's Attorney, directed prosecution efforts to obtain a conviction. Others on her staff, principally assistant prosecutor Benjamin Hahn, aided in presenting the case against Atkins. Should they win a conviction, the prosecutors

The trial court proceedings in the Daryl Atkins murder case took place in the York County-Poquoson Courthouse located in the historic district of Yorktown, Virginia.

were prepared to argue for the death penalty. In Addison's view, the death penalty was the only just outcome. The senseless murder of Eric Nesbitt by a man whose recent history was marked with increasingly violent crimes demanded that Atkins forfeit his life for the life he had taken. For Nesbitt's family and friends, justice would be served only if Atkins paid the ultimate price. As Addison frequently pointed out, Atkins had already been sentenced to life in prison for his previous crime spree. Another life term would not add to the sentence he would actually serve. Unless Atkins received the death penalty, his killing of Eric Nesbitt would be without personal consequence.

Defense attorneys George Rogers and Bryan Saunders, of course, saw things much differently. To them the record was not clear as to the identity of the person who shot Eric Nesbitt. Atkins and William Jones told conflicting stories of the events of that night with each claiming the other pulled the trigger. Their statements were obviously self-interested—only the actual murderer would face possible execution. The physical evidence convincingly supported neither Atkins's nor Jones's versions. Under these circumstances, sending Daryl Atkins to death row would be terribly unjust. There remained too much doubt about the identity of the actual killer, doubt that would never be completely resolved. In addition, Rogers and Saunders believed that Atkins's mental retardation made him less blameworthy for his actions. He had the intellect of a child, and in America young children are not executed. The defense attorneys could certainly sympathize with the Nesbitt family, but executing Atkins would only compound the killing. It would certainly not bring Eric back to life. Confining Daryl Atkins to prison for the rest of his natural life would protect society from any future violent actions. A harsher penalty would accomplish nothing.

AFTER MONTHS OF PREPARATION and numerous pre-trial skirmishes over evidence and procedure, the prosecution and defense readied to present their arguments and evidence before a court presided over by sixty-year-old Judge Prentis Smiley Jr. Smiley, a life-long Virginian, had the demeanor of a man steeped in the state's history and culture. He was born in Bristol, received his undergraduate degree from Lynchburg College, and his law degree from the College of William and Mary. He engaged in the private practice of law from 1964 to 1995 in Yorktown and Williamsburg. The General Assembly elected him circuit court judge for a term of eight years beginning in April 1995. Smiley, a white-haired jurist with a serious but courteous manner, enjoyed a reputation for demanding relevance, being intolerant of unnecessary courtroom delays, and being sensitive to the needs of jurors who served in his courtroom. Perhaps more than anything else, Smiley was not afraid or hesitant to make decisions. In both appearance and demeanor, Smiley in every way fulfilled the expected role of a judge. His duty would be to ensure that the Atkins trial was conducted consistent with legally correct procedures and to answer any questions of law that were raised.

The first step in the proceedings was to present Daryl Atkins with the charges against him and to hear his formal response to each. After the accusations were read, Atkins pled guilty to the crimes he had previously admitted, including the abduction and robbery of Nesbitt, but he pled

Virginia Circuit Judge Prentis Smiley Jr., who presided over the numerous trial court proceedings against Daryl Atkins from 1996 through 2008.

not guilty to the capital murder charge and to one count of using a firearm in the commission of a murder.

Judge Smiley then led Atkins through a long litany of questions to establish that he was ready for trial. These questions probed Atkins's understanding of the charges he faced, the potential penalties that could flow from those charges, his access to defense counsel, and whether his guilty pleas were freely and voluntarily entered. Having determined that Atkins was properly prepared, Smiley moved the proceedings to the more formal stages of the process.

The Sixth Amendment to the U.S. Constitution guarantees that "In all criminal prosecutions, the accused shall enjoy the right to a speedy and public trial, by an impartial jury of the State and district wherein the crime shall have been committed." With the scope of the trial now narrowed to the disputed murder accusation and a related weapons violation, a jury to hear the case now needed to be assembled.

A jury is essentially a fact-finding body with the responsibility of evaluating the evidence presented by both sides. Taking this evidence into account and following the judge's instructions, the jury must answer the single factual question that dominates all criminal trials: Is the defendant guilty of the crimes charged beyond a reasonable doubt?

The "reasonable doubt" benchmark defies easy definition and is often difficult for jurors to understand. Although reasonable doubt is a high standard for prosecutors to satisfy, it does not mean that jurors must be totally certain of the defendant's guilt. After all, there are relatively few exercises in the judgment of human affairs that yield absolute conclusions. There is always a possibility of error, no matter how slight. Instead, the courts have interpreted the standard to mean that when a juror reaches an abiding conviction, to a moral certainty, that the defendant is guilty, the prosecution has met its obligation. Jurors, then, must be convinced of the truth of the charges to a reasonable and moral certainty in order to return a verdict of guilty.

It should not be surprising that the selection of individuals to exercise this judgment and determine the fate of the defendant is a very critical stage of the process. The procedures for choosing jurors are carefully spelled out in the law to ensure fairness. Strict adherence to the jury selection rules is particularly warranted in capital cases.

Juries are supposed to be representative of the community. Although no single jury can perfectly reflect the demography of a jurisdiction, the people serving on juries in any locality over a significant period of time should constitute a reasonable cross-section of the community. In order to achieve this goal, courts begin with a list of residents who are legally eligible to participate in jury service. Most jurisdictions use voter registration rolls as their initial source of names. This is convenient because the same age, residency, and citizenship factors are normally used to establish both voter and jury service eligibility. Local jurisdictions may supplement the voter registration lists with names taken from other sources such as tax rolls, public utility records, and lists of those holding driver's licenses. When juries are needed, courts randomly call eligible citizens to report for service.

Because juries are drawn from a specific geographical area, the people chosen to serve tend to reflect that community. Daryl Atkins and William Jones abducted and robbed Eric Nesbitt in the city of Hampton. As they drove toward the location where the murder would take place, they traveled through the city of Newport News. But when they killed Eric Nesbitt they did so just inside the York County limits. Consequently, Daryl Atkins would stand trial before a jury that represented the population of the York County/city of Poquoson area rather than the cities of Hampton or Newport News.

This was a matter of no small significance. York County's population was decidedly different from the cities of Hampton or Newport News. When the Atkins jury was selected, only 13.5 percent of York County residents were African American; whereas, the populations in Hampton and Newport News were, respectively, 45 percent and 39 percent black. The median family income in York County was $58,000, whereas in Hampton it was $39,500 and in Newport News $36,600. The poverty rate in York County was 3.5 percent, but it was three to four times higher in Hampton and Newport News. More than a third of adults in York County had college degrees, but only about 20 percent did in the cities of Hampton and Newport News. There were political differences as well. Voters in York historically supported Republican candidates, and Hampton and Newport News voters generally favored Democratic Party candidates. As a consequence, any jury drawn in the York circuit would likely be whiter, more affluent, better educated, and more conservative than juries selected in either Hampton or Newport News.

Once prospective jurors are called for service, they are questioned by the judge and, in most states, by the attorneys for each side. This process, called *voir dire,* is designed to identify jurors who have beliefs or conflicts of interest that would make their participation on a particular trial inappropriate. As the questioning proceeds, the attorneys are free to challenge any potential juror for "cause." When lawyers do so, they are claiming that the would-be juror possesses a bias or some other disqualifying characteristic. If, for example, the questioning reveals that a potential juror has a relationship with the defendant, holds racially prejudicial views that would likely affect how the juror would decide the case, or might somehow profit from the case outcome, one of the attorneys would likely challenge for cause. When such a challenge is made, the judge decides whether to retain or dismiss the juror from participating in that particular case. Because it is vitally important to eliminate those individuals who cannot be impartial, challenges for cause are generally unlimited in number.

In addition to challenges for cause, the attorneys have the ability to excuse a limited number of potential jurors without giving a reason or obtaining the agreement of the judge. These juror strikes are called "peremptory challenges." Attorneys use them to eliminate potential jurors who are likely to favor the other side.

The U.S. Supreme Court, however, has imposed some exceptions to the traditionally unrestricted use of peremptory challenges. Beginning in

Batson v. Kentucky (1986), the justices developed a rule against either the prosecution or the defense using peremptory strikes to eliminate potential jurors on account of race. And with *J.E.B. v. Alabama ex rel. T.B.* (1994) a similar ban was imposed against dismissing jurors because of their sex. Attorneys may enter an objection if they believe the opposing lawyers have exercised a peremptory challenge based on either of these impermissible factors. If in response to the objection legitimate reasons for the dismissal cannot be convincingly offered, the judge can reject the peremptory challenge.

Virginia law requires juries of twelve individuals in serious criminal cases. But because the Atkins trial was projected to take at least a week, a total of fourteen jurors would be selected. The two additional jurors would serve as alternates, pressed into full service if illness or some other factor prohibited a regular juror from completing the trial. The two alternates would be selected by lot from among the fourteen at the beginning of the trial. Only the attorneys would be informed of their identities; not even the alternates would know. They would fully participate, and only at the end of the trial, when jury deliberations were about to begin, would the alternates learn of their status and be excused.

From the approximately fifty potential jurors called, twenty-four randomly selected individuals participated in the opening *voir dire* process. Standard questions were asked concerning such subjects as previous contact with any of the participants in the trial, exposure to press accounts of the crime, personal or family member experiences as crime victims, and any personal burdens that might be caused by serving for a week as a juror.

In addition, in death penalty cases jurors' attitudes and beliefs about capital punishment come into play. The law demands that capital punishment sentencing verdicts be based on individualized considerations of aggravating and mitigating factors. The U.S. Supreme Court, in decisions such as *Witherspoon v. Illinois* (1968), has held that jurors must be open to the possibility of voting in favor of either execution or a lesser penalty depending upon their evaluation of the evidence. A juror who admits an inability to support the death penalty under any circumstances or the contrary belief that all convicted murders should be executed is incapable of applying the law.

Much of the Atkins case *voir dire* was devoted to the death penalty question. Several potential jurors were dismissed for cause because of their capital punishment beliefs. Some of the excused individuals expressed strong moral objections to the death penalty; others adhering to the biblical command of "an eye for an eye" thought it would only be right for Atkins to forfeit his life if he were convicted. Such individuals were dismissed because their beliefs would not allow them to follow the dictates of the law in determining an appropriate sentence should Atkins be convicted.

New jurors, replacing those challenged for cause, were subjected to the same lines of questioning. This continued until twenty-four individuals were identified who possessed no disqualifying characteristics. At this point, the prosecution and defense were each given five peremptory challenges to excuse jurors whose answers revealed possible sympathies for the other side. Upon completion of this process, fourteen people remained—eight men and six women. These individuals would constitute the jury that would determine Daryl Atkins's fate.

Throughout the subsequent legal proceedings race was always a simmering issue, but never one that took center stage. Upon the completion of the peremptory challenge process, George Rogers objected to the prosecution excusing a nineteen-year old black woman, claiming that the strike was racially motivated. Eileen Addison, however, convinced Judge Smiley that nonracial factors, including the woman's youth and some factual discrepancies in her *voir dire* responses, accounted for the prosecution's decision to dismiss her. In the end, only one of the fourteen jurors was African American.

WITH THE JURY IN PLACE, opening arguments began on Tuesday, February 10. Daryl Atkins was at the defense table with his attorneys. "Nattily dressed," as one writer reported, Atkins projected a non-threatening image. Throughout the trial he sat quietly, occasionally rocking in his chair. He appeared rather distant, rarely saying anything to his attorneys. Mary Sloan and members of her family had come from upstate New York to attend the trial. True to their earlier promise, a group of uniformed Air Force personnel also attended the daily sessions out of respect for their fallen colleague. Members of Atkins family were also present, including his parents and grandparents.

Eileen Addison was the first to address the jurors. She carefully outlined the issues in the case and how she intended to demonstrate beyond a reasonable doubt that all the elements of capital murder were present. In doing so she also began to lay the groundwork for the penalty phase by emphasizing the senseless brutality of the crime, at one point asking the jurors, "Have you ever heard the phrase 'riddled with bullets?'"

Daryl Atkins at his 1998 trial for the murder of Eric Nesbitt.

For the defense, George Rogers emphasized the presumption of innocence and hammered away at prosecution's burden to prove guilt beyond a reasonable doubt. The evidence, he argued, would not conclusively establish that Atkins was the triggerman. Rogers conceded that Atkins had participated with Jones in the killing, but claimed that the evidence pointed to William Jones as the one who took Eric Nesbitt's life, not Daryl Atkins.

Among the conflicts that occurred on the second day of the trial was a dispute over the admissibility of the thirty-one-page statement Daryl Atkins had given to Investigator Troy Lyons shortly after he was arrested. In that statement Atkins admitted to participating in the robbery and abduction, but claimed William Jones had committed the actual murder. In substantial detail, Atkins had described his account of how the murder had taken place.

Defense attorneys wanted to introduce the statement as evidence. If they succeeded in doing so, they could get into the record Daryl Atkins's account of what happened at the murder scene without putting him on the witness stand. If Judge Smiley disallowed the introduction of the statement, they could advance their theory of the crime only by having Atkins testify. That could prove to be a very dangerous move. If Atkins took the witness stand, he would have to undergo cross-examination by the prosecutor. It would be almost impossible for Atkins to do well under the interrogation of a skilled litigator like Eileen Addison. If the statement to Lyons could be introduced, however, Atkins would not have to take the stand and cross-examination could be avoided.

The prosecution, of course, moved to block the statement from being entered into evidence. If the defense was to present Atkins's account of the crime to the jury, the prosecution wanted the opportunity to cross-examine him. In order to accomplish its objective, the prosecution argued that admitting Atkins's statement into evidence would violate the "hearsay rule."

The hearsay rule is a complicated evidentiary doctrine. Its meaning is difficult for non-lawyers to grasp. It is based on the premise that assertions of the truth made out of court are inherently unreliable. In order to ensure credibility, factual assertions should be made under oath, in court, and be subject to cross-examination. Thus, the hearsay rule bars out-of-court assertions from being introduced as proof of what is being asserted. According to the prosecution, Atkins's statement to Lyons was clearly hearsay. Atkins had represented to Investigator Lyons that Jones was the real killer. That out-of-court assertion should not be used in court as evidence to support the conclusion that Jones was the murderer. Instead, Atkins should be required to make his accusations against Jones in open court and under oath.

Hearsay is not generally admissible in court. It is excluded for numerous reasons. Among them are that the hearsay is not given under oath, that the hearsay cannot be cross-examined, that the introduction of hearsay violates the principle that the defendant should be able to confront his accusers in open court, and that the jury has no opportunity to observe the demeanor of the person who provided the hearsay statements.

Judge Smiley agreed with the prosecution's position over defense objections. If the defense wanted to make the claim that Jones was the real killer, it would have to provide a witness to testify to that fact in court, under oath, and be subject to cross-examination. Smiley's ruling meant that Daryl Atkins, the only person other than Jones to witness the murder, would have to take the witness stand.

EILEEN ADDISON deftly presented the prosecution's case. Between Tuesday and Thursday she introduced witnesses and physical evidence to reconstruct the crime and the circumstances surrounding it, all orchestrated to prove Daryl Atkins's guilt.

Addison began by calling Eric Nesbitt's mother, Mary Sloan, to the witness stand. Sloan gave the jury a description of her son, including how he grew up, his youthful activities, and his decision to join the military. She explained why he had taken the second job at the auto parts store and told the jury she had last seen her son at a family reunion two weeks before he was killed. At one dramatic point in her testimony, Addison showed her the photograph taken at the Crestar ATM machine and asked if she recognized anyone in the picture. She identified her son Eric as the person wedged between Atkins and Jones, and the man who had a gun pointed at him. Sloan's testimony not only portrayed a positive image of her son, but also began to build an understanding of the terror Eric must have experienced as the events of the night unfolded.

Addison followed with two witnesses who provided information related to the scene of the crime. Garland Clay described to the jury how he spotted Nesbitt's body face down on the side of Crawford Road. Phillip Atkins, Daryl's grandfather, was called to explain that he lived not far from where the murder occurred. He testified that Daryl had visited his home on several occasions. This testimony allowed the inference that Atkins was well acquainted with the location of the murder, lending support to William Jones's story that it was Atkins who selected the murder site.

Next came witnesses who described events that took place in the twenty-four-hour period before the killing. Mark Armitage, Eric's Air Force friend, told of spending time with Nesbitt at the squadron picnic just hours before he died. Eric's supervisor, Sergeant George Duncan, also explained his last interactions with Nesbitt in the afternoon before the murder. He also verified that there was no damage to the driver's-side door of Nesbitt's truck when Eric left the picnic. And Vivian Brown, who closed the Advance Auto Parts store with Eric less than two hours before he was killed, explained how he had watched to make sure that she got safely to her car. Each of these witnesses not only testified to the last interpersonal contacts Nesbitt had before he was abducted, but also continued to build for the jury a sense of the worth of the young man whose life was taken. Hoping to move the jurors' attention off these witnesses as quickly as possible, Rogers and Saunders responded with minimal cross-examination.

At the end of Tuesday's session and continuing into Wednesday, Addison moved to cover the events of the crime itself. Deputy Troy Lyons, chief investigator for the case, carefully went over the steps in the investigation beginning at the time he was called to the crime scene. The testimony indicated how the investigation and prosecution moved from step to step based on the evidence that was uncovered prior to the arrests of Atkins and Jones.

This was followed by testimony provided by individuals who had seen Atkins in the Riverside Hospital emergency room shortly after Nesbitt's death. Nurse Jacquelyn McIntyre recapped how she had been the first to approach Atkins when he entered the ER with a bloody towel wrapped around his wounded left ankle. She related how Atkins told her that a man just outside the hospital had assaulted him. Atkins, however, offered a much different story to Anthony Tutone, the Newport News police officer who questioned Atkins in the emergency room. According to Tutone's testimony, Atkins claimed to have been the victim of an attempted robbery almost two miles from the hospital and that he had hopped all the way to the ER for treatment. Contradictions such as these began to whittle away at Atkins's credibility even before he took the witness stand. Finally, emergency room physician Ozita Cooper outlined the treatment Atkins received at the hospital before he was released.

Forensic pathologist Dr. Leah Bush, the assistant chief medical examiner who had conducted the autopsy of Eric Nesbitt's body, gave the most compelling testimony of Wednesday's session. Bush methodically reviewed her findings for the jury. She explained that eight shots had been fired into Nesbitt's body. Several of the bullets exited from their point of entry and struck other sections of the body, resulting in eighteen separate bullet holes and significantly expanding the damage caused. Bush showed how none of the gunshots were immediately fatal, but that Nesbitt likely lived for several minutes until the profuse bleeding caused a drop in blood pressure to the point that life could not be sustained. She supported her detailed description with photographs and drawings. Although none of the evidence was helpful in identifying the triggerman, Bush clearly conveyed to the jury the brutality of the assault on Eric Nesbitt's life.

Also on Wednesday, the jurors left the courtroom to get a first-hand view of Nesbitt's truck. Police towed the Nissan pickup to a secured entryway to the courthouse. The jurors were able to examine the vehicle from any perspective they wished. Some knelt to look into the vehicle, others touched the truck at various points. Of primary interest were the areas where police had collected blood samples or found ballistics evidence. A few of the jurors even sat in the truck to get a better perspective of what had occurred on the night of the killing. Undoubtedly members of the jury attempted to understand what Eric Nesbitt must have felt as his abductors seized control of the truck and later drove him to that desolate Crawford Road location. Daryl Atkins observed the actions of the jurors from a slight distance, where he was placed behind a covered railing so that the jurors would not be able to see the leg irons that prohibited any means of escape.

Addison then moved to perhaps the weakest part of her case against Atkins. For the remainder of Wednesday's proceedings and into Thursday, she would present expert testimony pertaining to the physical evidence that was collected by investigators. While to this point the prosecutor's basic arguments were well supported, the scientific evidence, particularly with respect to the blood samples, was vulnerable to alternative explanations. It was here that the defense hoped to introduce sufficient doubt to convince the jury that the prosecution failed to meet the high standard for proving guilt in a criminal case.

First up was Richard Martin, a crime scene investigator for the Newport News police department, who searched Nesbitt's truck after it had been towed from the King James Motel. Contrary to the story William Jones would tell, Martin had no trouble opening the driver's-side door from the inside of the vehicle, but could not open it from the damaged outside. He described a bullet he had found on the floorboard of the truck and a bullet hole in the transmission hump. He explained procedures used to collect blood samples from the vehicle. No weapon was recovered from the truck, but Martin did find a twenty-ounce bottle of Mountain Dew and a bag of Tostito chips—both unopened.

John Ward, a firearms expert from the state crime laboratory in Norfolk, stated that bullets were recovered from the truck's passenger-side floorboard and transmission hump, Nesbitt's body, and Atkins's leg. All came from the same .38-caliber handgun. Six shell casings were also found and each was consistent with the same weapon. The lack of powder burns on Nesbitt's body were consistent with shots fired from not closer than two to five feet.

Next came the most important, yet perplexing, of all the physical evidence—the blood found in Nesbitt's truck. Three experienced Commonwealth of Virginia forensic scientists provided the jury with their expert analysis. A stain and splatter expert testified that blood was found on the passenger-side door, door frame, floorboard, seat, and backrest. Blood was also discovered on the inside of the driver's-side door. Importantly, the samples collected from the passenger seat and backrest were determined to be projected blood. He also testified that no blood was found adjacent to the bullet hole in the transmission hump. A second expert explained DNA testing to the jury and verified that the blood samples taken from Nesbitt's pickup truck had been properly handled for scientific testing. The third forensic scientist testified that DNA test results indicated at a high probability that the blood taken from the inside of the driver's-side door belonged to Atkins, but Nesbitt's blood was found on the passenger door and door frame, passenger seat, and backrest. The drops of blood on the passenger floorboard were not able to be tested. None of the results provided any grounds to suspect that the blood in the truck belonged to anyone but Nesbitt and Atkins.

Most of Thursday's court session was devoted to the two witnesses most critical to establishing Daryl Atkins as the actual killer of Eric Nesbitt. The first was William Jones, the only other witness to the crime. And the second was Stephen Burton, who had shared the same cell block with Atkins.

Eileen Addison's questioning led William Jones through a narrative account of his relationship with Daryl Atkins and a step-by-step description of the events surrounding Eric Nesbitt's murder. Jones spoke in a soft, quiet voice, requiring several of his answers to be repeated so that that jury could hear them. Jones's testimony was perfectly consistent with what he had told prosecutors months before. It was Daryl Atkins who secured the gun, Daryl Atkins who initiated the carjacking and ATM theft, Daryl Atkins who said he knew of a place near his grandfather's house and had directed Jones to drive to the secluded spot at Crawford and Tower, and Daryl Atkins who had fired the shots that killed Eric Nesbitt. At no point that evening had Jones held the gun. At the murder scene Atkins ordered Nesbitt out of the truck, allowed Nesbitt to take about two steps, and then he opened fire while Nesbitt pleaded for his life. Jones explained that he was surprised to hear the gunfire, tried unsuccessfully to open the truck door, and finally crawled out the window. He then rushed to stop Atkins, at which point the two struggled over the control of the gun. During that time the weapon accidentally discharged with the shots striking Atkins in the lower left leg. Jones then explained how he delivered Atkins to the hospital emergency room and proceeded to move from motel to motel over the next few days in order to avoid being arrested.

George Rogers aggressively cross-examined Jones, seizing on every item in his testimony that might have been inconsistent with any statements made in the past. He also attacked Jones's claim that he had no first-hand knowledge of the murder site prior to the night Nesbitt was killed. Jones did not significantly waiver with the pressure of Rogers's questions. He remained wedded to the story he had just told the court.

Rogers vigorously attacked Jones's motivation for testifying, attempting to undermine his credibility with the jury. He accused Jones of agreeing to testify only to reduce the prison sentence he would receive for his crimes. The prosecutor's pledge to drop the robbery, abduction, and two weapons charges was dependent upon Jones's providing testimony against Atkins. Rogers implied that the story Jones told the court was filled with lies and exaggerations designed to cultivate the favor of the prosecutor in order to satisfy the conditions of his plea agreement. With his scheduled sentencing just two weeks away, Jones knew it was now time to curry favor with the prosecution by providing damning testimony against Atkins. Rogers directly accused Jones of being the real killer. Jones, however, did not budge from his claim that Atkins had pulled the trigger.

Rogers had at least succeeded in providing the jury with a reason why Jones might be motivated to lie: if he satisfied the prosecution with his testimony, Jones would have some of his pending charges dismissed and receive the recommendation of the Commonwealth for leniency at sentencing. Addison moved to confront this issue directly. The plea bargain was not saving Jones from a harsh sentence. It required him to plead guilty to first-degree murder, a crime punishable by up to life in prison. Jones was not saving his own life by testifying against Atkins. Regardless of whether or not Jones cooperated with the prosecution, there was insufficient evidence to support a capital murder charge against him.

In response to Addison's question, "why are you testifying?" Jones replied, "One thing, just so Mr. Nesbitt's family know what really happened. And the other is because of my mother. She told me to. And my father, before he died, told me to testify." Jones explained that it was already well known among the prison population that he was testifying against a fellow inmate. That alone put his life in jeopardy. "Like I said, I wanted to testify to tell … their family the real truth of what happened; my Mom, let her know, ease some of the pain; won't ever bring him back, but help them a little."

Although Jones stood up reasonably well against Rogers's cross-examination, the jury could not help but recognize that that his testimony was offered in exchange for a plea bargain deal. Addison needed something to combat the implication that Jones was lying for his own benefit. With the physical evidence not definitively supporting either Jones or Atkins, it was imperative for Addison to find some corroboration for Jones's testimony that Atkins committed the murder. She found that corroboration in the testimony of Stephen Burton.

Burton testified that between December 1996 and March 1997, Atkins and he lived in the same cell block in the York County jail. In January, the two inmates struck up a conversation during which they discussed the various charges each faced. According to Burton, Atkins said "that he had put a boy out of a truck in York County, that he had shot at a boy to scare him. … And he had mentioned later on that he had shot himself in the leg but he was too—excuse my French—fucked up to remember it because he had been drinking and doing drugs…. That he had freaked out…. I mean, he laughed about it. He laughed about the robbery like it was nothing that mattered. Just basically a big joke."

Burton also claimed that Atkins expressed no worries about a conviction. The only evidence the police had, he said, was the ATM photograph. They didn't have the gun, because he "had thrown a weapon off a bridge past the tunnel." But if "he was convicted of the crime … he wouldn't go down by himself, that he would take his boy down with him." According to Burton, Atkins made it clear that "his boy" was William Jones.

Burton's testimony was particularly damaging to Atkins. Although Atkins's words that he "shot at a boy to scare him" stopped short of an admission of murder, it did put the gun in Atkins's hands at the site of the crime. Atkins's statements, as quoted by Burton, provided a possible explanation for the disappearance of the murder weapon, although the testimony of both Atkins and Jones was not consistent with any reasonable opportunity for Atkins to dispose of the weapon in the way Burton described. Furthermore, Atkins's purported threat to take Jones down with him was enough to prompt jurors to question Atkins's accusations that Jones was the real triggerman.

Defense counsel Rogers immediately attacked Burton's credibility. He pointed out that Burton had initially been charged with cocaine violations, but that the charges were later dropped. Even the grand theft charges for stealing the television set and video recorder had been reduced to petty theft. Clearly Rogers was implying that Burton's testimony was not believable, that he had only come forward in response to the prosecution's agreement to reduce the charges against him. To Rogers and Saunders, Stephen Burton was nothing but a "jail house snitch."

Addison responded that the cocaine charges were dropped because there was insufficient evidence to justify the case going forward. She also pointed out that the plea bargain arrangement that reduced the grand theft charges to petit theft contained no requirement that Burton cooperate or testify in the Atkins case.

At this point the prosecution rested its case.

IT WAS NOW TIME for Rogers and Saunders to present the defense. Their task was a difficult one. Addison and her assistants had assembled a strong case. They had laid out a theory of Nesbitt's murder that certainly seemed compelling. In addition, they had built in the jury's mind a strong, positive image of Eric Nesbitt, engendered sympathy for the victim's family, showed the extremely violent nature of the crime, and demonstrated how the evidence suggested that Daryl Atkins was the murderer. To this point, the defense had not been able to weaken the prosecution's case significantly. Still, the defense had hope.

The prosecution had presented numerous witnesses over a three-day period, yet very little of that evidence was directly related to the question of who killed Eric Nesbitt. The scientific evidence was very inconclusive and, at times, ran contrary to William Jones's account of the crime. Nothing in that scientific evidence implicated Daryl Atkins any more than it pointed to William Jones as the killer. The only witnesses to the killing were Atkins and Jones. If the jury believed William Jones, Daryl Atkins would likely face a death sentence.

Clearly, Jones held the upper hand. His testimony accusing Atkins presented a plausible account of the crime. He held up reasonably well under cross-examination. But Rogers established that Jones had definite incentives to lie on the witness stand, and most likely the jury did not fully believe Jones's altruistic claim that he was motivated to testify in order to do the right thing and to please his parents. While subject to considerable question, much of the damage to Jones's credibility was repaired by Stephen Burton's corroborating testimony. And finally, there was the ATM photograph. It vividly showed Daryl Atkins with the gun pointed at Eric Nesbitt. It would not be easy to remove this image from the minds of the jurors.

The best option available to the defense was to introduce an alternative theory of the crime. Specifically, to show that it was just as probable that William Jones had been the triggerman. Because the hearsay rule blocked the defense from introducing Atkins's statement to Investigator Lyons identifying Jones as the murderer, the only viable option was to put Daryl Atkins on the witness stand.

The Fifth Amendment to the U.S. Constitution specifies that a criminal defendant is under no obligation to take the witness stand at his own trial. In most criminal cases defendants are best advised to exercise their right not to testify, thereby removing the danger of making any damaging statements. In this case, however, there was little other choice.

If Atkins could present persuasive testimony implicating Jones, the degree of doubt in the jurors' minds might be raised to a critical level, causing them to question whether the prosecution had satisfied its burden of proof. The odds of success were not great. While Atkins might be capable of telling his story on direct examination, Addison would have the right to cross-examine him. Most criminal defendants have difficulty standing up to the searching questions of an able prosecutor. Daryl Atkins seemed especially vulnerable to an aggressive cross-examination by an experienced Commonwealth's Attorney. Still, what else could the defense do? If Atkins did not present his version of the story, the jury would undoubtedly return a verdict of guilty.

On Friday morning, the fifth day of the trial, Daryl Atkins took the stand on his own behalf. He was the only witness the defense would call.

In response to questions posed by George Rogers, Atkins briefly described his background and then quickly turned his attention to the night of the murder. His version of the story veered dramatically from Jones's account, beginning with what had occurred on their last trip to the 7-Eleven for beer. From that point forward, according to Atkins, the events of the evening were all directed by Jones. Atkins simply followed along.

According to Atkins, both he and Jones left the apartment with intent to rob, but it was Jones who had borrowed and was carrying the .38 semi-automatic handgun. When they reached the convenience store, Jones flagged down Eric Nesbitt and took control of the truck at gunpoint. Once in control of the vehicle, Jones took the wheel, giving the gun to Atkins with instructions to keep it trained on Nesbitt. Atkins grabbed Nesbitt's wallet and removed $60 in cash. While he was doing so, Jones saw the ATM card and decided to drive to the bank and force Nesbitt to make a withdrawal.

After removing $200 from the account, Jones and Atkins decided to tie Nesbitt up and leave him somewhere. Jones said he knew of a place, but didn't say where. He just drove north on the interstate highway. When Jones turned onto Crafford Road, Atkins was in an area he had never been before. Jones stopped the car and demanded that Atkins return the gun to him. He also ordered Atkins and Nesbitt to switch seats so that Daryl was in the middle and Eric in the passenger seat. Jones then drove a little farther until they reached the point where Tower Lane intersected Crawford.

Jones got out of truck and ordered Nesbitt also to exit. Nesbitt complied, but then crouched in a defensive posture. Jones ordered him to stand up straight, and when he did, Jones opened fire. Atkins testified that he saw flashes of light coming from the gun and heard the shots. He quickly slid from the middle to the passenger side of the seat, but suddenly felt a burning sensation in his left leg just above the ankle. He had been shot by a bullet that entered the truck. Shortly thereafter the shots stopped. Jones got back in the truck and drove off. Jones said he did not know how a bullet had hit Atkins in the leg, but he drove Atkins to the emergency room for treatment.

Atkins ended his testimony by explaining that he had made a statement to Investigator Lyons shortly after his arrest in which he admitted to the robbery and abduction of Eric Nesbitt but said that Jones had done the killing. The description of the crime given to Lyons at that time, Atkins said, was the same as the testimony he was now giving in court. Atkins finally repeated that he had never fired the gun that night.

Atkins's version of the crime was now on the record. On all crucial points it stood in stark contrast to what Jones told the jury. For the defense the question now was, could Atkins survive Addison's cross-examination with his story intact.

For Addison, the goal on cross-examination was to discredit Atkins. There were many inconsistencies in the stories he had told since the time of the murder, and she needed to exploit each of them. She wanted to establish that William Jones was a more believable witness than Daryl Atkins.

At the beginning of cross-examination, Atkins asserted that he told the truth to Investigator Lyons immediately after his arrest in 1996 and that he had just told the truth in his direct testimony. This declaration set the stage nicely for Addison to demonstrate that Atkins's statements were filled with lies and inconsistencies. First, in his statement to Lyons Atkins said that he was shot as he jumped in front of the gun to save Nesbitt's life, but had now claimed in court that he was hit by the bullet while still sitting in the passenger seat of the truck. Under cross-examination Atkins admitted that this statement to Lyons was untrue. Second, Akins told Lyons that he had no intention of engaging in robbery when he walked to the 7-Eleven. But his testimony on direct examination indicated that both he and Jones intended to engage in robbery in order to get beer money. Third, Atkins lied to Lyons when he denied ever having the gun in his hand that night and when he claimed it was Jones who pointed the gun at Nesbitt at the ATM. Obviously, Atkins was unaware of the Crestar ATM photos when he made these statements to Lyons. Fourth, Atkins previously claimed either that he did not know where the gun came from or, alternatively, that Jones brought it to the apartment that day. But in his court testimony he acknowledged that it came from Mark Dallas.

Addison pursued other lies and inconsistencies. Atkins, for example, admitted lying to Nurse McIntyre in the emergency room when he said he was shot right outside the hospital and to Officer Tutone, to whom he claimed to have been shot in a holdup attempt two miles from the emergency room. Atkins's various accounts also had inconsistencies about what had occurred both at the ATM and at the scene of the murder.

At end of the cross-examination, Atkins acknowledged many of the mistruths he previously had told, but continued to assert that his court testimony was the full and accurate story of what had happened. He held fast to his position that it was William Jones and not he who killed Nesbitt.

Addison's cross-examination had been effective. She had shredded Atkins's credibility. Her questioning brought to light a long series of inconsistencies and mistruths in the various statements Daryl Atkins had given. As is the case in many criminal trials lacking conclusive physical evidence, the jury's decision would rest on matters of credibility. Which version of Eric Nesbitt's murder would be believed? Would the jury accept the account of William Jones, whose testimony was given in return for a plea bargain arrangement? Or, would the jury give credence to the testimony of Daryl Atkins, whose record of providing truthful information was seriously compromised? Issues of credibility and standards of reasonable doubt would dominate the closing arguments of the prosecution and defense.

With the evidence fully presented, Judge Smiley now turned his attention to the jury. Earlier in the trial one male juror had been dismissed when he communicated to Smiley that he had developed a lingering feeling of having had previous contact with Daryl Atkins, perhaps at his workplace. He admitted that he had checked his company records to see if that had been the case. The attorneys and the judge agreed that it would be best if the juror were excused. With thirteen jurors remaining, one of the two alternates had to be removed. By lot, a male juror was selected, leaving six men and six women to judge the case.

For the next twenty minutes, Judge Smiley instructed the jurors. Their responsibility was to consider the evidence and, after deliberation, choose among three alternatives: (1) guilty of capital murder, (2) guilty of murder in the first degree, or (3) not guilty. He then covered important legal points regarding credibility, reasonable doubt, the characteristics that distinguished capital murder from first-degree murder, and the presumption of innocence. He also emphasized that the burden of proof rested exclusively on the prosecution. The defense carried no such responsibility.

The attorneys now had their final opportunities to persuade the jurors. Closing arguments were next.

"LIES, LIES, AND MORE LIES," Addison exclaimed as she began her closing argument. Her strategy was to attack Atkins's credibility as forcefully as possible. He simply was not to be believed. Between fifteen and seventeen times under cross-examination he admitted to lying or changing his story. His final version of the crime was inconsistent with the physical evidence. The prosecution had presented some seventy pieces of physical evidence, including photographs, autopsy reports, ballistics tests, and blood analysis. None of the physical evidence had been successfully challenged by the defense. Atkins's criminal history, which now included convictions on almost two dozen felony counts, further demonstrated that his word should not be trusted.

Addison asked the jury whether Atkins's story made sense. Take, for example, Atkins's claim that just before arriving at the crime scene, Jones stopped the truck and ordered Nesbitt to change seats with Atkins. Atkins and Nesbitt, he said, got out of the truck while Atkins passed the gun to

Jones. The two then reentered the truck with Nesbitt in the passenger seat and Atkins in the center. Why would Nesbitt comply with Jones's demand? He was terrified of what might happen to him. He was in an isolated, wooded area. He was a well-trained, physically fit military man and an experienced outdoorsman. Why wouldn't he have attempted to flee the moment he stepped out of the truck as Atkins passed the gun to Jones? He could have easily disappeared into the nearby woods and eluded his abductors. Addison would later say that even she would have attempted to escape under those circumstances. Yet Atkins expected people to believe that Nesbitt passively complied with Jones's orders.

If Atkins was telling the truth about sliding over to the passenger side of the truck during the shooting, how did Nesbitt's blood get projected onto the passenger seat and backrest? And what about Atkins claim that he was shot while sitting in the truck? One bullet was lodged in Atkins ankle, but the second bullet passed through his leg. If this second bullet was the one that ultimately pierced the transmission hump why was there no blood splatter surrounding the entry point? "Use your common sense, ladies and gentlemen," Addison pleaded.

William Jones, however, had come forward to give truthful testimony, Addison claimed. Most of what he remembered from the night in question was perfectly consistent with the physical evidence. There was no evidence to support the theory advanced by the defense that William Jones pulled the trigger.

Addison ended her argument by demanding justice. She held up the photograph of Eric Nesbitt's assaulted body and declared, "Your decision here today, ladies and gentlemen, is to determine who is telling the truth because that's the point of this case.... This young man, who was shot eight times, eight times, while he begged for his life. Justice for Eric Nesbitt. You decide who told you the truth in this courtroom and who pulled the trigger."

On Atkins's behalf, George Rogers argued that the trial could be reduced to a single question: was there proof beyond a reasonable doubt that Daryl Atkins was the triggerman? The evidence is inconclusive, he claimed. No one can prove who shot Eric Nesbitt. The only two individuals present at the murder were blaming each other. The chief prosecution witnesses were not credible. Stephen Burton had originally been arrested for cocaine and grand theft violations. Then the Commonwealth reduced those charges to petit theft, and Burton suddenly became a witness against Atkins. Likewise, William Jones's testimony was motivated by "a sweetheart deal" with the prosecution. He was initially charged with capital murder, but those charges were reduced to first-degree murder, and other outstanding criminal violations were to be dismissed, conditioned on his testimony against Atkins. Can Jones really be believed under these circumstances?

Unlike Jones, who refused to say anything for a full year, Daryl Atkins readily cooperated with the York County sheriff's department and admitted his participation in the abduction, robbery, and murder of Eric Nesbitt. But he declared from the very beginning and has continued to maintain that Nesbitt did not die by his hand.

Much of the physical evidence did not match the prosecution's version of the crime. Jones, for example, testified that the shooting took place several feet outside the vehicle with Nesbitt cowering in a self-defensive posture. If that were truly the case, how did Nesbitt's blood get on the truck door, passenger seat, and backrest? And if, as Jones claimed, Atkins was shot in a struggle outside the truck, why was Atkins's blood found on the inside of the driver's-side door? Is not that more consistent with Atkins's claim that he was shot inside the vehicle? Also, Jones described how he crawled out of the driver's-side window because the door could not be opened. Yet crime scene experts testified that the door could easily open from the inside.

Other physical evidence, according to Rogers, was much more consistent with the story Daryl Atkins told the jury. Atkins was sitting in the truck at the time of the shooting. This was supported by the location and path of the bullet wound to Atkins's lower left leg. The trajectory lined up perfectly with a shot being fired from outside the truck, passing through Atkins's leg, and continuing into the transmission hump. This evidence was totally inconsistent with Jones's story that the two men struggled over the gun and the weapon accidentally fired twice while pointed downward toward Atkins's ankle.

We may never know the full truth about what happened that night, Rogers concluded. One thing is clear, however. The evidence does not support Atkins's guilt beyond a reasonable doubt. The prosecution had failed to meet its burden and the jury should return a verdict of not guilty.

Addison had the last say. In a short rebuttal argument she emphasized that Stephen Burton was not required to testify as a condition of his plea bargain arrangement and that, while Jones hoped for leniency at sentencing, his story should be believed because it matched most of the physical evidence.

The presentation of testimony, evidence, and arguments came to an end midway through the fifth day of the trial. Judge Smiley instructed the jury of six men and six women to retire to a private conference room to begin their deliberations. The attorneys who had battled in court for a full week, the families and friends of the victim and the accused, and Daryl Atkins, whose life hung in the balance, had nothing left to do but wait.

The wait, however, was not long. Before the end of the day on Friday, after three and one half hours of discussion, the jury announced that it had reached a decision. The jurors were ushered back into the courtroom and their verdict was read:

> We, the jury, find the Defendant guilty of capital murder, as charged in Indictment Number One. We, the jury, find the Defendant guilty of use of a firearm in the commission of a murder, as charged in Indictment Number Four.

As the verdict was announced Daryl Atkins looked straight ahead without any emotional expression. For the Atkins family there was sadness and fear of what the ultimate sentence might be. For Mary Sloan there was a sense of relief, as she leaned forward and held her face in her hands while her husband Dan put his arm around her. For Nesbitt's friends from Langley Air Force Base, several of whom had maintained a presence in the courtroom throughout the trial, there was a sense that justice had been done.

Judge Smiley accepted the verdict from the jury. Wasting no time, he ordered the penalty phase of the trial to begin on Saturday morning, the very next day.

BIBLIOGRAPHIC NOTE.

The account of the guilt phase of Daryl Atkins's trial is based primarily on the transcripts and court records of those events. It is supplemented by information included in press reports of those days of the trial, especially the work of reporters Mathew Paust and Deborah Straszheim whose work appeared in the Hampton Roads *Daily Press.*

For further reading on juries and jury trials, see Normal Thompson, *Unreasonable Doubt* (Columbia: University of Missouri Press, 2006); Reid Hastie (ed.), *Inside the Jury: The Psychology of Juror Decision-Making* (New York: Cambridge University Press, 1993); Robert M. Krivoshey (ed.), *Juries: Formation and Behavior* (New York: Garland Publishing, 1994); Leonard W. Levy, *The Palladium of Justice: The Origins of Trial by Jury* (Chicago: I.R. Press, 1999); Seymour Wishman, *Anatomy of a Jury* (New York: Times Books, 1986); Harry Kalven Jr. and Hans Zeisel, *The American Jury* (Boston: Little Brown, 1966); Stephen J. Adler, *The Jury* (New York: Times Books, 1994); William L. Dwyer, *In the Hands of the People* (New York: St. Martin's Press, 2002); Randolph N. Jonakait, *The American Jury System* (New Haven, Conn.: Yale University Press, 2003); Hiroshi Fukurai, *Race in the Jury Box* (Albany: State University of New York Press, 2003); Benjamin Fleury-Steiner, *Jurors' Stories of Death* (Ann Arbor: University of Michigan Press, 2004); Bryan C. Edelman, *Racial Prejudice, Juror Empathy, and Sentencing in Death Penalty Cases* (New York: LFB Scholarly Publishing, 2006).

Sentencing

ON SATURDAY, FEBRUARY 14, 1998, Daryl Atkins stood before the same jurors who found him guilty of capital murder the previous day. The jurors would now determine his sentence. There were only two alternatives: life in prison without parole and execution.

The Commonwealth of Virginia and the death penalty have a long history. Virginia was not only the site of the first public execution in the American colonies, but it continued to use the death penalty throughout its history. Between 1608 and 1976, Virginia executed 1,277 defendants, more than any other state.

Data from the early twentieth century in Virginia illustrate conditions that influenced the U.S. Supreme Court's decision in *Furman v. Georgia* (1972) to impose a nationwide ban on executions. Between 1908 and 1962, Virginia put to death 240 criminal defendants. Eighty-five percent of these condemned criminals were African American. Even more disturbing, sixty-two defendants received the death penalty for rape, attempted rape, or robbery, all crimes less serious than murder. All sixty-two of those executed for these crimes were black. The state's laws allowed for near complete discretion on the part of juries and required no automatic appellate review.

Between 1975 and 1977, the Virginia legislature totally revamped the state's capital punishment laws in response to *Furman*. First, the state significantly reduced the number of crimes for which death was a possible punishment. Second, the law removed execution as the only penalty for a capital crime; it now permitted life in prison as an alternative. Third, the state adopted bifurcated trial procedures for capital cases, with the first stage focusing on guilt and the second stage, if necessary, concentrating on an appropriate sentence. Fourth, the state guided jurors in capital case sentencing by defining the use of aggravating and mitigating factors. And fifth, the law provided for an automatic appeal to the state supreme court of all death penalty sentences. Two decades later, Virginia tightened sentencing options by removing parole eligibility for any person sentenced to life in prison for a capital murder committed after January 1, 1995.

With a new capital punishment law in place, the death penalty was again a sentencing option. Although prosecutors quickly took advantage of the new procedures, there were several years of trials and appeals before a convicted murderer was put to death. Virginia's moratorium on executions, which began in 1962, officially ended when Frank Coppola, a former police officer convicted of a 1978 home invasion, robbery, and murder, was put to death in the electric chair on August 10, 1982.

The statutory changes had a considerable impact on capital punishment patterns. Between 1977 and 1999, there were 9,235 murders with known offenders in Virginia. Only 119 of the accused murderers received a death sentence. The odds of a capital offender receiving a death sentence, therefore, were quite low. With a capital punishment rate of 0.013 per solved murder, Virginia was significantly below the national average of 0.022 for states that used the death penalty.

Under the new procedures, the influence of race moderated from the pre-*Furman* years. From 1995 to 1999, the years immediately surrounding the Eric Nesbitt murder and Atkins's trial, white defendants arrested for murder were indicted on capital charges at a higher rate than blacks. From the first post–*Gregg v. Georgia* (1976) execution in 1982 through 2007, Virginia executed more white offenders (fifty-one) than African Americans (forty-four). The proportion of all death sentences handed out to black defendants, however, remained higher than would be expected based on the proportion of African Americans in the state population.

Some death penalty trends, however, were not running in Daryl Atkins's favor. Between 1976 and 2008, Virginia was second among the states in the number of capital offenders executed and had the fourth highest execution rate per capita of the death penalty states. The state's 98 executions, however, were dwarfed by the 405 individuals put to death in

Texas. Also, during the time between Eric Nesbitt's murder and the beginning of the Atkins trial, Virginia executed fourteen convicted murderers, a rate of almost one per month.

On the other hand, the officials of York County could not be described as having an abnormal zeal to impose the death penalty. Atkins was the first case since capital punishment was reinstated in which York County prosecutors had asked for the death penalty. In addition, with the removal of parole possibilities, juries were less hesitant to sentence capital offenders to life in prison. Prior to this statutory change, death was the only option for which jurors could be confident that the murderer would never be released back into society.

Prior to 1995, Virginia exclusively used the electric chair to carry out its executions. The law, however, was amended to give condemned offenders a choice between electrocution and lethal injection. On January 24, 1995, Dana Ray Edmonds, a black man convicted of killing a white shopkeeper in Danville twelve years earlier, became the first person executed by lethal injection. Following Edmonds's death, lethal injection became the primary method of execution in Virginia. Of the next seventy-three capital offenders put to death, only four selected electrocution.

THE TASKS FOR BOTH the prosecution and defense were clearly laid out under Virginia law. To obtain a death sentence, Eileen Addison had to convince the jury beyond a reasonable doubt of the presence of at least one aggravating circumstance. State law only specified two factors as aggravating circumstances:

1. Future Dangerousness. There is a probability, based upon evidence such as the defendant's prior history or the circumstances of the crime, that the defendant would commit criminal acts of violence that would constitute a continuing threat to society.
2. Vile Crime. The defendant's conduct, based on evidence, was outrageous or wantonly vile, horrible, or inhuman in that it involved torture, depravity of mind, or aggravated battery to the victim.

During the sentencing phase Bryan Saunders took the lead role for the defense. He and co-counsel George Rogers pursued a two-pronged strategy.

First, they intended to attack the prosecutor's evidence of aggravation with the goal of convincing the jury that there was insufficient evidence to establish the existence of such factors beyond a reasonable doubt. And second, they wanted to demonstrate the existence of mitigating circumstances that would persuade the jurors to be lenient and to spare the life of Daryl Atkins.

The prosecution was first to present its case. Addison's goal was to convince the jury that there was ample evidence to establish both a vile crime and future dangerousness. She would use evidence of the wanton nature of the murder that was previously presented during the guilt phase, as well as new material to establish the probability of future dangerousness.

She began her presentation to the jurors by focusing on the crimes Atkins had committed in the months leading up to Nesbitt's murder. The objective was to show, based on Atkins's formal record and testimony from some of his victims, a pattern of escalating violence suggesting a high probability of future criminal activity.

The first witnesses to testify were Dennis Tuinei and John Hultquist, two of the four victims who had been robbed at gunpoint while they used a payphone in April 1996. Both identified Daryl Atkins as one of the three men who had confronted them. Tuinei described how he had been forced to lie face down on the pavement while one of the men held a gun to his head and Atkins searched him for valuables. He also stated that Atkins struck him over the head with a bottle during the course of taking his pager and $5 from his pocket. Hultquist described that he, too, was made to lie on the ground while he was robbed of $22.

Because Atkins had earlier admitted to participating in the crime, defense attorney Saunders used his cross-examination of the witnesses to minimize the seriousness of Atkins's role. In response to his probing, Tuinei and Hultquist acknowledged that Atkins was not the person who held the revolver and that he did not appear to be the leader of the group. Hultquist also responded that Atkins at no time physically assaulted him.

Next to the witness stand was Kevin Phillips, the pizza deliveryman who was robbed at gunpoint. Addison's questions carefully led Phillips through the events of June 28, 1996, when he attempted to deliver an order to a residence on Sacramento Drive in Hampton. Phillips explained how it felt to have a gun placed at the back of his head, how he was made to crawl back to his car, and how, after being robbed, he was driven to a swampy area by two of the robbers who openly debated whether to shoot him. Phillips also related how he had to crawl through the swamp when his attackers gave him five seconds to escape before they threatened to open fire.

Once again, Saunders attempted to minimize the damage by getting Phillips to admit that Daryl Atkins was not the man who held the gun during the robbery and abduction. Little more could be accomplished because Atkins had already pled guilty to crimes stemming from this incident.

Among Atkins's past victims, Amanda Hamlin, the woman shot by Atkins in August 1996 as she finished mowing her lawn, was the most effective prosecution witness. Hamlin described to the jury her surprise at being suddenly "slapped up behind the head" with a gun as she was about to dismount her mower. She went on to explain how Atkins dragged her to the front lawn and struck her to the ground. Hamlin not only feared that she would be shot but also had deep concern for the safety of her daughter who was in the house. When Atkins started to leave she thought she was safe, but he returned almost immediately and shot her in the abdomen. The result was a twenty-one-day hospital confinement, a colostomy, and continuing psychiatric treatment.

Rather than risk extending the jury's attention on the crime or compounding the effects of Hamlin's powerful testimony, the defense waived its right to cross-examine.

Next Addison presented victim impact evidence, intended to demonstrate the seriousness of the Nesbitt murder by its effect on the victim's friends and family. Two witnesses testified. The first was Mark Armitage, perhaps Eric Nesbitt's closest friend at Langley Air Force Base. Armitage explained that he and Nesbitt worked together nearly every day and frequently socialized together after their shifts. He explained that his wife, Sarah, was also a close friend to Nesbitt. When Investigator Troy Lyons informed them of Nesbitt's death, Sarah, then nine-months pregnant, cried for days.

The court's attention then focused on the testimony of Mary Sloan, Eric Nesbitt's mother. Addison first questioned Sloan about her son, eliciting information to show the jurors Eric's values and character. Sloan described her son's role in the family as the eldest of six children and how his siblings admired him. She explained Eric's love for the outdoors, his participation in sports, his attainment of the Eagle Scout rank, and his volunteer work for the town's fire department and rescue squad. She gave an account of Eric's decision, shortly after high school graduation, to serve in the U.S. Air Force. Sloan went on to describe her shock on the day the Air Force Death Notification Committee drove up to her home. She explained how devastating Eric's death had been for the family and provided detailed accounts of the effect of the murder on each of her surviving children.

Again, there was little the defense could offer in response. Bryan Saunders stood, expressed his deep sympathy to the family for their loss, and announced that he had no questions for the witness.

Finally, the prosecution asked the Court to allow the introduction of all the evidence presented during the guilt phase of the trial in support of the "vile crime" aggravating factor. The defense objected, preferring the judge to require the prosecution to reestablish each point and element of evidence previously used. Judge Prentis Smiley, however, held that the prosecution had the right to have the evidence reintroduced without requiring the jury to sit through the testimony of witnesses they had already heard earlier in the week.

Thuerefore, evidence of the circumstances of the murder was automatically made a part of the prosecution's case for capital punishment. This included scientific evidence, photographs of the body, and the medical examiner's autopsy report. Thus, the jury was free to consider the circumstances surrounding the abduction and robbery of Eric Nesbitt at gunpoint, the number of times he had been shot, and the medical examiner's vivid description of the condition of the body. The prosecution hoped this evidence would convince the jury that the murder was barbaric and the assault on Eric Nesbitt's body was far in excess of what was necessary to kill him.

At this point the prosecution rested its case for capital punishment. Addison and her assistants were confident that they had established both aggravating circumstances.

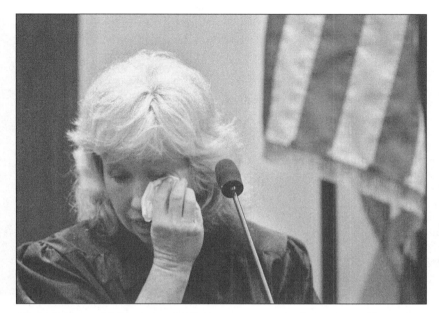

Mary Sloan provided emotional testimony on Eric Nesbitt's murder and how it affected the family.

The defense had accomplished little on cross-examination to blunt the efforts of the prosecution to establish aggravation. The victims of Atkins's earlier crimes along with the friends and family of Eric Nesbitt combined to present a strong case for the prosecution. The defense's only hope was to argue that mitigating factors were also present and that they were sufficiently compelling to outweigh evidence supporting the death penalty.

Saunders and Rogers's most viable option was to argue, consistent with the Supreme Court's *Penry v. Johnson* (1989) decision, that Atkins's limited intellectual ability significantly reduced his criminal culpability. It would be a difficult task. Atkins's ineffective testimony during the guilt phase had been rejected unanimously by the jurors, indicating a lack of any significant jury support for his cause. Furthermore, Atkins's appearance and demeanor was not consistent with stereotyped images of a person suffering from mental retardation. Through the first five days of the trial he sat quietly at the defense table generally looking bored and uninvolved, but exhibited no behavior that a juror might construe as odd.

But the defense was not without support for its retardation argument. In the early stages of preparing a defense to the capital murder charges, the court, upon the motion of the defense attorneys, appointed Dr. Evan Stuart Nelson to complete a psychological assessment of Daryl Atkins and to advise the defense on the presence of any mitigating circumstances. Evans earned his doctorate in clinical psychology from the University of North Carolina in 1991. He served an internship at the Indiana School of Medicine and did a residency at Virginia's Central State Hospital. Dr. Nelson specialized in forensic psychology and had given expert evaluations in many capital cases. Most of his evaluation work had been on behalf of the accused. About a month before the Atkins trial began, Nelson submitted a letter to Bryan Saunders summarizing his evaluation findings. The results provided strong support for a conclusion that Daryl Atkins suffered from mental retardation. Nelson's expert testimony would constitute the cornerstone of the defense argument for leniency. In fact, Dr. Nelson would be the only witness the defense called.

Nelson first summarized for the jury the extent of his evaluation. He interviewed Atkins in jail on two occasions. He also had discussions with Atkins's father and mother, and talked to jail officials. He reviewed background information including medical histories, school files, and criminal records. He examined all the pretrial statements made by William Jones and Atkins, and he reviewed Eric Nesbitt's autopsy report. And most importantly, Dr. Nelson administered a full WAIS-III intelligence test.

The results of the WAIS-III intelligence test provided the most compelling evidence for the defense. Nelson's evaluation classified Daryl Atkins as mildly mentally retarded. His full-scale IQ score of 59 placed him in the bottom first percentile of adult Americans, considerably below an IQ score of 70 that customarily distinguishes normal intelligence from mild retardation. According to Dr. Nelson a person with an IQ of 59 could likely qualify for some Social Security disability programs. Nothing in the testing process suggested that Atkins had suffered brain damage nor did his response patterns suggest that he was faking his answers in order to achieve a low score. Nelson did acknowledge that Atkins might have scored slightly higher on the test if he was not suffering from mild depression. There was no doubt in Nelson's mind, however, that Daryl Atkins had significantly sub-average intelligence.

According to Nelson's evaluation, Atkins's behavior over the years was consistent with an individual having a low intellectual capacity. His academic career beginning in second grade showed repeated failures and barely passable work. He was made to repeat the second and tenth grades. Despite the fact that Atkins failed each of his classes in eighth grade, he was promoted to the ninth. He only performed at a satisfactory level when placed in very highly structured classes. Prior to dropping out of high school Atkins's overall performance was no better than a D+ average.

Like many retarded juveniles, Atkins ultimately realized that he would never achieve approval based on his academic work. Instead, he turned to a peer group for acceptance. Atkins, unfortunately, gravitated toward individuals who abused drugs and alcohol and engaged in criminal behavior. Possessing a typical tendency of retarded people to follow rather than to lead, Atkins soon was on a trajectory that would lead ultimately to the murder of Eric Nesbitt.

Nelson assessed Atkins as having several risk factors for future violent behavior, including his age, prior record of violence, and history of substance abuse. However, prison conditions requiring highly structured behavior without access to drugs and alcohol significantly reduced those odds. Consistent with this, Atkins's incarceration record since his arrest revealed no serious disciplinary infractions and no acts of violence. Nelson's results indicated a probability that Atkins could lead a life in prison that would not pose a significant likelihood of future dangerousness.

Assistant Commonwealth's Attorney Benjamin Hahn conducted the cross-examination of Dr. Nelson. Under Hahn's questioning, Nelson noted that Atkins could understand the criminality of his conduct and had the ability to behave appropriately if he chose to do so. Hahn continued to press the prosecution's theory that Atkins's actions were caused by his voluntary drug and alcohol consumption rather than his low intelligence levels. Nelson acknowledged that Atkins's test results indicated an antisocial personality disorder, and that this condition when coupled with drugs and alcohol increased the probability of aggressive criminal violence. But he maintained that Atkins was less culpable for his actions because his intellectual deficits imposed a limited understanding of the world around him and made him more susceptible to outside influences. Like many retarded individuals, Atkins was a follower, not a leader. In all of his successful crimes, Atkins was part of a group. When he executed a crime on his own, as in the attempted robbery of Amanda Hamlin, he failed. At no point during cross-examination did Nelson waver from his view that Atkins would likely do well in a highly structured prison environment.

With the defense resting its case, the attorneys for both sides met with Judge Smiley to discuss the instructions that would be given to the jury before they began their deliberations. Once agreements were reached, the sentencing moved into its final stages with the closing arguments from the prosecution and the defense.

Eileen Addison's remarks were brief. She argued that the Commonwealth had met its obligation of proving aggravating circumstances beyond a reasonable doubt. The vile nature of the crime was amply proven by the medical examiner's report and the autopsy results. Eric Nesbitt's life was taken in a most brutal and violent way. There was also no reasonable doubt, she argued, over future dangerousness. Atkins's activities in last several years represented a consistent escalation in the frequency and violence of his criminal acts.

Bryan Saunders emphasized to the jurors that they had a choice. Even if they found evidence of aggravation, the jury could still be merciful. There was no reason to compound the loss of life by recommending the death penalty. Life in prison without parole would guarantee that Daryl Atkins would never again hurt an innocent person. He had already served sixteen months of incarceration. While placed in the highly structured prison environment, Atkins had shown that he could live successfully without resorting to crime or violence. "I ask you," Saunders concluded, "to impose a life sentence without the possibility of parole."

After receiving their final instructions from Judge Smiley, the jurors retreated to deliberate in private. They were not gone long. In only one hour and forty minutes the jury of six men and six women returned. The clerk read the jury's findings:

We, the jury, on the issue joined, having found the Defendant guilty of the capital murder of Eric Nesbitt occurring in the commission of a robbery, and having unanimously found, after consideraticn of his history and background, that there is a probability that he would commit criminal acts of violence that would constitute a continuing serious threat to society, and that his conduct in committing the offense is outrageously or wantonly vile, horrible, or inhuman in that it involved aggravated battery to the victim beyond the minimum necessary to accomplish the act of murder, and having considered the evidence in mitigation of the offense, unanimously fix his punishment at death.

The jurors found the presence of both aggravating factors and did not consider Atkins's low intelligence levels to be sufficient mitigation to warrant leniency.

Reaction to the jury's decision was predictable. Upon hearing the verdict, Daryl Atkins lowered his head, but said nothing. Eric Nesbitt's mother, Mary Sloan, admitted to reporters, "It's another grim day, but it's slightly less grim than August 16, 1996." Eileen Addison, the prosecutor, offered, "It's always sad, but I don't see what else could be done under the circumstances."

The defense attorneys maintained their position that it was William Jones who did the actual killing and not their client. "The defense is still convinced," George Rogers declared, "there is no proof beyond a reasonable doubt that Daryl Atkins pulled the trigger."

Rogers and Saunders were not about to give up. Judge Smiley would not impose an official sentence for several weeks. In the interim, probation officers would conduct a complete background report on Atkins. Smiley would use the report to help determine if the recommended death sentence was appropriate and just. There was still a possibility, although remote, that Judge Smiley would not accept the jury's decision and that he would invoke his power to replace the death penalty with a life sentence. If all else failed, the case would automatically be appealed to the Virginia Supreme Court.

WILLIAM JONES HAD satisfied his part of the bargain. In accordance with the agreement, on September 5, 1997, Jones pled guilty to murder, robbery, abduction, and three counts of firearms violations. He had cooperated with the prosecution in building a case for capital murder against Daryl Atkins. His testimony at the trial was crucial in convincing the jury that the story offered by Daryl Atkins was not believable. In return for his cooperation and truthful testimony, prosecutors had promised to ask the court to reduce the charges to murder and one count of weapons violations. But they could not control the sentence that Judge Smiley might impose even if the charges were reduced. A non-capital murder charge could still result in a life behind bars.

On February 26, 1998, twelve days after the jury recommended a death sentence for Atkins, William Jones appeared before Judge Smiley for sentencing. Timothy Clancy and Leslie Smith, Jones's attorneys, hoped to persuade Smiley to be lenient. The defense offered several witnesses to bolster its case.

Investigator Lyons detailed the role Jones had played in bringing Daryl Atkins to justice. He explained that Jones was cooperative and truthful throughout the prosecution of Atkins, providing critical information about the events surrounding the Nesbitt murder.

Leigh Hagan, a University of Missouri-trained forensic psychologist, reported that Jones had an IQ of 81 and had been impaired by voluntary consumption of alcohol and drugs. He also described Jones as a socially immature person who tended to associate with younger individuals. He claimed that the death of Jones's father had prompted the young man to reevaluate his life. That reassessment led Jones to agree to cooperate with the prosecution.

Next came Mary Rodgers, Jones's mother, who described why she urged her son to testify: "I told him to put me in Mrs. Sloan's place.... That he should at least let the family know what happened to their child. That's the only thing he could do now. He couldn't bring him back or anything like that. But he could at least tell the truth." Rodgers also pointed out that Jones had a large supportive family, several of whom were present in the courtroom, including his sons, six-year-old Khyre and four-year-old Pyre.

Finally, William Jones took the witness stand. He said he was ashamed to walk shackled into court in front of his family and friends. "As far as Eric Nesbitt, it's a tragedy that I have to live with now on. And now on.

Not even if I ever get out, even if I don't, I still have to live with it. I got to live with his death. I got to live with my involvement in it. I got to live with my kids out there growing up and not having a father. I got to live with my mother, back there crying and looking at me, like, what is my son doing up there? You know, I got to—I just take responsibility for what I have done." Addison asked Jones if he thought he deserved leniency, and he responded, "Sometimes, not all the time, for the simple fact that I was the oldest.... Nothing in this world can excuse my behavior ... [M]y behavior put me here, not nobody else forced me, but my behavior."

Judge Smiley did not seemed moved. He noted that Jones's testimony did not match the physical evidence. He seemed particularly concerned with Jones's statement that Atkins shot Nesbitt about five feet from the truck. How then, he asked, did Nesbitt's blood get splattered over the truck seat and backrest? Jones admitted that he had no answer, but speculated that it must have happened while he was crawling out of the truck window and racing around the back of the truck to get to Atkins. During those moments, he lost sight of what Atkins was doing.

With the testimony finished, Addison argued for leniency. She claimed that the prosecution of Atkins would not have been successful without Jones's full cooperation and truthful testimony. His participation allowed the Commonwealth to convict the true triggerman. Clancy followed with a request that the court take into account not only Jones's cooperation, but also his expression of remorse and responsibility, his drug and alcohol history, and his low IQ.

The prosecution and defense joined in a recommendation that the court vacate the abduction, robbery, and two firearms charges. Clancy urged the judge to find Jones guilty of felony murder and sentence him to twenty-four years. Under such a sentence he would not leave prison until he was fifty-two years old.

Judge Smiley would have nothing of it. Although he "very reluctantly" agreed to the joint request to vacate the abduction, robbery, and firearms charges, he was not persuaded to be lenient on the sentencing. "[I am] without any ability to erase the six-day jury trial that we had on Daryl Atkins and the evidence that was elicited at that hearing, which had a lasting effect on anyone who was present, the memory of which may never be erased from the court's mind.... You are guilty. You have pled guilty. You have admitted you're guilty."

On the charge of using a firearm in the commission of a murder, Smiley sentenced Jones to three years imprisonment. On the murder charge, the judge found Jones guilty and sentenced him to life in prison. Rather than leniency, Judge Smiley had imposed the most severe sentence permissible.

As a practical matter, Jones's life sentence was no less severe than he would have received if he had not cooperated with the prosecution. He was essentially given no credit for his testimony against Atkins. This result clearly disappointed defense and prosecution attorneys. Clancy claimed Judge Smiley's action would make future defendants much more reluctant to cooperate with prosecutors. Addison also took exception to some of the judge's comments, expressing satisfaction with the truthfulness of Jones's testimony against Atkins and confidence that the true killer of Eric Nesbitt had been convicted of capital murder.

TWO MONTHS LATER, on April 28, Daryl Atkins stood before Judge Smiley to learn his fate. His attorney, George Rogers, made one last appeal for mercy, knowing full well, however, that judges rarely reject a jury's recommendation. Rogers reiterated his position that the forensic evidence was not conclusive and that the testimony of William Jones was not credible. Jones was influenced by his own desire to be spared from the death penalty, Rogers asserted. His story likely was slanted in order to please the prosecution and guarantee that his plea bargain arrangement would be honored. Rogers even reminded Smiley that the judge himself had expressed doubts about the veracity of this testimony when he harshly sentenced Jones.

"Don't allow your beloved Commonwealth of Virginia to execute Daryl Atkins on the false words of William Jones," Rogers pleaded. "That, your honor, would not be justice."

Once again, Judge Smiley was neither convinced nor sympathetic. He reminded those present that the jury, not the judge, determines the facts in the case, and that the jury had rejected Daryl Atkins's version of what had happened that night. He also expressed agreement with the jury's conclusion concerning the horrible nature of the crime and Atkins's future dangerousness. Finally, nothing in the background report compiled by the probation office provided any reason for the judge not to follow the jury's recommendation.

Judge Smiley then sentenced Daryl Atkins to death for the murder of Eric Nesbitt. In addition, he imposed two life sentences for armed robbery and abduction, as well as five years in prison on each of three counts of weapons violations.

Judge Smiley set August 20, 1998, as the execution date. This was just a formality, however. State law required an automatic appeal to the Virginia Supreme Court and other procedural avenues were available to the defense as well. Prosecutor Addison predicted it would be eight years before the execution would take place, an estimate that proved to be considerably short of accurate.

For the time being, however, the question of who killed Eric Nesbitt had been settled. Upon hearing the news, Mary Sloan reported the family's sense of relief that justice had been served.

Following Judge Smiley's decision, Daryl Atkins was transferred from the Yorktown jail to the custody of state corrections officials. He was first assigned the to Mecklenburg Correction Center, an intake and evaluation facility, and then to Sussex State Prison in Waverly, home of Virginia's death row. Daryl Atkins officially became Virginia Inmate #255956.

APPEALS ARE HEARD using a much different format than occurs at the trial level. There is no jury. There are no witnesses and no primary evidence is introduced. The question in an appealed criminal case is generally not whether the defendant is guilty or not guilty. Appeals are considered by a panel of judges. The court is interested in one central question: did reversible errors occur in the lower court proceedings? That is, were there mistakes at the trial? And were those mistakes of such significance that the outcome of the case should be set aside?

Lawyers for each side of the case present their views in two ways. First, they submit written arguments in documents called briefs. The party that lost the case in the court below, called the appellant or petitioner, argues that the decision of the lower court should be invalidated because serious errors were made. The winning party, called the appellee or respondent, argues in its brief that the lower court proceeded correctly or that if errors occurred they were harmless. Second, in many cases, the attorneys also have the opportunity to present oral arguments. The attorney for each side stands before the court to argue the case and answer questions posed by the judges.

After the completion of the oral arguments, the judges retreat to their conference room to discuss the case privately and reach a decision. One of the judges is given the task of drafting a statement, or opinion, explaining the court's ruling. That draft is circulated among the other members of the court for approval or suggested revisions. Judges who do not agree with the decision of the majority are free to write opinions expressing their own views. When the process of writing, revising, and circulating the opinions has been completed, usually weeks or even months after the oral arguments were presented, the court's decision is announced. The decision will either affirm what the lower court did or reverse the outcome of the case with instructions on how the errors should be corrected.

George Rogers and Bryan Saunders continued to act on behalf of Daryl Atkins as the case moved to the Supreme Court of Virginia. They alleged that a host of errors had occurred in the Atkins case. These challenges ranged from broadside attacks on the constitutionality of the Virginia death penalty laws to technical mistakes they claimed happened during both the guilt and penalty phases of the Atkins trial. They persisted in their argument that the evidence presented at the trial fell short of establishing Atkins's guilt beyond a reasonable doubt. The defense faced discouraging prospects in pressing these arguments to the state supreme court. Since 1977 the Virginia high court had affirmed 93 percent of all cases in which the death penalty had been imposed by the circuit court.

The Commonwealth's position was represented by the Capital Litigation Unit of the state attorney general's office. This unit was created in 1995 in response to the increasing numbers of appeals sought by convicted murderers and the growing complexity of death penalty law. The department specialized in handling appeals against the state filed by death penalty defendants. The unit quickly developed a reputation for effective representation of the state's interests in upholding jury decisions and reducing delays in sentence implementation. Defense attorneys and capital punishment opponents have frequently expressed criticism of lawyers who staff this effort. They perceive the unit as being overly zealous in its defense of capital punishment verdicts, too eager to reduce procedural safeguards, and too committed to a hasty imposition of death sentences. Critics of the unit have referred to it as "The Death Squad."

At the time of Atkins's appeal to the Virginia Supreme Court, five attorneys staffed the Capital Litigation Unit. Taking the lead in opposing the appeal filed by Rogers and Saunders was Pamela Anne Rumpz, a veteran appellate attorney and death penalty specialist, trained at the University of Detroit Law School. She had been recruited to the Capital Litigation Unit from a position in the Arkansas attorney general's office.

The Virginia Supreme Court issued its decision in the case of *Daryl Renard Atkins v. the Commonwealth of Virginia (Atkins I)* on January 8, 1999, with the final version of its opinion published on February 26. The decision was unanimous, with the court's opinion written by Justice Lawrence Koontz, who had served at various levels of the Virginia judiciary for more than thirty years.

The court rejected without discussion a number of Atkins's complaints on the grounds that the issues raised had been definitively settled in previous cases. Other assertions of error were considered at greater length, but also rejected. Among those were defense claims that the prosecution rejected a prospective black juror for racial reasons, that the trial court erred in admitting blood sample evidence from the murder scene without requiring a blood sample from Jones, that Judge Smiley had erred in refusing on hearsay grounds to allow into evidence a statement Atkins made to Deputy Lyons, and that the evidence presented was insufficient to establish Atkins's guilt beyond a reasonable doubt. In the end, the court agreed with Rumpz that the Atkins's trial suffered no errors of sufficient significance to require a reversal of the jury's finding that he was guilty of capital murder. The guilty verdict was upheld.

One aspect of the sentencing phase, however, did disturb the justices. It concerned a seemingly technical issue dealing with the verdict form given to the jury. In criminal cases, the jury is provided a form on which to record its decision. This form normally lists all of the relevant options from which the jurors must choose in deciding the case. When the jury completes its deliberations it certifies which of the available outcome options it has selected. The prosecution and the defense may suggest or draft a proposed verdict form. If the recommendations of the two sides are not compatible, the differences are worked out between the lawyers and the judge during the conference on jury instructions and a final version is approved.

Eileen Addison drafted a verdict form for the prosecution that contained six possible outcomes the jury could reach after deliberating on an appropriate sentence: a recommendation of either death or life in prison based on finding that future dangerousness had been established beyond a reasonable doubt; a recommendation of either death or life in prison based on a finding that vile crime alone had been proven; and a recommendation of either death or life in prison based on a finding that both aggravating factors had been proven. Although worded differently, the version offered by the defense included these options plus a seventh: a recommendation of life in prison based on a finding that neither future dangerousness nor vile crime had been established beyond a reasonable doubt.

After some negotiating back and forth over which form to use, Judge Smiley ultimately agreed to use a modified version of the draft provided by the prosecution. Although Smiley's verbal instructions to the jury correctly outlined all available options, the verdict form did not include the option that neither of the aggravating factors had been proven. After deliberating, the jurors returned a recommendation of death after finding that both aggravating factors were present.

The defense lawyers claimed the jury's sentence recommendation should be invalidated because the verdict form did not allow the jurors the option of finding that neither aggravating factor was present. The state responded that the jury's finding that both future dangerousness and vile crime had been proven clearly implied that the jurors rejected the notion that neither aggravating factor was present. Therefore, the absence of that option on the form was a harmless mistake having no bearing on the outcome.

The justices of the state high court concluded that the jury must be presented with a verdict form that includes all available options open to them and that it is the trial court's obligation to make sure this requirement is met. The prosecutor's claim that the competing drafts of the verdict form were essentially the same "simply was not accurate," the court's opinion read. "Clearly, it is materially vital to the defendant in a criminal case that the jury have the proper verdict form." The fact that the judge's verbal instruction and the options on the written form were in conflict introduced additional confusion. Consequently, the justices set aside the death sentence. Daryl Atkins's conviction for capital murder, therefore, stood, but a new penalty phase of the trial would have to be held.

THE SECOND PENALTY PHASE posed challenges for both Prosecutor Addison and defense attorneys Rogers and Saunders. A new jury would be selected to determine Daryl Atkins's fate. At the first trial, before the jurors ever confronted the question of sentencing, they were exposed to three and a half days of testimony and evidence upon which they concluded that Atkins was guilty of capital murder. The new jury would not sit through a guilt phase. They would not know all the details of the crime. They would not observe Daryl Atkins on the witness stand performing poorly under the sharp cross-examination of the prosecution. In addition, for both sides the stakes seemed higher. The appellate reversal undoubtedly stung Addison and her assistants, especially after so thoroughly convincing the trial jury that their account of the murder of Eric Nesbitt was true. The decision of the Virginia Supreme Court rejuvenated the defense, giving them a second opportunity to save their client from death by lethal injection.

Addison would now have to present a much more extensive case for death than she had done at the first penalty phase. She would have to introduce evidence of the wantonly vile nature of the crime that was unnecessary in the first sentencing hearing where the jurors were already well acquainted with the circumstances leading to Nesbitt's death. To bolster her case, she intended to increase the information she would present to demonstrate Atkins's escalating tendency to engage in violent criminal behavior and the impact the crime had had on Nesbitt's family and friends. And finally Addison needed to counter Dr. Evan Nelson, whose expert testimony supported the conclusion that Atkins suffered from mental retardation.

To accomplish this last objective, Addison secured the services of Dr. Stanton E. Samenow, a Yale- and University of Michigan-trained clinical psychologist. Samenow, an expert on antisocial behavior and the author of several scholarly volumes, was well known in forensic circles for his work on the criminal mind, work that often went against the grain of conventional thinking. Samenow articulated the view that psychologists tend to overemphasize the importance of environmental and other outside influences. Instead, he believed, individuals control their own behavior. Although often prompted by distorted thinking processes, people freely chose to engage in criminal acts and they are responsible for them.

Defense attorneys Rogers and Saunders, on the other hand, realized that their first attempt to obtain leniency for Atkins had failed badly. The first jury returned a recommended death sentence after less than two hours of deliberation. Without a guilt phase in this second proceeding, the defense would be unable to inject any doubt about Atkins's role in the crime. The jury would begin with the fixed reality that he had been convicted. The case for the defense would have to focus on providing mitigating evidence to offset whatever material the prosecution offered to establish the presence of aggravating factors.

The defense would again use the expert testimony of Dr. Nelson to establish Atkins's mental deficiencies, hoping the new jury would be more inclined to see his intellectual deficits as a mitigating factor. They would also use the testimony of family members to counter any impression that Atkins was a hardened criminal without any positive attributes. And finally, the defense was in a better position to argue that Atkins did not pose a threat of future violence. By the time the new penalty hearing would take place, Atkins would have been jailed for a total of three years and his prison disciplinary record was clean. This provided strong predictive evidence that Atkins could perform well in the highly structured prison environment. There was no need for the state to take his life.

Several months prior to the new penalty phase, Judge Smiley ordered a psychiatric evaluation of Daryl Atkins to determine if he was competent to participate in the hearing. Robert S. Brown Jr., a forensic psychiatrist from

Charlottesville, was appointed to conduct the testing. Brown reported back to Judge Smiley on June 30, 1999. The evaluation was based on a review of court, school, and prison records, consultations with the attorneys, past psychological tests, and a four-hour, face-to-face session with Atkins.

Dr. Brown reported Atkins understood the reason for his visit and the nature of the upcoming hearing. Atkins was soft-spoken, polite, and reserved; he participated voluntarily in the interview but his answers were short. Atkins suffered no psychological, emotional, or sexual abuse as a child. He admitted a history of alcohol and drug abuse. He was not currently suffering from any serious illnesses or injuries, and he was not taking any prescription medication.

Atkins lived in a single cell in Sussex Prison. He spent his days watching television, smoking cigarettes, and listening to music. He regularly read *Vibe* and *Playboy* magazines as well as the Bible. He normally fell asleep at about 7:00 in the morning and awoke at 2:00 in the afternoon, an unusual sleep pattern. He expressed great confidence in his lawyers and enjoyed visits from them as well as from members of his family.

Brown's mental evaluation indicated that Atkins was fully alert and well oriented. He demonstrated a sixth-grade reading level. He could make simple change and could recite the months of the year in order, although omitting March and September. Atkins demonstrated a basic ability to learn and remember. He exhibited no delusions or hallucinations. He could do simple, but not complex intellectual tasks.

According to Brown's analysis, Atkins suffered from chronic mild depression. The depression, of course, was understandable given that he was facing possible execution. Atkins held a belief that his sentence was unjustly harsh. In his view a fair sentence would be five years in prison. Brown also diagnosed Atkins as suffering from an antisocial personality disorder, a condition consistent with his extensive criminal record. As to mental ability, Brown agreed with Dr. Nelson's judgment that Atkins was mildly mentally retarded.

In spite of these mental difficulties, Brown concluded that Atkins had the capacity to understand the upcoming resentencing hearing and that he was competent to assist his attorneys in the preparation and presentation of his case.

THE NEW SENTENCING hearing for Daryl Atkins began on August 17, 1999, in the same Yorktown courthouse as his earlier trial. It was the third anniversary of Eric Nesbitt's death. Once again, Judge Prentis Smiley presided. And once again Eileen Addison and her staff for the prosecution faced off against defense attorneys George Rogers and Bryan Saunders.

The jury selection phase proceeded efficiently, although there were skirmishes over the use of peremptory challenges. Addison attacked the defense for using four of its five strikes to eliminate men. Rogers and Saunders objected to the prosecution eliminating a potential black juror. Judge Smiley rejected each of these objections, finding adequate race- and gender-neutral reasons for the strikes. The new jury consisted of eleven women and three men, including two alternates. There were no African American members.

Judge Smiley instructed the jurors that Daryl Atkins had been convicted of the capital murder of Eric Nesbitt by a previous panel. Their only task was to recommend an appropriate sentence. The jury had only two options: life in prison without parole and death. In order for the death penalty to be considered, the prosecution carried the burden of proving beyond a reasonable doubt the existence of at least one of the two aggravating factors recognized under Virginia law: future dangerousness and vile crime.

Addison first called witnesses to explain the impact that Eric Nesbitt's murder had on family and friends. Mary Sloan was the first to take the stand. She had come to Yorktown with her husband and three of her children. In great detail Sloan repeated for the new jury a sympathetic review of her son's character, life, and accomplishments, emphasizing the role he played as the eldest of six children in a close-knit family. She described the horror she experienced the day she was outside in her yard and watched the Air Force Death Notification Committee van turn into her driveway. She also related how crushed her other children had been by Eric's murder. Sloan's testimony was powerful. One reporter covering the event wrote, "Several jurors, as well as the court reporter and clerk, wiped away tears as they listened to Sloan testify..."

Four more witnesses followed. Mark and Sarah Armitage, Eric's best friends at Langley Air Force Base, explained the deep loss and emotional pain they suffered when Investigator Lyons informed them of the murder.

George Duncan, Eric's supervisor at Langley, testified about what it was like to assemble Eric's personal belongings and escort his body back to the family in Gilbertsville. And Vivian Brown recalled the last time she saw Eric on the night they closed the Advance Auto Parts store together just hours before he would be killed.

The testimony was quite effective. The prosecution successfully painted a picture of Eric Nesbitt as a young, promising man, hardworking and eager to please others. He was an important figure in the lives of his family members, coworkers, and friends. His loss was senseless and tragic. The defense, wanting neither to extend the jury's attention on these matters nor to appear unsympathetic to the losses suffered, did not seriously cross-examine the witnesses.

Next, Addison called two witnesses to establish the vile nature of the crime. Troy Lyons, who headed the investigation of the Nesbitt murder, was the first to take the stand. Addison's questioning led Lyons through the steps taken by the sheriff's department beginning with the original call he received to go to the murder scene.

Lyon's testimony was followed by that of Dr. Leah Bush, the assistant chief medical examiner who conducted the autopsy. Bush's testimony was especially important. She described in vivid detail the gunshot wounds Nesbitt suffered and how he ultimately bled to death. Importantly, Bush's description made it clear that eight bullet wounds at relatively close range constituted an aggravated assault that went well beyond what would have been necessary to kill Nesbitt. This fact helped establish the brutality of the crime.

Finally, Addison turned her attention to the future dangerousness factor. As she had at the first sentencing hearing, the prosecutor presented evidence of Atkins's past crimes and called some of his victims as witnesses. Testifying were Dennis Tuinei, Shane Stoops, and John Hultquist, three of the four men robbed at gunpoint by Atkins and others late one night after they used a public telephone; Kevin Phillips, the pizza delivery driver, also robbed at gunpoint and made to crawl through a swamp to escape; and most importantly, Amanda Hamlin, shot in the stomach in a botched robbery attempt that led to the conviction of Daryl Atkins on aggravated maiming charges.

At the end of the prosecution's case, Addison had presented ample evidence that Daryl Atkins senselessly took the life of a good, young man, causing a loss felt deeply by his family and friends. The crime was one of brutal and excessive violence that was the culmination of a series of escalating criminal acts. These factors formed the foundation of the prosecution's argument that the Nesbitt murder was particularly vile and that Atkins presented an unacceptable risk of future dangerousness.

Could Rogers and Saunders now present mitigating evidence that would offset the impact of the prosecution's witnesses?

Although Judge Smiley had made it clear that the issue of Atkins's guilt was a closed question, the defense on several occasions attempted to show that there remained some doubt about Atkins's role in the murder. This included another try by Rogers and Saunders to introduce the thirty-one-page statement Atkins had given to Investigator Lyons. Smiley consistently turned away these efforts. He would not allow the defense to pursue any line of questioning that was designed to produce jury leniency based upon a residual sense of doubt pertaining to Atkins's guilt.

The defense called two family members to testify about Atkins's early years. The first was Phillip Atkins, Daryl's father. The purpose was to highlight the conditions under which Daryl had been raised. Phillip explained how much Daryl had been affected by his parents' divorce and how difficult it was for him to grow up under those circumstances. He described how Daryl's intellectual deficits caused difficulties in school and how he had been drawn into a bad set of friends who set him on the wrong course in life. Daryl was a follower, his father said, and William Jones was a bad influence on him.

Next came the testimony of Virginia Banks Atkins, Daryl's step-grandmother, who explained how devastating Daryl's arrest had been on her and the other members of the family. These matters had come as a shock because the family was not aware that Daryl had been involved in criminal behavior. Ms. Atkins explained that she prayed daily for her grandson and for Nesbitt's family. At the end of her direct testimony, she turned to the jury and pleaded: "But I am very sorry for what's happened, for whatever part my grandson played.... But I ask you if you could just find it in your heart to forgive Daryl for anything that he have done and to give him life without parole, I will be most gracious for your consideration."

Having presented witnesses that could speak to the more human side of Daryl Atkins, the defense then turned to Dr. Evan Nelson to present the results of his intelligence testing. As he had at the original sentencing hearing, Nelson explained his credentials, the technicalities of IQ testing, and the sources of information he had consulted in evaluating Daryl Atkins. Under the direct questioning of Bryan Saunders, Nelson told the jury that the testing of Atkins revealed a full-scale IQ of 59, well into the range of mild mental retardation. This intelligence level was consistent with Atkins's failing academic record as well as his social history as a follower susceptible to the undue influence of others.

Finally, Nelson explained that Atkins would not pose a threat of future dangerousness if given a sentence of life in prison without parole. During his long months in jail Atkins had no disciplinary problems and had not engaged in any violence. He did quite well living in a highly controlled environment where he was denied drugs and alcohol. There was no reason to believe that this would change in the future.

On cross-examination, assistant prosecutor Benjamin Hahn aggressively questioned Nelson. Hahn hammered away at two themes. The first related to Atkins's responsibility for the crime. In response to Hahn's questions Nelson testified that there was no evidence that Atkins did not appreciate the criminality of his actions or was unable to control his behavior on the night of the murder. He understood it was wrong to shoot Eric Nesbitt. There were no signs that he suffered from delusions or irrationality at the time of the crime, nor was he under the influence of any extreme mental or emotional disturbance. His intoxication that night was voluntary.

Second, Hahn attacked Nelson's diagnosis of mental retardation. He elicited from Nelson testimony that although Atkins did poorly in school, he was never diagnosed as mentally retarded. His case was referred to a school system screening committee, but the committee saw no need to recommend full evaluation of his intelligence levels. Although Atkins was placed in the lowest academic classes and spent one year in a highly structured setting for underperforming students, he was never assigned to a special education curriculum. This line of questioning was designed to convince jurors that Atkins, while mentally slow, was not retarded, that he was responsible for his actions, and any academic failings were due to his own lack of motivation and the influence of drugs and alcohol.

On redirect examination, Bryan Saunders reinforced the retardation argument by guiding Nelson through a review of Atkins's academic performance, emphasizing that his failures began very early and continued unabated. Over the course of his school years his scores on standardized tests never rose above the twentieth percentile. He barely passed the required state literacy examinations. Drugs and alcohol may have compounded his lack of progress in high school, but he had established a long record of being unable to do standard academic work well before his substance abuse and teenage disengagement began.

On rebuttal the prosecution countered Nelson's account with testimony from its own expert, Dr. Stanton Samenow. Samenow had interviewed Atkins on two occasions, administered various mental ability tests, and reviewed school records and other documents. He would later briefly discuss his experiences with Daryl Atkins in a revised edition of his book, *Inside the Criminal Mind* (2004). Samenow agreed with Dr. Nelson's conclusions with respect to Atkins's mental state at the time of the crime: he was able to appreciate the criminality of his conduct, he had the ability to conform his conduct to the requirements of the law, his intoxication was voluntary, and he was under no extreme mental or emotional distress.

Samenow's conclusions about Daryl Atkins's mental abilities, however, were quite different from those of Dr. Nelson. When asked by Prosecutor Hahn about his reaction to Nelson's retardation diagnosis, Samenow directly responded, "I sharply disagree with it." Instead, Samenow said of Atkins, "He is of average intelligence, at least."

In response to Hahn's questioning, Samenow led the jury through the evidence supporting his opinion that Atkins was not retarded. His discussions with Atkins revealed a young man who used vocabulary and syntax inconsistent with mental retardation. He correctly used, for example, words like "orchestra," "decimal," and "parable." He had awareness of current events, including the ability to identify the president and immediate past president of the United States and the governor of Virginia. He knew that John F. Kennedy was president in 1961. He could do simple monetary exchanges, complete number sequence tests, and create reasonable stories from photographs. Atkins even claimed to know some chemistry and possess the ability to do mathematics through reciprocal fractions. His dismal academic record was due to a lack of motivation and concentration as well as very poor study habits. In addition, the results of intelligence tests that Samenow administered were not consistent with Nelson's findings.

Samenow also drew conclusions from Atkins's adaptive behavior. Atkins claimed that he could wash his clothes and cook, even discussing a favorite chicken recipe. He knew how to ride the bus system. Although he never had a job and always lived with his parents, these were voluntary choices and not a result of retardation. The events on the night Nesbitt was killed required planning and forethought every step of the way, abilities not commonly found among the mentally impaired.

According to Samenow's test results, however, Atkins met all the criteria for having an antisocial personality disorder. This diagnosis was consistent with Atkins's record of criminal behavior that included increasingly violent actions culminating in the killing of Eric Nesbitt. Atkins had a reckless disregard for others. Samenow concluded that Atkins's past conduct and his personality disorder placed him at high risk for future violent conduct.

The second day of the hearing ended with the completion of Stanton Samenow's direct testimony on behalf of the prosecution. The next morning it was Bryan Saunders's chance to strike back.

Saunders's cross-examination hit hard at what the defense considered a faulty evaluation of Atkins's mental ability. In response to repeated questions, Samenow acknowledged that his examination of Atkins did not meet all of the established guidelines for conducting full mental evaluations. Samenow administered only certain questions pertaining to intelligence rather than a full WAIS-III battery of questions. In addition, he used outdated test questions during a portion of his evaluation. The defense took the position that these defects made the results invalid, but Samenow responded that he modified his testing procedure in order to maximize individualized information pertinent to the Atkins situation.

Furthermore, Samenow noted that ethical guidelines only require administering all test items when a full evaluation is being conducted. Samenow's purpose was not to repeat Nelson's full evaluation but to use sample questions to see if they matched Nelson's results.

Saunders also used his cross-examination to call into question Samenow's interview techniques and the breadth of his evaluation. For example, under Saunders's questioning Samenow admitted that at times he pushed Atkins to give correct answers to various items. Samenow also acknowledged that he took Atkins at his word for his life-skill competencies. He did not contact friends or family members, for example, to verify Atkins's claim of using a washing machine or being able to cook. Often retarded people overestimate their abilities in order to be more favorably viewed by others. Atkins's claim of being able to work with reciprocal fractions, for example, might be an example of this tendency. By accepting without corroboration Atkins's descriptions of his own abilities, the defense charged, Samenow risked reaching an inaccurate estimate of Atkins's adaptive behavior levels.

Benjamin Hahn then used his final opportunity to direct questions to Samenow in an attempt to repair some of the damage the defense had inflicted during cross-examination. Samenow testified that school records supported his position that Atkins had the ability to pass his academic classes, but chose not to do so. High school attendance records showed, for example, excessive absences and tardiness. Notes inserted in his school records by teachers repeatedly showed that Atkins's problems were due to poor attitude and motivation, not a lack of mental ability. Based on his almost thirty-five years of experience, Samenow had confidence in his opinion of Atkins's intellect. Also, Samenow reiterated his conclusion that Atkins posed a danger. Atkins had expressed no remorse for his crime. Even if confined to prison for the rest of his life, he could be a threat to fellow inmates and corrections personnel.

The conclusion of Samenow's testimony brought an end to the presentation of evidence to the jury. Judge Smiley then gave the jurors their instructions, advising them that they must choose one of the two penalties available to them, death or life in prison without parole. Before they could consider a death sentence, the jurors were required to find the presence of at least one aggravating factor beyond a reasonable doubt. In addition, they could use any other information as mitigation that might prompt them to decide on the more lenient of the two available sentences. His instructions were carefully presented over the course of more than an hour. Judge Smiley clearly wanted no repeat of a reversal by the state supreme court.

Addison's closing argument to the jury was short and to the point. She acknowledged that the jurors faced a difficult, emotionally draining decision, but their sworn duty was to apply the law of Virginia. The requirements for capital punishment were clearly met. The shooting of Eric Nesbitt was a wantonly vile crime and Atkins's long history of criminal behavior predicted future dangerousness.

George Rogers spoke at greater length. He discussed Atkins's criminal past, stressing that Daryl was almost always a follower rather than the architect of a crime. He reviewed Atkins's broken home, difficult childhood, and dismal academic performance. Rogers drew a stark contrast between the thorough evaluation of Atkins's intelligence levels by Dr. Nelson and the less systematic evaluation provided by the prosecutor's expert, Stanton Samenow. He chided Samenow for failing to follow the required rules for valid intelligence testing, accusing him of "cherry-picking" questions and using outdated items. Nelson's test results, he argued, were much more credible, and those results indicated the presence of mental retardation.

Additionally, Rogers emphasized that sending Daryl Atkins to prison for life without the possibility of parole would mean he would never be free to hurt innocent people again. Furthermore, his prison record already demonstrated that he could control his behavior and live by institutional rules when placed in a carefully controlled environment. A life sentence would remove any possibility of future dangerousness.

"Punish Daryl by keeping him in maximum security for as long as he shall live," Rogers concluded. "I beg you not to have Daryl's death on your mind for as long as you each shall live."

Eileen Addison had the final word. Her rebuttal statement asked for justice. She believed that the maximum crime deserved the maximum penalty. And she asked the jurors to consider what Eric Nesbitt had experienced:

I'm going to ask you in your deliberations to do something that Daryl Atkins has not done, and that is to put yourself in Eric Nesbitt's place for the last hour of his life. The Eagle Scout, the volunteer fireman, the rescue worker, the airman with a promising career, but most importantly a loving friend, a big brother, and a son.... Imagine how he felt that last hour.

Force yourself, as painful as that will be, to do what his mother and his brothers and sisters and his friends have had to do repeatedly for the last three years and imagine what he went through. Being abducted, being taken to that ATM machine, look at those pictures and try to imagine the terror he felt and what he felt on that 18-mile trip from Hampton to York County, and what he might have thought of those last few minutes after he had been shot eight times.

With the end of the closing arguments, Judge Smiley gave the jury the last of their instructions and sent them to deliberate. Their work did not take long. In about two hours the jurors returned with their verdict. They had found the presence of both aggravating factors and insufficient mitigating grounds for leniency. The recommendation was death.

Daryl Atkins heard the jury's recommendation and expressed no apparent reaction.

Two months later, on October 26, 1999, Judge Smiley accepted the jury's recommendation and officially sentenced Daryl Atkins to death. George Rogers had argued on Atkins's behalf that there was too much doubt concerning who was the actual killer of Eric Nesbitt to justify the execution of Atkins. He implored Smiley to spare his client's life. Judge Smiley, however, responded that there was nothing sufficient to justify a rejection of the jury's determination.

Atkins's family was shrouded in sadness, but expressed faith in God that their son's life ultimately would be spared. As Daryl Atkins was led from the court by corrections officials, Judge Smiley uttered, "Good luck to you, sir. May God have mercy on your soul."

THE ATKINS CASE, of course, did not end with the second imposition of the death sentence. State law required the sentence automatically to be reviewed by the state supreme court.

Once again George Rogers and Bryan Saunders represented Daryl
Atkins on appeal to the Virginia Supreme Court. They alleged eight different errors that occurred at the trial level that, in their opinion, merited
reversal of the death penalty. These alleged errors included the use of
rules that limited the arguments the defense could make, racial discrimination in jury selection, the judge's inappropriate application of the
hearsay rules, and a lack of sufficient evidence to prove Atkins's future
dangerousness or the vileness of his crime. In addition, Rogers and
Saunders raised the issue of proportionality. State law prohibited sentences that were disproportionate or excessive. They argued that a death
sentence imposed on a mentally retarded defendant is both excessive and
disproportionate.

Pamela Rumpz of the state attorney general's office for the second time
represented the Commonwealth. She urged the justices to reject each of
the claims made by the defense lawyers.

On September 15, 2000, the Virginia Supreme Court issued their ruling in *Daryl Renard Atkins v. Commonwealth of Virginia (Atkins II)*. The
opinion was written by Justice Cynthia Kinser, a former prosecutor who
had served on the court for three years. In her statement, Justice Kinser
noted that several arguments raised by the defense were matters of established law that the court would not revisit, were objections raised and
rejected earlier in *Atkins I,* or rested on claims that had no factual basis.
These issues were dismissed with relatively brief explanations of each.

The opinion, however, devoted considerable attention to the proportionality claim, the most serious issue raised by Atkins's attorneys. Given
his extensive criminal record and the brutality of Eric Nesbitt's murder,
there were ample grounds to conclude that Daryl Atkins posed a future
danger and that his act was wantonly vile. Kinser cited a number of
previous instances where the death penalty had been given in cases presenting similar factual scenarios. The defense, however, asserted the claim
that Atkins's mental retardation made him less culpable and therefore a
comparison to previous cases was inappropriate.

The court acknowledged that retardation was recognized by the state
and by the U.S. Supreme Court's *Penry* decision as a legitimate mitigating

factor. At the trial level the defense was given ample opportunity to present evidence of Atkins's IQ test results and adaptive behavior skills. The jury heard testimony from expert witnesses offered by both the prosecution and the defense. The opinions of the experts were frequently in conflict. It was the jury's responsibility to evaluate the credibility of the experts' opinions, to determine the strength of their evidence, and ultimately to reach an individualized assessment of Daryl Atkins's claimed retardation. Justice Kinser wrote:

> The jury was instructed in the present case to consider any evidence in mitigation of the offense and the jury obviously found that Atkins's IQ score did not mitigate his culpability for the murder of Nesbitt.... The question of Atkins's mental retardation is a factual one, and as such, it is the function of the factfinder [the jury], not this Court to determine the weight that should be accorded to expert testimony on that issue.

This analysis led the majority to conclude, "[W]e perceive no reason to commute Atkins's sentence of death and will affirm the judgment of the circuit court."

Five members of the court agreed with this conclusion. Two dissented from the ruling, Leroy Rountree Hassell, the court's only African American member, and Lawrence Koontz, who had written the opinion in *Atkins I* vacating the first death sentence. Both justices focused on the retardation issue.

Justice Hassell forcefully expressed his view that the retarded should be shielded from the death penalty. Unlike the majority who were unwilling to substitute their own evaluations for the findings of the jury, Hassell was quite willing to give his own independent analysis of the evidence. For Hassell, the evidence was clear. Dr. Evan Nelson, after conducting a full evaluation of the defendant, including a complete battery of intelligence tests revealing an IQ of 59 and evidence provided by others substantiating deficits in adaptive behavior, judged Daryl Atkins to be mildly mentally retarded. For Hassell, this evidence was compelling.

In vivid contrast Hassell found the evaluation provided by the prosecution's expert, Dr. Stanton Samenow, to be deficient. Hassell attacked the validity of Samenow's analysis for what he believed were defective testing procedures and a failure to consult others in order to verify the accuracy of Atkins's self-described adaptive behavior levels. Hassell explained:

> I simply place no credence whatsoever in Dr. Samenow's opinion that the defendant possesses at least average intelligence. I would hold that Dr. Samenow's opinion that the defendant possesses average intelligence is incredulous as a matter of law. Indeed, I am perplexed that Dr. Samenow, who did not administer a complete IQ test to the defendant and admittedly asked the defendant questions based upon bits and pieces of outdated tests to supposedly evaluate the defendant, would opine that this defendant possesses at least average intelligence.

Noting that his decision was based not on the Supreme Court's *Penry* decision, but on the requirements of the Virginia state code, Hassell concluded, "I believe that the imposition of the sentence of death upon a criminal defendant who has the mental age of a child between the ages of 9 and 12 is excessive, considering both the crime and the defendant." Recognizing, however, that Atkins's criminal history justifies the conclusion that he would constitute a danger to society, Hassell supported commuting the sentence to life in prison without the possibility of parole.

Justice Koontz joined Hassell's dissenting opinion, but also wrote separately to express his own views. Significantly, Koontz's short opinion looked beyond the specific facts in the Atkins case and stated a more general proposition:

> [I]t is indefensible to conclude that individuals who are mentally retarded are not to some degree less culpable for their criminal acts. By definition, such individuals have substantial limitations not shared by the general population. A moral and civilized society diminishes itself if its system of justice does not afford recognition and consideration of those limitations in a meaningful way.... [T]he execution of a mentally retarded individual rather than the imposition of a sentence of life without the possibility of parole is excessive. I would not permit such a result in Atkins' case even though his crime was vile and his guilt undeniable.

After the state supreme court rendered its ruling, lawyers for Atkins asked the justices to reconsider, but the request for a rehearing was denied. With the decision of the Virginia Supreme Court now final,

Atkins had exhausted his opportunities in the state system. He had been found guilty of capital murder and condemned to death by two different juries. Both the conviction and the sentence had now been reviewed and affirmed by the state supreme court.

The only appellate opportunity remaining was a petition to the U.S. Supreme Court. But the odds that the justices of the nation's highest court would even grant Daryl Atkins a full hearing were minimal indeed.

BIBLIOGRAPHIC NOTE.

Data on the use of capital punishment in Virginia are available from the Bureau of Justice Statistics of the U.S. Department of Justice and the Death Penalty Information Center. The discussion of procedures used in Virginia capital offense cases at the time of the Atkins trial and factors affecting capital case outcomes relies in part on studies conducted by the Virginia's Joint Legislative Audit and Review Commission, especially its *Review of Virginia's System of Capital Punishment,* December 10, 2001.

The accounts of the Jones and Atkins sentencing decisions and the rulings of the Virginia Supreme Court rest largely on the official court transcripts and opinions, supplemented by press accounts of those actions. Reactions to the 1998 sentencing of Daryl Atkins were reported in an article by Tom Fredrickson in the Hampton Roads *Daily Press.* The discussion of the reactions to the sentencing of William Jones and Daryl Atkins's 1999 death sentence decision relies in part on the accounts of *Daily Press* reporter Patti Rosenberg published in the days surrounding those events. Also helpful was the work of Greg Weatherford on the Virginia Capital Litigation Unit that appeared in the *Roanoke Times,* April 20, 1997.

Dr. Stanton E. Samenow's work on criminal behavior can be found in: *Inside the Criminal Mind,* revised edition (New York: Crown Publishers, 2004); *Straight Talk about Criminals* (Northvale, N.J.: Jason Aronson, 1998); *Before It's Too Late* (New York: Three Rivers Press, 2001).

Examples of other work on criminal sentencing: Robert Emmet Long (ed.), *Criminal Sentencing* (New York: H. W. Wilson, 1995); Douglas W. Kieso, *Unjust Sentencing and the California Three Strikes Law* (New York:

LFB Scholarly Publishing, 2005); Bryan C. Edelman, *Racial Prejudice, Juror Empathy, and Sentencing in Death Penalty Cases* (New York: LFB Scholarly Publishing, 2006); Lois G. Forer, *A Rage to Punish: The Unintended Consequences of Mandatory Sentencing* (New York: Norton, 1994); Tamasak Wicharaya, *Simple Theory, Hard Reality: The Impact of Sentencing Reforms on Courts, Prisons, and Crime* (Albany: State University of New York Press, 1995); Robert Satter, *Doing Justice: A Trial Judge at Work* (New York: Simon and Schuster, 1990).

Approaching the Supreme Court

AFTER LOSING A CASE disappointed litigants occasionally threaten to appeal "all the way to the United States Supreme Court." Such a claim is normally more bluster than reality. Appealing a case to the Supreme Court is no easy matter, even if a party has the financial resources and the legal talent to do so. The odds of the justices giving full consideration to any particular appeal are dauntingly low. The barriers to obtaining Supreme Court review are both jurisdictional and discretionary.

Article III of the Federal Constitution gave birth to the federal court system by declaring that "The judicial Power of the United States, shall be vested in one supreme Court, and in such inferior Courts as the Congress may from time to time ordain and establish." When the federal judiciary came into being state court systems had already been successfully operating for many years.

The federal courts were not designed to supplant the state judiciaries. Rather the delegates at the Constitutional Convention limited the jurisdiction of the federal courts to legal disputes relevant to the new national government. The existing state courts would coexist with their new federal counterparts, continuing to hear and decide matters of state law.

Rules regarding the jurisdiction of federal courts are complex and subject to congressional regulation, but Article III generally authorizes the federal courts to hear cases only if at least one of two requirements are met. First, federal courts can accept a case if its resolution requires an interpretation or application of the U.S. Constitution, federal statutes, or treaties with other nations. Such disputes are said to present a "federal question." Second, a federal court can hear a dispute if it involves certain parties. For example, lawsuits brought for or against the federal government or any of its officers or agencies qualify to be heard in federal court. So too do legal disputes between two or more states or those involving foreign ambassadors, ministers, and counsels. Diversity cases, those lawsuits between citizens from different states or legal actions involving a foreign state or citizen, are also eligible. The vast majority of lawsuits do not meet these requirements. Instead, they are based exclusively on state law. As such they are barred from entry to the federal courts.

Generally speaking, then, legal disputes arising from an interpretation of state law are heard by state courts, and cases involving an application of federal law are heard by the federal courts. Yet the work of federal and state court systems are not so neatly separated. For example, a common criminal case may involve both state and federal questions. If the police arrest an individual for violating state drug distribution laws, it would normally be a matter of exclusive state jurisdiction. However, if the accused claims that the police gathered evidence against him in violation of the search and seizure provisions of the Fourth Amendment of the U.S. Constitution, a federal question has also entered the case. The state judge hearing the criminal accusations would not only have to apply the state's controlled substance laws, but would also have to reach a decision on the federal constitutional claim. In cases like this one, the accused drug dealer may have the right, based on the federal constitutional claim, to appeal to the federal courts.

The U.S. Supreme Court sits at the top of the federal judicial hierarchy. It functions primarily as an appellate tribunal. The cases it hears have already been decided at the lower court level. In fact, the justices generally will not hear cases unless all lower court options have been exhausted. For the standard federal case, this means that the dispute has already been heard twice before the Supreme Court will consider it. First, the federal district court will have heard the case in an original trial; and second, the trial court's decision will have been reviewed by one of the federal courts of appeals. For disputes that start out in state court, but also involve a federal question, the U.S. Supreme Court will not be open to take the case until all remedies at the state level—all the way up to the state's highest court—have been attempted. Slightly more than 80 percent of cases decided by the Supreme Court are appeals from the federal courts of appeals and about 13 percent from the state supreme courts. The remainder of the Court's cases comes from other courts.

Although a case may meet the jurisdictional requirements, it still may never be heard by the Supreme Court. In its early years the U.S. Supreme Court was obliged to hear and decide all the cases brought to it that met the standard procedural requirements. As the decades went by, however, demands on the justices became far more than they could reasonably handle and many of the cases brought to them concerned issues of little import that already had received ample review in the lower courts. As a result Congress at various points passed legislation giving the justices increasing control over their own docket. By 1988, this process had run its course. With only a few exceptions, the justices now exercise almost total discretion over the cases they hear. Parties wishing Supreme Court review of lower court decisions must petition the justices to hear the appeal. The justices are free to accept these cases or decline to hear them. In refusing to hear a case, the justices permit the lower court decision to stand without indicating approval or disapproval of that ruling.

The Court decides which cases to hear through the writ of *certiorari* procedure. A writ of *certiorari* (literally, "to be informed of") is a judicial order calling for the lower court records to be submitted to the justices for review. An aggrieved party who wants the Supreme Court to review a lower court ruling will petition for a writ of *certiorari*. If the Court grants the writ, the case is placed on the Court's docket. When the justices deny the petition, they are declining to hear the case.

Consistent with a practice adopted by the Court in 1925, the decision to grant or deny a *certiorari* petition is determined by the "rule of four." That is, it takes the votes of four justices to accept a case for Supreme Court review. It is the only significant matter the justices decide that requires the vote of less than the majority of the full nine-member court.

The process begins when the party seeking Supreme Court review submits a petition for a writ of *certiorari* and pays the required filing fee. Forty copies of the petition, produced according to very exact paper quality and formatting requirements, must be filed with the Supreme Court clerk within ninety days of the final ruling of the lower court, although extensions are possible. Along with appropriate documentation, the petition must include the questions presented to the Court for adjudication, the legal provisions relevant to the case, a statement outlining the Court's jurisdiction, a description of the case facts, and most importantly the reasons why the justices should grant the petition.

Petitioners who are indigent can apply for *in forma pauperis* status. If granted, these petitioners do not have to pay the filing fees and are given allowances from the rigid filing requirements. Most *in forma pauperis* petitions are filed by prison inmates challenging the legality of their incarceration. These submissions outnumber the regular "paid" petitions by a 4–1 margin.

Once the petition is filed, the opposing party, known as the respondent, has thirty days to provide a brief arguing that the Court should not grant a writ of *certiorari*. The respondent, for example, might challenge the Court's jurisdiction over the case or may argue that the questions and issues raised by the petitioner are insufficiently compelling to justify the Supreme Court's full attention. The briefs filed by the parties for or against the writ of *certiorari* grant are limited to 9,000 words.

The petitioner then has the right to file a short reply brief (3,000 words) responding to arguments made in the respondent's opposition brief. In addition, both sides may file supplemental briefs at any time should circumstances merit. The usual reason for filing a supplemental brief is that decisions have been handed down, laws have been passed, or other events have occurred since the original filing that have relevance to the appeal.

The volume of cases brought to the Supreme Court has steadily increased over time. In the 2006–2007 term of the Court, for example, nearly 9,000 new cases were filed. Almost all were writ of *certiorari* petitions. Each of those petitions, of course, came with briefs submitted by both sides, as well as supporting documentation. In some instances, additional briefs favoring or opposing the grant of *certiorari* were filed by the federal government, state governments, or private organizations that are not parties to the litigation but have an interest in the outcome of the case. These are known as *amicus curiae,* or "friend of the court," briefs.

Because of this high demand, the Supreme Court expends much of its resources simply deciding what cases to decide. To avoid being overwhelmed, the Court has developed measures to process the petitions as efficiently as possible. The justices' law clerks, in addition to their other duties, play a key role in this process. Each of the associate justices is entitled to four law clerks and the chief justice five. The clerks are recent law school graduates with especially strong academic records, usually from prestigious universities, who spend a year as an assistant to a justice. Before coming to the Court, most have already served as a law clerk for a lower federal court judge.

Since the 1970s the justices have cooperated in a "*certiorari* pool" arrangement in which all of the clerks spend a portion of their time screening petitions. As the petitions are filed they are assigned to a single law clerk who analyzes the materials, writes a legal memorandum summarizing the petition, and offers a recommendation to grant or deny the writ. The memorandum is then distributed to each of the justices, who use it as a guide for determining how much additional and independent study to give the petition. The process cuts the initial screening workload significantly. Among recent justices, only John Paul Stevens has elected not to participate in the *certiorari* pool arrangement. The clerks in his office independently evaluate all incoming petitions.

The next stage of the process is initiated by the chief justice, who periodically distributes a "discuss list." This consists of a list of recently filed *certiorari* petitions that the chief justice believes to have sufficient substance to merit deliberation. As the list is circulated, each justice has the option of adding cases to the list, but no justice can remove list entries. Each petition placed on the list, therefore, has at least one justice who thinks it merits consideration by the whole Court.

When all of the justices have had a chance to react to the list, the Court will consider the petitions at its next conference. Any petition that has not been placed on the discuss list is automatically rejected. The rest receive the collective attention of the Court. The normal procedure is for each justice in order of seniority to present his or her views on the petition and whether the writ should be granted. Any petition receiving the support of four or more justices is granted, those receiving fewer votes are rejected.

After these decisions are made, the Court announces the outcomes. Ordinarily this consists of a single sentence without any explanation or justification of the Court's decision. On occasion, however, a justice dissenting from a *certiorari* denial will write an opinion expressing the minority viewpoint.

Cases for which *certiorari* has been granted will be decided by the Court. This does not mean, however, that the case will receive full-dress treatment. Some of the accepted cases will receive a summary decision. That is, the justices will issue a ruling without the benefit of additional briefs or oral arguments. This is often the case if an intervening change in the law or recent decision in another case makes the outcome sufficiently clear based on the petition documents alone.

Cases meriting full consideration are placed on the Court's oral argument calendar. In issuing the writ of *certiorari,* the Court may elect not to consider all of the issues presented by the petitioner. In some instances the justices will limit their consideration to specific issues and instruct the attorneys for both sides to restrict their arguments to those particular questions. Granting a writ of *certiorari* in a given case may not be an independent event. Rather, the justice may select cases with an eye to developing a more coherent annual docket. For example, several cases involving similar issues may be accepted in order to give a more complete response to issues pertaining to a given area of the law.

In the end, gaining access to the Supreme Court is a difficult process with a low probability of success. *In forma pauperis* petitions, granted at a rate of about two-tenths of 1 percent, are much less likely to be successful than paid petitions, which are approved at about a 4 percent rate. These differences reflect the fact that many *in forma pauperis* petitions are written by prison inmates without legal counsel and often present frivolous arguments. After all is said and done, from the thousands of petitions that are filed annually the justices will decide with full opinions only about seventy to ninety cases.

The way in which the Court processes writ of *certiorari* petitions tells us a great deal about how the justices go about their work. But it does not tell us much about how the justices determine which cases to hear and which ones to reject. What criteria does the Court use? What factors sway a justice to vote for or against a petition for full review? The rules of the Court do provide some guidance, but they are far from satisfactory.

The Supreme Court's Rule 10 states quite clearly, "Review on a writ of *certiorari* is not a matter of right, but of judicial discretion. A petition for writ of *certiorari* will be granted only for compelling reasons." This rule, simply stated, means that the justices freely determine which cases to hear and which to decline.

While disavowing that they either control or fully measure the Court's discretion, the rules suggest two kinds of cases the justices are likely to accept. First, the Court takes seriously its duty to encourage national uniformity by settling conflicts when lower courts interpret federal law differently. Thus, the justices are more likely to accept a case if an interpretation of the law used by a court of appeals or a state supreme court is incompatible with the way the same legal provision is being treated by other circuits or states. And second, the justices will be predisposed to accept cases that present important questions of federal law that have not been previously addressed by the Supreme Court.

These suggestions may be helpful, but they hardly are definitive. They do not reveal how the justices discriminate among the many petitions that claim lower court conflicts. And they certainly provide no defining characteristics of those legal questions the justices might consider to be important.

Court scholars have devoted considerable resources to evaluating just what factors the justices actually take into account in building the docket. The results have indicated that the Court really does care about reducing inconsistencies in the ways the lower courts interpret federal law. There is a much higher probability of the Court accepting an appeal if it presents an issue over which there is significant disagreement among lower court judges.

In addition, the justices have their own policy preferences and tend to accept or reject *certiorari* petitions based on whether the case may serve as a vehicle for advancing those interests. For example, a justice who is concerned about a particular legal issue may look for a *certiorari* petition that presents an opportunity for the justices to address it. The justices have a tendency, although not an overwhelming one, to review lower court decisions with which they do not agree. Consistent with this tendency, the justices reverse the decision of the lower court in roughly 60 percent of the cases they decide.

The Court is also deferential to certain parties when they support or oppose a *certiorari* petition. Most prominent in this regard is the government of the United States. If federal authorities want the justices to accept a certain case, the Court is much more likely to do so. At bottom, however, the justices accept the cases they want to accept and decline the issues they do not want to hear. Beyond the normal jurisdictional requirements, there is no limitation on the justices' freedom to shape their docket.

THE U.S. SUPREME COURT held the last hope for Daryl Atkins to avoid the death penalty. To be successful he had to fight two legal battles. First, Atkins had to convince the Court to accept his case for a full hearing. The probability of getting even that far was intimidatingly low. But if those odds were beaten and the justices agreed to hear his appeal, Atkins would face the second legal hurdle of persuading the Court to spare his life.

Approaching the Supreme Court meant that the rules of the game would change. To this point the guilt and sentencing issues had been litigated in the state courts focusing on Virginia state criminal law and procedure. The U.S. Supreme Court would have interest in these matters only to the extent that a federal question was involved. Unless Atkins could provide a compelling reason to question whether Virginia's criminal justice system was depriving him of his life in a manner contrary to the U.S. Constitution, the justices would likely deny review.

To move from the state judiciary to the federal system required new legal expertise. While George Rogers and Bryan Saunders had considerable experience with Virginia's trial and appellate courts, the federal judiciary was a much different matter. Consequently, two new lawyers assumed control of the appeal for Atkins: Charles E. Haden and Robert E. Lee Jr. Haden, a Hampton attorney, was well experienced in federal appellate court matters. Lee was the executive director of the Virginia Capital Representation Resource Center, an organization devoted to providing legal assistance to defendants facing capital punishment sentences. After receiving his law degree from the University of Virginia in 1992, Lee began a career devoted to opposing the death penalty. He had worked as an attorney for the Mississippi Capital Defense Resource Center before returning to Virginia. Haden became counsel of record in the attempt to obtain Supreme Court review, and Lee's organization provided the primary legal resources to make the case.

In Lee and Haden's analysis Judge Prentis Smiley's application of the hearsay rule constituted the most vulnerable aspect of the state's actions to impose the death penalty. In their opinion, Smiley's decision, upheld by the Virginia Supreme Court, violated Atkins's constitutional rights by denying him the ability to offer meaningful evidence of mitigation. This issue would become the centerpiece in their argument for Supreme Court review.

Lee and Haden believed that the statement Atkins made to Investigator Troy Lyons was crucial to establish sufficient mitigation to save Daryl Atkins's life. Atkins admitted to Lyons that he had participated in the crime and expressed a willingness to cooperate with the authorities. The Atkins legal team believed that these comments reflected remorse. Had the jury believed that Atkins was truly remorseful they likely would have been more lenient in determining the sentence.

Introducing the statement itself or questioning Lyons about it was prohibited because the statement was hearsay, an unsworn assertion of the truth made outside of court. Furthermore, since the statement included Atkins's claim that William Jones was the real murderer, introducing this information at the sentencing stage would reargue the already decided question of guilt. The trial court and the state supreme court found no reason to make an exception to the hearsay rules. The Virginia code was clear: mitigating evidence relevant to sentencing is "subject to the rules of evidence governing admissibility."

To Lee and Haden, however, this was a mechanistic application of the hearsay rule. An exception should be allowed in order to establish mitigation. At the very least, information about that portion of the statement that dealt with the remorse issue should be admitted, even if the claim against Jones was excluded. If this evidence had been introduced and if it had persuaded even one juror to vote for life in prison, Daryl Atkins's life would have been spared. Applying the hearsay rule in such a harsh fashion, they argued, violated the Due Process Clause of the Fourteenth Amendment of the U.S. Constitution: "Nor shall any State deprive any person of life, liberty, or property, without due process of law." By denying Daryl Atkins the opportunity to introduce evidence relevant to mitigation the Commonwealth of Virginia was depriving Atkins of his life without due process of law.

On February 1, 2001, Lee and Haden submitted their formal petition for writ of *certiorari*. They asserted that the hearsay issue in Atkins's case was a fundamental question of fairness in capital sentencing hearings. The rule, as applied by the Virginia courts, seriously compromised the U.S. Supreme Court's mandate that a trial court cannot refuse to consider any constitutionally relevant mitigating evidence. Because other death penalty states had similar procedural barriers to establishing mitigation, the issue was of much broader importance than simply affecting the life of Daryl Atkins. The Court should grant *certiorari*, Atkins's lawyers argued, in order to remove doubts about the application of various rules of evidence that might block the opportunities of all capital defendants to persuade jurors to be lenient.

The Commonwealth of Virginia filed its opposition brief on March 8. Pamela Rumpz, the state's experienced appellate advocate from its Capital Litigation Unit, once again represented Virginia. Rumpz's basic argument was that Atkins's petition did not present a question worthy of the Supreme Court's attention. The Supreme Court of Virginia had held that "no exception to the hearsay rule applied which would allow Lyons to testify about the content of Atkins' statement." This ruling was based on an interpretation of state procedural rules. "Despite Atkins' efforts to dress his evidentiary claim in a cloak of constitutional dimensions," she wrote in the state's brief, "at bottom the claim is purely one of state law." The U.S. Supreme Court has always left such rules up to the individual states, and it should follow that course in this case as well. Because the state courts made no ruling on federal law, no federal grounds for appeal existed.

Contrary to his petition, Rumpz argued, Atkins could have avoided the hearsay problem by testifying under oath at the sentencing hearing and making himself available to cross-examination. Although the judge would rightfully not allow the introduction of evidence seeking solely to establish residual doubt about his guilt, Atkins could have testified about the non-guilt aspects of his statement. He did not even try to do so.

With the *certiorari* petition submissions now completed for both sides, it was now up to the justices to decide whether Atkins's case merited a full review by the Supreme Court.

DARYL ATKINS'S FUTURE depended not only upon the strength of his own legal case, but it was also tied to the fate of Ernest Paul McCarver, a convicted murderer sitting on death row in North Carolina. His case shared many similarities with the situation faced by Daryl Atkins, as well as Johnny Paul Penry before him. McCarver's appeal to the Supreme Court was progressing only slightly ahead of Atkins's petition.

Ernest McCarver's background ensured with near inevitability that his life would not be successful. Ernest and his older brother Lee were born to parents with a penchant for criminal behavior. When his father and mother were sent to prison on burglary charges, two-year-old Ernest and three-year-old Lee were placed in foster care. After his mother and father completed their sentences, they returned to their criminal ways, often taking Ernest and Lee with them during their burglaries. As the brothers grew older they were shuttled among their parents, their poor and sickly grandmother, and an orphanage. In 1975, McCarver's father regained custody of Lee, but he left Ernest in the orphanage claming that he was not Ernest's biological father. Later the three reunited and resumed their thefts. At various times in his childhood, Ernest was sexually and physically abused. He was frequently ill, received little formal education, and suffered bouts of depression.

When Ernest was seventeen he began working as a dishwasher at the K & W Cafeteria in Concord, North Carolina. He and his brother were befriended there by Woodrow Hartley, who also worked at the restaurant. McCarver sporadically worked at the cafeteria over the next six years. Along the way he continued to have difficulties with the law, including being convicted of eight counts of felonious larceny and one count of forgery. In March 1984 he was placed on probation for these crimes, but soon after was sent to prison for violating the restrictions placed on his activities. McCarver suspected three men as possible sources of the information upon which his probation was revoked. One of them was Woodrow Hartley.

Upon release, McCarver, then 26, took work as a roofer. He had difficulties financially and frequently lived in his car. On January 1, 1987, McCarver needed money and was also unstable emotionally. The mother of his new daughter had told him that she was leaving him to marry another man. From his days at the cafeteria, he knew that Woodrow Hartley arrived at work early, well before other employees, in order to open the restaurant. He also knew that on paydays Hartley would often carry

Convicted murderer Ernest McCarver petitioned the Supreme Court to prohibit executions of the mentally retarded.

significant amounts of money. McCarver thought Hartley offered an opportunity to make some quick cash and also provided a way for him to strike back at Hartley for whatever role he may have played in the parole revocation. Calling Hartley an "easy target," McCarver enlisted the help of a fellow roofing worker, Jimmy Rape, to carry out the plan.

At about 4:20 on the morning of January 2, McCarver and Rape drove to the cafeteria to await Hartley's appearance. At about 5:00 a.m. Hartley arrived at the restaurant. Minutes later McCarver and Rape entered the cafeteria through a back door. As Rape stayed in the background, McCarver struck up a conversation with his old friend. Rape then approached the seventy-one-year-old Hartley from behind, held him in a headlock, and attempted to strangle him. As the struggle progressed, Hartley's ribs were broken and he fell to the floor. McCarver took a knife from his pocket and stabbed Hartley three times in the chest. One of the wounds cut the aorta, and Hartley quickly died.

McCarver and Rape promptly left the cafeteria and drove to their assigned roofing job. Their robbery efforts did not yield what they had hoped. Their total take was only about $19. The most valuable item they stole was a 1902 silver dollar, for which they received $7 at a local pawn shop. Another restaurant employee who was just arriving for work saw McCarver leave the building carrying a knife and found Hartley's body. McCarver and Rape were arrested at their job site later that day. McCarver waived his *Miranda* rights. In response to police interrogation, he confessed to the crime. McCarver was charged with murder and robbery with a dangerous weapon.

In a pretrial competency hearing, McCarver provided chilling responses to a battery of psychological tests: "I like to kill," he said. "The happiest time of my life was when I killed that man. At bedtime I dream of killing."

After an earlier conviction had been overturned on procedural grounds, a jury in 1992 found McCarver guilty on both the murder and robbery charges. At the penalty phase of the trial the defense alleged seventeen mitigating factors. These centered on McCarver's troubled childhood, lack of adequate parenting, sexual and physical abuse, chronic depression, and a history of substance abuse. In addition, a clinical forensic psychologist who evaluated McCarver found that he had the intellectual and emotional capability of a ten- or twelve-year-old with a diminished capacity to appreciate the criminality of his actions. His personality was abnormal in several respects due to the lack of nurturing he received as a youth. Initial tests placed his IQ at 74, within the five-point margin of error for determining mental retardation. At a future point, long after his trial and sentencing, another IQ test placed McCarver's IQ at 67.

The prosecution argued the presence of three aggravating factors recognized under North Carolina law: that the murder was committed to avoid arrest, that the murder occurred during the commission of a robbery with dangerous weapon, and that the murder was especially heinous, atrocious, or cruel.

The jury concluded that the first two of these aggravating factors were proven beyond a reasonable doubt. They further decided that the aggravating factors outweighed the mitigating circumstances and recommended a sentence of death. The trial court judge accepted the death penalty recommendation and also sentenced McCarver to forty years in prison on the robbery charge. In September of 1995 the North Carolina Supreme Court affirmed the conviction and sentence. An attempt to convince the U.S. Supreme Court to review the case failed the next year.

McCarver's attorneys continued to work on his behalf, searching for other ways to save his life or at least to delay the execution for as long as possible. After some unsuccessful maneuverings in state court, McCarver petitioned the U.S. district court for relief. His attorneys argued, among other things, that he did not receive adequate legal representation at his trial and therefore his Sixth Amendment right to counsel had been violated. The district court rejected the argument, the Fourth Circuit Court of Appeals upheld that rejection, and the U.S. Supreme Court refused yet another request for review.

McCarver's execution was scheduled for 2:00 a.m. on March 2, 2001. As that day approached there was a flurry of activity on his behalf. A glimmer of hope came from the state legislature, which began considering a bill that would prohibit the execution of the mentally retarded. It was questionable, however, if the proposed law would be enacted prior to the scheduled execution. And even if it were enacted in time, it was not certain that the law would be retroactive. Nevertheless, on February 26, four days before the execution date, McCarver's attorneys convinced state superior court judge Leon Stanback to issue a stay of execution until the legislative issue was resolved. North Carolina authorities, however, promptly went to the state supreme court, whose justices dissolved the stay the next day.

With only three days remaining, McCarver's representatives made two final moves. First, they requested the intervention of the U.S. Supreme Court. And second, they petitioned North Carolina governor Michael Easley to use his executive powers to intervene.

On March 1, the governor announced that he would not stop the execution. "I deeply appreciate the sincerity and thoughtfulness of the arguments presented to me in favor of clemency," Easley said. "However, they are outweighed by the fact that this brutal murder was planned and orchestrated by Mr. McCarver and motivated by his desire for revenge against a former co-worker. Such evidence strongly supports the jury's recommendation of death and the decision of numerous appellate judges to affirm the sentence. The victim was an elderly and hard-working man who did nothing to deserve his fate. I do not see evidence sufficiently compelling to stop the fate that a jury of his peers recommended and that the courts have upheld."

Preparations for the implementation of the sentence proceeded. On the evening of March 1, Ernest McCarver had his last meal and spent some time saying goodbye to his brother and daughter. Unexpectedly, however, a last-minute reprieve came from the U.S. Supreme Court. That evening, just six hours before McCarver's scheduled execution, Chief Justice William Rehnquist on behalf of the Court issued a stay of the execution. The emergency action was temporary. The stay would be in effect only to give the justices time to consider McCarver's latest petition challenging his sentence. If his request that the Supreme Court give his case a full hearing was rejected, the stay of execution would terminate automatically and the execution would be rescheduled.

On March 26, 2001, however, the Supreme Court granted the requested writ of *certiorari*. The justices would hear McCarver's case. They did so with one significant limitation. Their review of his death sentence would be restricted to a single question: whether the application of the death penalty to the mentally retarded violated the cruel and unusual punishment provision of the Eighth Amendment to the U.S. Constitution. It was clear that the Supreme Court, or at least four of its justices, wanted to reconsider the 1989 *Penry* decision.

THE SUPREME COURT'S grant of *certiorari* to the *McCarver* appeal radically altered the legal environment for Daryl Atkins. In light of the *Penry* ruling, relegating retardation to a mitigating circumstance, Atkins's limited intellectual ability offered little hope on appeal to the Supreme Court. The issue of his mental retardation as a mitigating factor had received a full hearing at the trial court level and the jury had found it wanting. The Virginia Supreme Court found no reason to disturb that conclusion. But the *McCarver* case changed everything. Now a real possibility emerged that Atkins's retardation claim might be resurrected.

It was important for Lee and Haden to act quickly. They needed to amend their previous filing before the justices had a chance to deny *certiorari*. On March 29, 2001, just three days after the Court accepted the *McCarver* case and only two weeks after the complete submission of Atkins's *certiorari* papers, Lee and Haden submitted a supplement to their earlier petition. In it they requested two things. First, they moved to amend their original petition to add a new issue, alleging that the execution of the mentally retarded violates the Cruel and Unusual Punishment Clause of the Eighth Amendment.

"Petitioner's execution would violate the Eighth and Fourteenth Amendments to the United States Constitution," they argued, "because petitioner is retarded and there is now a national consensus against executing the mentally retarded." Since the *Penry* decision, sixteen states had joined Georgia, Maryland, and the federal government in banning such executions. This, of course, was the same issue that the Court planned to address in *McCarver*.

Their second point took the form of a backup plan. If the justices would not permit Atkins to amend his *certiorari* petition to add the retardation issue, they asked the Court to hold the Atkins case as pending until *McCarver* was decided. This second request, if granted, would keep Atkins's execution at bay for about a year while the *McCarver* case was being heard and decided. If the Court used *McCarver* to strike down the death penalty for retarded persons, it would give Atkins's attorneys new legal options to pursue.

On April 4, Pamela Rumpz responded. In her opposition to the petitioner's new filing, she argued that the writ of *certiorari* petition should be denied without accepting the new issue and without delay. Atkins raised the retardation issue in the state supreme court only as a mitigating factor in an attempt to establish that the death penalty in Atkins's situation was disproportionate under Virginia law. Atkins did not argue in the lower court that executing mentally retarded people violated the Eighth Amendment to the U.S. Constitution. Furthermore, the state supreme court rejected Atkins's pleas exclusively on state law grounds; the Virginia justices did not reach a decision on the federal constitutional right because they were not asked to do so. There were no grounds, she argued, for the U.S. Supreme Court to review a decision by the Virginia Supreme Court that did not address the position the petitioner was now asserting.

Furthermore, before Atkins should be allowed to raise a claim of retardation, the lower courts should first authoritatively decide on the extent of his mental impairment. The prosecution and defense had presented conflicting evidence at the trial court level regarding the presence

of mental retardation. The court made no definitive ruling on his intellectual ability. The retardation question is a factual one that should be
resolved first at the trial level. Only if Atkins is found to be retarded
should he be able to allege a right that pertains to intellectually impaired
persons.

Six days later, Lee and Haden filed their response to the state's opposition. They argued that the retardation issue had been presented at the
state appellate level. The state supreme court considered and rejected the
argument. Although the majority did not elaborate on the issue, it was
discussed at length in the two dissents.

There was no immediate reaction from the Court. As the final weeks of
the Court's 2000–2001 term came to an end in June there was still no word
on the justices' action on Atkins's revised petition for review. At this point
it was almost assured that nothing would be decided until late September
2001 when the justices would assemble for their pretrial conference before
the beginning of the next term.

In the interim, however, the political and legal landscape again
changed. On August 4, 2001, Governor Michael Easley of North Carolina
signed into law a bill that would ban the imposition of capital punishment on the mentally retarded. Within days of this event, the attorney
general of North Carolina wrote to the U.S. Supreme Court, informing
the justices that the new law had retroactive effect. Ernest McCarver was
eligible to take advantage of the new law's opportunity to provide evidence of his retardation in order to avoid the death penalty. In light of
these events, the state asked the Court to dismiss the McCarver appeal.

On September 25, after the justices met in preparation for the beginning of the new term, the Court announced that McCarver's petition for
certiorari would be "dismissed as improvidently granted." That same day
the Court also announced that it had granted Daryl Atkins's petition for
review and allowed him to proceed *in forma pauperis*. And only six days
later, on October 1, the justices officially instructed lawyers for Atkins and
the Commonwealth of Virginia to confine their arguments to the following question: "Whether the execution of mentally retarded individuals
convicted of capital crimes violates the Eighth Amendment?" The justices
had effectively swapped McCarver for Atkins.

The state of Virginia was not happy. Within two days Rumpz filed a motion for the Court to dismiss the writ issued to Atkins. Again she argued that the Court should not accept the case because in the lower courts Atkins had not raised the federal constitutional question regarding the execution of the mentally retarded. Even Justice Leroy Hassell's dissent in the Virginia Supreme Court decision criticized the majority for not taking up the constitutional issue. Under these circumstances she asked the Court to dismiss the case.

On October 29, the Court rejected the motion to dismiss. The case was scheduled for oral argument on February 20, 2002.

The Atkins camp, of course, was delighted by this turn of events. The justices were clearly ready to reconsider *Penry*. The fact that they went out of their way to make sure the issue remained on the docket after the McCarver case became moot encouraged death penalty opponents. But the issues had now changed. Atkins was no longer arguing a rather technical evidentiary point of law in the hope of reversing his sentence. The issue now was much broader and had greater significance. The Atkins appeal ceased to be of interest exclusively to people with a single focus on the death penalty itself. Now those concerned with the legal rights of the retarded, and in fact the entire disability community, had a great deal riding on the Court's decision. The *Washington Post* projected that the Court's ruling was "bound to be one of its most significant decisions" of the term.

BIBLIOGRAPHIC NOTE.

Materials on the Supreme Court and its procedures can be found in a number of publications. An excellent example is Lawrence Baum, *The Supreme Court*, 9th ed. (Washington D.C.: CQ Press, 2007).

The rules of the Supreme Court, which include the procedures it follows in deciding *certiorari* petitions, are available on the Court's Web site at: www.supremecourtus.gov.

Scholarly examinations of the Supreme Court's decision making on writ of *certiorari* petitions include H. W. Perry Jr., *Deciding to Decide: Agenda-Setting in the United States Supreme Court* (Cambridge: Harvard University Press, 1991); Gregory A. Caldeira and John R. Wright, "The

Discuss List: Agenda-Setting in the Supreme Court," *Law & Society Review* 24 (1990) 807–836; Gregory A. Caldeira and John R. Wright, "Organized Interests and Agenda-Setting in the Supreme Court," *American Political Science Review* 82 (December 1988): 1109–1127.

For a look at the work of Supreme Court law clerks, see Todd C. Peppers, *Courtiers of the Marble Palace: The Rise And Influence of the Supreme Court Law Clerk* (Palo Alto, Calif.: Stanford University Press, 2006); Artemus Ward and David L. Weiden, *Sorcerers' Apprentices: 100 Years of Law Clerks at the United States Supreme Court* (New York: New York University Press, 2006).

The discussion of the *McCarver* case in this chapter relies heavily on the trial and appellate court records of the case, official statements of the governor of North Carolina, and an abundance of legal and political commentary on the issues disputed.

Persuading the Justices

THE JUSTICES HAD SERVED NOTICE that they were interested in answering only one question presented in Atkins: Does the execution of mentally retarded capital offenders violate the Cruel and Unusual Punishment Clause of the Eighth Amendment? Providing a definitive answer to this question would require the justices to confront two major claims advanced by Atkins and opposed by the Commonwealth of Virginia. First, there are characteristics shared by all mentally retarded persons that make it appropriate to treat them as a class rather than as discrete individuals. And second, the standards of the American people have evolved to a point that a national consensus against executing the mentally retarded now exists.

Justices have a general reluctance to overturn precedent, but holding in favor of Daryl Atkins undoubtedly would require the reversal of the precedent set just thirteen years earlier in *Penry v. Lynaugh* (1989). The *Penry*-approved system of individualized sentencing would be replaced by a constitutional ban on executions of the mentally retarded.

The Court's decision not to address procedural matters such as the hearsay issue but instead to focus exclusively on the cruel and unusual punishment question required changes in the Atkins legal team. Robert Lee, the executive director of the Virginia Capital Representation Resource Center, became the attorney of record for the case. Lee brought on board Mark E. Olive, a Florida attorney with twenty-five years of experience representing death penalty defendants in trial and appellate courts. Just two years earlier he had appeared before the Supreme Court in *Weeks v. Angelone* (2000), arguing on behalf of a man convicted of killing a Virginia state trooper. Olive had a long association with Lee and with the Virginia Capital Representation Resource Center.

While Olive added additional capital punishment experience, the Atkins team lacked one crucial element—someone with expertise in the area of mental disabilities. There was one natural choice: James W. Ellis, a professor of law at the University of New Mexico and recognized as perhaps the nation's leading academic lawyer in the field of mental retardation law.

For three decades Ellis had been an advocate for the legal rights of the mentally disabled. His interest in the field began in 1969 when, as a conscientious objector and recent graduate of Occidental College, he was assigned to work at the Yale Psychiatric Hospital as an alternative to military service. His experience interacting with patients at the hospital inspired a life-long interest in mental disabilities. With his service completed, Ellis began his legal studies at the University of California at Berkeley. In 1974, as a recent law school graduate, Ellis accepted a position at the Bazelon Center for Mental Health Law in Washington, D.C., where he further advanced his training in the field. Two years later he joined the faculty at the University of New Mexico law school, specializing in constitutional law and the rights of the mentally disabled. His approach was decidedly interdisciplinary, often collaborating with New Mexico special education professor Ruth Luckasson, another nationally known expert on retardation issues.

Ellis's efforts were not confined to the classroom. He regularly published legal research articles on mental retardation and provided expert opinion to state agencies on the rights of the disabled. He was very active in national advocacy groups for the retarded, especially the American Association on Mental Retardation, an organization for which he served a term as president, and The Arc. Ellis authored *amicus curiae* briefs in support of the mentally disabled in more than a dozen appeals to the Supreme Court, including the *Penry* case. There was no one who was more experienced or knowledgeable in the field of mental disability law. If a national consensus had emerged against the death penalty for the retarded, James Ellis had played a major role in creating it.

Of the decision to invite Ellis to join the Atkins legal team, Robert Lee explained, "It's kind of like if you're in the World Series. You're in the bottom of the ninth and you get to pick anyone you want to come to the plate. Jim has just been a leader in disabilities law virtually all of his professional life. There was an obvious expertise and awareness of the history of this issue that is truly unparalleled." Additionally, Ellis joined the efforts on behalf of Atkins already well prepared for the battle. He had authored an *amicus curiae* brief for a coalition of mental health organizations for McCarver's case.

University of New Mexico law professor James W. Ellis argued Daryl Atkins's case before the U.S. Supreme Court.

Described by students and colleagues as brilliant, humble, and generous with a quick wit and an unsurpassed command of his subject matter, the fifty-six-year-old Ellis was well qualified to tackle the case. But he had one important shortcoming. Ellis had always worked behind the scenes. He had never previously argued before the Supreme Court. In fact, he had never argued before any court. "Not even a traffic ticket in police court," he often acknowledged. Ellis's lack of appellate oral argument experience did not concern Atkins's other lawyers. They were convinced that they had now joined forces with the best mental retardation lawyer available.

Admitting that he "obviously needed a lot more preparation than lawyers ordinarily do," Ellis assembled a team of his New Mexico law students and colleagues to assist him. He also received advice and support from the NAACP legal defense office. He met with Daryl Atkins in Sussex prison to get a first-hand impression of the man he now represented. He collaborated with Lee and Olive in developing the case. He not only had the resources of his own New Mexico team and the Virginia Capital Representation Resource Center, but also the encouragement of other lawyers active on behalf of the disability community.

Ellis's preparation was guided by what he saw as the central message coming from the *Penry* decision. The justices in that case had refused to extend blanket capital punishment protection for the retarded because of insufficient evidence that a national consensus had developed against such executions. Only two states at the time barred the infliction of the death penalty on the mentally retarded. *Penry,* according to Ellis, was an invitation from the justices to "bring us more states." And Ellis intended to do just that. His team dug into the post-*Penry* statutory and historical records of all fifty states to catalog the legislative, political, and public opinion changes that had occurred. They also assembled information on the ways other nations dealt with retarded offenders. The goal was to collect the strongest evidence possible that a national consensus had emerged since *Penry,* thus offering a compelling case that executing Daryl Atkins and other retarded defendants would violate the Eighth Amendment's Cruel and Unusual Punishment Clause.

The *Atkins* case for Ellis was not just another appeal before the U.S. Supreme Court. It was an opportunity to create new constitutional protections for the entire class of mentally disabled people. To Ellis the retarded were so deficient in understanding and so lacking in culpability that it was "inconceivable" that a state could justifiably take their lives regardless of the crimes committed.

Pamela Rumpz continued to represent Virginia, backed by the resources of the state attorney general's office. Unlike Ellis, Rumpz was an experienced appellate litigator. This was not her first time before the justices. Three years earlier she successfully defended the state's position in the capital murder case of *Strickler v. Greene* (1999). Rumpz hoped for a similar outcome in the Atkins case.

ANY CASE ACCEPTED for full review by the Supreme Court involves high stakes. Although the life of Daryl Atkins was hanging in the balance, the ramifications of the decision would extend far beyond the fate of a single convicted murderer. The Supreme Court would use Atkins's appeal to give additional shape and meaning to the Cruel and Unusual Punishment Clause of the Eighth Amendment. Its ruling carried the potential to dramatically affect the lives of scores of people already on death row and the many more with low intelligence levels that would commit capital offenses in the future.

All attorneys presenting cases before the Supreme Court understand the need to attract the support of a majority of the nine justices. This is not an easy task. Appeals involving simple or unimportant issues have been weeded out by the *certiorari* process. What remains are difficult, often ideologically charged and controversial issues over which the individual members of the Court may have very different views. The attorneys must carefully plan their strategies and arguments to garner the votes of at least five justices.

James Ellis and Pamela Rumpz would submit their arguments to a very experienced set of jurists. As a group the justices averaged more than sixteen years of service on the high court. Each had heard many death penalty cases. Five had participated in the *Penry* decision that the Court was now about to reconsider.

Given their long judicial histories, it should not be surprising that the members of the Court had each developed relatively strong positions on the constitutional rights of the criminally accused and on the death penalty itself. The array of these ideological positions nearly ensured that the Court would not reach consensus. A divided vote was taken as a given, but which side would attract the required five votes for victory was not at all certain. Most experienced Court observers were reasonably confident in predicting how seven of the justices would vote, but the votes of two members of the Court were clearly in play.

Pamela Rumpz could feel relatively confident about three justices: Chief Justice William Rehnquist and Associate Justices Antonin Scalia and Clarence Thomas.

William Hubbs Rehnquist was the Court's most senior member, having been nominated to be an associate justice by Richard Nixon in 1971. After serving in the Army Air Corps during World War II, the Milwaukee native received his bachelor's, master's, and law degrees from Stanford University and an additional master's degree in government from Harvard. Rehnquist apprenticed for a year as a law clerk to Justice Robert Jackson and then settled in Phoenix where he mixed private practice with conservative Republican politics. When Nixon was elected in 1968

Rehnquist joined the administration as an assistant attorney general, his only significant political post before joining the Court. After laboring fourteen years as an associate justice and establishing a record of supporting conservative legal positions on the bench, President Ronald Reagan elevated Rehnquist to replace the retiring Warren Burger as chief justice in 1986. In spite of his generally unswerving conservative posture, Rehnquist's leadership of the Court was well received by the other justices no matter their own individual philosophies.

In scores of capital punishment cases Rehnquist had consistently voted to support the authority of the state to impose the death penalty. In the *Penry* case, he joined the majority refusing to endorse a blanket death penalty exemption for the mentally retarded, supporting instead the recognition of retardation as an individually considered mitigating factor. There was little reason to suspect that the seventy-seven-year-old Rehnquist would now change his position.

Antonin Scalia was also predicted to be a firm vote in favor of Virginia. The sixty-five-year-old jurist had been on the Court for sixteen years, appointed by President Reagan in 1986 to take the associate justice position vacated by the elevated William Rehnquist. A conservative Catholic born in New Jersey, Scalia was the first Italian American justice. He came to the Court after a career as a legal academic. Trained at Georgetown University and Harvard Law School, Scalia held law faculty positions at the University of Virginia and the University of Chicago following seven years in private practice. Before being elevated to the Supreme Court Scalia served four years on the U.S. Court of Appeals for the District of Columbia.

Scalia's opinions reflected great intellectual capacity, a biting wit, and strong conservative leanings. He interpreted the Constitution based on the text itself in the light of the nation's history and traditions. Criminal defendants could not expect much sympathy from Antonin Scalia. He had a strong record of favoring law enforcement interests over the claims of the accused. He joined Rehnquist in the *Penry* majority rejecting the notion that a clear national consensus had emerged against applying the death penalty to retarded individuals. It was unlikely that Scalia would change his mind on the Atkins appeal.

The final safe vote for the state would likely be cast by Clarence Thomas. It had been eleven years since the nation's second African American justice had survived a bitter confirmation battle to take his position on the Court. Thomas was born into poverty conditions in rural Pin Point, Georgia. Deserted by his father, Thomas was profoundly influenced as a child by his grandfather who instilled in him discipline and Catholic religious principles. He received his education at the College of the Holy Cross and Yale Law School. He served in the U.S. Department of Education and chaired the Equal Employment Opportunity Commission under Presidents Reagan and Bush. After one year on the U.S. Court of Appeals, George H. W. Bush named him to the high court to replace the retiring Thurgood Marshall.

Thomas's record on criminal cases, and especially on death penalty appeals, was unswervingly conservative. A vote for Daryl Atkins from the fifty-three-year-old Thomas was highly improbable.

James Ellis and the other lawyers supporting Daryl Atkins had strong reasons to be optimistic about four of the justices: John Paul Stevens, Ruth Bader Ginsburg, David Souter, and Stephen Breyer.

John Paul Stevens, the oldest of the justices at eighty-one years, was the most liberal member of the Court. His father was a wealthy Chicago businessman in the hotel and insurance fields. Stevens received his undergraduate education at the University of Chicago, majoring in English. Following service in the U.S. Navy in World War II, he studied law at Northwestern, after which he won a coveted law clerk position with Justice Wiley Rutledge. For the next two decades he engaged in private practice, specializing in antitrust law. After serving five years on the United States Court of Appeals, Gerald Ford appointed him to the Supreme Court in 1975.

Stevens initially lived up to his reputation as a moderate Republican justice, but over the years he steadily moved to the left of his colleagues on the bench. This was reflected in his death penalty decisions. Shortly after joining the Court, Stevens agreed with the majority in *Gregg v. Georgia* (1976) to reinstate capital punishment. It did not take long, however, for Stevens to alter his position. He gradually became the Court's most consistent vote against the death penalty, at times being the lone justice in dissent. He concluded in *Penry* that the execution of the mentally retarded violated the Constitution.

Ruth Bader Ginsburg, a Brooklyn native, became the second woman appointed to the Supreme Court when President Bill Clinton nominated her in 1993. She was the first Jewish justice since Abe Fortas resigned in 1969. Ginsburg attended undergraduate school at Cornell and then studied law at Harvard and Columbia. Her pre-nomination career, like that of Antonin Scalia, was primarily as a legal academic. She held professorships in the law schools at Rutgers and Columbia. Her reputation, however, was based largely on her work for the American Civil Liberties Union where she headed the organization's Women's Rights Project. In that capacity she participated as an attorney in several landmark Supreme Court rulings dealing with gender issues. She often has been described as the Thurgood Marshall of the women's movement.

Before joining the Supreme Court, Ginsburg sat on the Court of Appeals for the District of Columbia for thirteen years, serving alongside Antonin Scalia during part of her tenure there. Her judicial voting record leaned decidedly in the liberal direction, but contrary to the fears of her conservative critics she did not espouse extreme ideological views. On death penalty issues, the sixty-eight-year-old Ginsburg generally favored the rights of the accused.

David Souter joined the Court in 1990, an appointee of George H. W. Bush. Souter left his home in New Hampshire to attend college and law school at Harvard University. In recognition of his academic achievement, he was named a Rhodes Scholar and studied at the University of Oxford in England. Shortly after returning to New Hampshire, he joined the state attorney general's office, ultimately becoming New Hampshire's attorney general in 1976. He began his judicial career in 1978, moving quickly from a New Hampshire trial court judge to the state supreme court and then to the U.S. Court of Appeals for the First Circuit. Only two months after joining the federal appeals court, however, President Bush nominated Souter for the Supreme Court.

Relatively little was known about David Souter when he was nominated. Although highly regarded by his associates, Souter's work as a lawyer and judge in a small New England state and his quiet, almost reclusive, demeanor gave him limited visibility. State Republican officials vouched for his ability and conservative ideology. On the Court, however, Souter proved to be much more liberal than his supporters anticipated. On death penalty cases he decidedly leaned toward the interests of the accused. There was every reason to believe that the sixty-two-year-old justice would be sympathetic to Daryl Atkins's plight.

Stephen Breyer was the final justice whose vote was predicted to favor Daryl Atkins. Justice Breyer, the junior member of the Court at that time, was appointed by President Clinton in 1994. Born in California, Breyer attended Stanford University and later studied at Oxford before beginning his legal training at Harvard. After earning his law degree, he served as a clerk for Justice Arthur Goldberg. He completed two years of service with the Justice Department and then began his professorial career at Harvard Law School and Harvard's Kennedy School of Government. In 1980 President Jimmy Carter named Breyer to the Court of Appeals for the First Circuit where he served until he joined the Supreme Court.

Breyer's reputation was one of moderate liberalism, more pragmatic than ideological. He likely would consider many different sources of information to determine if a consensus had developed over the imposition of capital punishment on the retarded. In the end, however, Court observers expected the sixty-three-year-old Breyer to extend Eighth Amendment protections to retarded capital offenders.

The records of these seven justices allowed clear expectations on how they would react to the Atkins case. But the remaining two members of the Court, Sandra Day O'Connor and Anthony Kennedy, were less predictable.

Justice O'Connor, the first woman to become a member of the Court, was appointed by President Reagan in 1981. She received her undergraduate and law degrees from Stanford University, graduating in the same law school class as Chief Justice Rehnquist. Eventually she settled in Arizona, practicing law for a short time and then becoming a state assistant attorney general. That experience, coupled with her active participation in Republican Party politics, led to her appointment and subsequent election to the Arizona state senate. In 1975 she became a state trial court judge and then joined the Arizona court of appeals in 1979.

For most of her tenure on the Supreme Court, O'Connor cast predictable conservative votes, particularly on issues involving the powers of state government. Her criminal rights decisions generally favored law enforcement interests. In the latter stages of her time on the bench she became a more centrist jurist often being the "swing vote" on issues such as affirmative action and privacy rights. The seventy-one-year-old O'Connor took a moderate approach to the death penalty. In the *Penry* case she found that the instructions given to the jury were sufficiently defective to void Penry's death sentence, but she was unwilling to endorse a constitutional ban against the execution of the mentally retarded as a class. Her vote in the Atkins case might well depend on whether she believed a national consensus against such executions had emerged in the thirteen years since *Penry* was decided.

Anthony Kennedy also frequently found himself in the ideological center of the Court. Kennedy was born into a Catholic family in which both parents were active in California Republican politics. His father was a prominent attorney and lobbyist in Sacramento. Kennedy received his undergraduate degree at Stanford and then left the state to attend Harvard Law School. He returned to California, ultimately taking over his father's law office. While practicing he taught constitutional law on a part-time basis at the University of the Pacific. In 1974, Ronald Reagan, an old California friend, convinced President Ford to nominate Kennedy to fill a vacancy on the Ninth Circuit Court of Appeals.

In 1987 President Reagan was faced with appointing a successor to retiring Justice Lewis Powell. After losing a bruising battle to obtain confirmation of the controversial Robert Bork and a failed attempt to elevate federal judge Douglas Ginsburg, Reagan turned to his old friend Kennedy. Kennedy was a faithful conservative who was not saddled with a controversial past or a history of indiscretions. His nomination was confirmed in the Senate by a 97–0 vote. Once on the Court, Kennedy followed a moderately conservative course, often playing the role of the swing vote along with Justice O'Connor. In the *Penry* decision, he voted with the conservative majority that the Eighth Amendment does not provide the mentally retarded a blanket protection from capital punishment. Although the sixty-five-year-old jurist's votes in death penalty cases usually supported

The votes of Justices Sandra Day O'Connor and Anthony Kennedy would likely tip the balance in the Atkins *case.*

the states' law enforcement interests, his position was not as rigidly held as the Court's other capital punishment supporters. Kennedy might have a natural tendency to lean toward Virginia's position in the Atkins case, but neither side could be confident about this vote.

These nine members of the Rehnquist Court had been together for eight years, an unusually long time for the Court to enjoy a stable membership. In some ways they were a diverse lot. Seven men, two women, one African American, three Catholics, two Jews, broad geographical representation, and a range of ideological perspectives. Yet they also had great similarities. The justices were educated in the nation's finest undergraduate colleges and law schools. All had legal careers, either in private practice, government service, or as legal scholars. All had significant judicial experience.

Court experts handicapping the case predicted four justices voting in favor of Atkins with three likely to side with the state. If these estimates were correct, Justices O'Connor and Kennedy would determine the outcome. Should James Ellis convince just one of them to agree with his arguments, Daryl Atkins's life might well be spared. The task for Pamela Rumpz appeared a bit more difficult. She would need both O'Connor and

Kennedy to join the three justices naturally leaning in her direction in order to obtain the required votes for Virginia's position to prevail.

ATTORNEYS HAVE TWO opportunities to influence the justices on the merits of their respective positions—through the submission of written briefs and by the presentation of oral arguments. The submission of the briefs occurs first. Unlike the *certiorari* briefs that clash over whether the Court should accept a case, these written arguments focus on the substantive legal questions that the justices must resolve. The briefs of the petitioner and the respondent may include as many as 15,000 words (about fifty pages). In addition, the petitioner is allowed to react to the respondent's arguments by filing a reply brief of up to 7,500 words. The rules of the Court admonish attorneys to keep their briefs "concise, logically arranged with proper headings and free of irrelevant, immaterial or scandalous matter."

Because the brief is in written form it has an impact throughout the decision-making process. Justices read the briefs in preparation for oral arguments and often reach tentative conclusions about the case at that time. The briefs may be consulted after the oral argument in anticipation of what may be discussed at the Court's conference. And the briefs are referred to once again by the justices and their law clerks during the opinion writing stage. Consequently, the writing of the brief offers attorneys their best opportunity to persuade the justices.

In addition to the briefs, the justices have access to a "joint appendix" that contains relevant information about lower court actions on the case. Among the documents included are the lower court docket entries, pleadings, jury instructions, opinions, orders, trial transcripts, and any other materials that provide reference information for the justices. Although the two sides are encouraged to cooperate in deciding which documents should be included, the primary responsibility for creating, printing, and submitting forty copies of the joint appendix rests with the petitioner.

The brief on behalf of Daryl Atkins was filed on November 29, 2001. Predictably, it stressed two major arguments. First, because of their diminished personal culpability the infliction of the death penalty on mentally retarded offenders violates the Eighth Amendment's ban on cruel and unusual punishment. Second, executing persons with mental retardation offends society's evolving standards of decency.

In order to demonstrate the personal culpability argument, the brief carefully walked the justices through the meaning of mental retardation. Retardation is defined first by a sub-average intelligence level, as measured by scientific IQ testing. The retarded score in the bottom 3 percent of the general population. Second, the retarded experience significant adaptive behavior problems that result in an inability to cope with the common demands of everyday life. And third, retardation manifests itself at birth or early childhood. Thus, the effects of an intellectual disability are compounded by a limited capacity to learn during an individual's most crucial period of personal development. This impairs normal emotional and adaptive growth.

The Supreme Court's capital punishment jurisprudence has emphasized the importance of personal culpability. The death penalty is appropriate only for persons who can act with deliberation. It is excessive if applied to those who have an underdeveloped ability to reason or who cannot make a fully reasoned choice. To be legitimate candidates for capital punishment defendants must be able to understand and evaluate the consequences of their actions. It is inappropriate to inflict death on individuals who are unable to comprehend why their life is being taken. The defendant also must be sufficiently mature to conform to society's basic norms. Children who commit murder, for example, are less mature and responsible for their crimes than adults. They have lower levels of understanding and control. The death penalty is proportionate only when the defendant's culpability and personal responsibility warrant the sanction of death.

These principles, Atkins's brief argued, lead to the conclusion that the retarded as a class should be ineligible for the death penalty. Those with mental retardation do not have the same capacity as others to make reasoned choices. They lack the ability to appreciate the consequences of their actions. Similar to young children, they do not have the requisite maturity, judgment, and personal responsibility to be held fully accountable for their actions. They often have only a partial ability to control their impulses, to think abstractly, or to engage in moral reasoning. In addition, the retarded are prone to be unduly influenced by others. These factors result in a level of personal culpability that is significantly lower than the imposition of the death penalty requires.

The execution of mentally retarded people serves no legitimate penal objective. Capital punishment is often justified because it promotes the interests of deterrence and retribution. Neither objective, however, is advanced by applying the death penalty to the mentally retarded. The retarded have limited ability to understand the consequences of their actions or the relationship between their behavior and subsequent punishment. Nor do the retarded have the capacity to learn from punishments imposed on others and to apply that information to their own decisions to commit crimes. Because the retarded lack these abilities, the death penalty has no deterrent impact on them.

Similarly, retribution interests are inapplicable. Retribution calls for the imposition of punishment proportionate to both the severity of the crime and the personal culpability of the offender. Because the retarded have low levels of personal culpability, it is grossly disproportionate to impose on them the most severe of all penalties.

The *Penry* policy of individualized consideration of retardation for mitigation purposes is insufficient to protect the rights of the retarded, argued Atkins's lawyers. Those with low intellectual abilities often engage in behavior to please others. During the investigation process this may include waiving rights that should not be waived or admitting to crimes that were not committed. The mentally retarded do not have the ability fully to assist their attorneys in the preparation of a defense. Jurors often do not understand retardation and its effects on personal culpability. Unlike children charged with crimes, the mildly retarded may look like normal adults. It is difficult for jurors to appreciate their limited intellectual abilities. Because of their lack of understanding, retarded defendants may act inappropriately in the courtroom, leaving jurors with the impression that these defendants lack remorse for their crimes or respect for the court. These factors contribute to making retarded individuals much more vulnerable to a death penalty verdict than those of normal intelligence.

The second major argument submitted on Atkins's behalf was that inflicting the death penalty on the retarded now offends our society's standards of decency. Because the Supreme Court in previous cases declared that state legislative actions constituted the most appropriate indicator of society's values, the brief for Atkins emphasized the movement of the states toward banning the execution of those with low intelligence levels. The majority in *Penry* rejected the conclusion that a national consensus had emerged against such executions because only two states, Georgia and Maryland, along with the federal government, had banned them. In the thirteen-year interim, however, sixteen states passed new laws exempting the retarded from the death penalty. Combining these eighteen states with the twelve who have abandoned the death penalty altogether leaves a minority of states that allow even the possibility of executing persons with mental retardation. The movement of the states in this regard has been so pronounced as to reflect a change in national norms.

Other indicators of change in national standards also exist. For example, public opinion polls show distaste among the general population for executing the retarded, and various organizations in the legal and mental retardation fields officially have opposed death penalty eligibility for those with significantly sub-average intelligence levels. And finally, the international community has expressed overwhelming rejection of the practice. These data clearly indicate that the people of the United States and those of other nations now reject the imposition of the death penalty on mentally retarded persons. As such, the penalty has become cruel and unusual punishment.

The Atkins brief ended with an argument that Daryl Atkins is mentally retarded. Dr. Evan Nelson's testing of his mental abilities clearly established that fact. Dr. Stanton Samenow's conclusions to the contrary were based on incomplete and inappropriate testing procedures that are not reliable. Given these factors, Ellis and his colleagues concluded, the decision of the Virginia Supreme Court affirming Daryl Atkins's death sentence should be reversed.

Pamela Rumpz's brief submitted on behalf of the Commonwealth of Virginia presented three basic arguments. The first was the jurisdictional position she unsuccessfully asserted during the *certiorari* process. Atkins had not raised an Eighth Amendment claim at the state court level, and the Virginia Supreme Court had not decided any Eighth Amendment issue. Therefore, she maintained, the U.S. Supreme Court should dismiss Atkins's appeal.

Such jurisdictional arguments are not often successful. If the Supreme Court has accepted a case, it has done so with the full intention of deciding the questions presented. Occasionally, however, the justices may have second thoughts about a case once they delve more deeply into it. They might find jurisdictional problems that they did not recognize previously. Or they might simply conclude that they do not want to decide an issue that initially seemed worth considering. In these situations the Court might use a jurisdictional objection to avoid making a ruling on the merits. Still, Rumpz's first issue was a long shot.

Her second argument spoke to the heart of the questions the justices wanted to address. She rejected the position that the Eighth Amendment required a blanket prohibition against the execution of retarded capital offenders. Her opposition to the arguments submitted by the Atkins legal team was two-fold. First, she denied the claim that a national consensus had emerged against such executions. And second, she claimed that retarded people, like all others, deserved to be treated as individuals, not as parts of a monolithic class sharing identical traits with all other class members.

As to the national consensus point, Rumpz attempted to erect a high threshold for determining whether such a consensus had developed. Quoting the Court in *Stanford v. Kentucky* (1989), she argued that placing an entire class of offenders outside the state's ability to punish by the death penalty "requires a 'national consensus so broad, so clear and so enduring' as to be beyond all legitimate question."

Rumpz argued that this standard had not been met. Of the thirty-eight capital punishment states, eighteen—less than half—had passed some sort of statute prohibiting the application of the death penalty to the mentally retarded. Twenty permitted such executions. This, she said, is not evidence of a national consensus.

Furthermore, several of the eighteen states that have adopted a prohibition have allowed certain exceptions. Eight of those states, for example, did not make their laws retroactive to cover convicted offenders on death row. The New York law generally imposed the ban, but made an exception for murders committed in prison. If there existed a broad national consensus that such executions violated the standards of civilized humanity, such limits and exceptions would never be placed in state laws. Rather, the bans would be absolute.

Rumpz further objected to Atkins citing the views of foreign governments and organized interest groups. The concept of a "national consensus" is supposed to reflect the values of Americans. When the people of the United States come to a conclusion and make their views known to their elected legislators, then there is evidence of the required consensus. "The purported standards of decency of other nations," she wrote, "are an inappropriate means of establishing the fundamental beliefs or national consensus of *this* Nation." So, too, are expressions of opinion by special interest groups that frequently are not representative of the American population.

Rumpz's second Eighth Amendment argument constituted a plea to treat those with limited intelligence as individuals. The retarded are distinct persons. They are not interchangeable, and they are not cut from the same pattern. Even those organizations advocating on behalf of the retarded consistently urge society to recognize their individual abilities and not to stereotype them as all being the same.

Especially heterogeneous are those individuals falling into the "mildly mentally retarded" category. Some function at a very high level. "These are adults, not children," she claimed. "They hold jobs, own houses, and live in stable cohabitation. It is demeaning to equate these adults with children" incapable of moral understanding and responsibility. Some retarded capital offenders have culpability levels deserving of the death penalty and others do not. *Penry* wisely concluded that the retarded should not be treated as a class, but should be assessed and judged on an individual basis.

Current statutory and constitutional safeguards are sufficient to protect the retarded, Rumpz contended. Before individuals can be tried they must be competent, able to assist their attorneys, understand the proceedings against them, and be sane. If the prosecution seeks capital punishment, the defendant must understand why the death penalty may be applied. The accused have full opportunities to present evidence in mitigation. If the jury finds that a convicted murderer's retardation level is insufficient mitigation to ward off the death penalty, the defendant can appeal or can request clemency from the governor. Judges and juries are fully capable of considering and giving effect to mitigating factors. More protection by way of the Eighth Amendment is not required.

Rumpz's third and final argument was that Daryl Atkins is not retarded. The issue of his mental ability was considered at his trial and sentencing, but this consideration occurred in the context of determining mitigation. Experts gave conflicting opinions about the extent of his mental deficiencies. No court answered the direct question of whether Atkins is in fact retarded. Even if the justices were to abandon *Penry,* Atkins's specific case would still have to be returned to the Virginia courts to determine if his intellectual abilities meet the legal definition of retardation.

Rumpz's three arguments, that the Court lacked jurisdiction, that the Eighth Amendment did not require a blanket ban on executions of the retarded, and that Daryl Atkins was not retarded, all led her to the same conclusion: the decision of the Supreme Court of Virginia should be affirmed.

Four weeks later, Ellis and his colleagues exercised their right to submit a short reply brief in response to the arguments advanced by the state. Their first task was to reinforce the position that a consensus against executions of the mentally deficient had emerged. The statutes of the eighteen states and the federal government withdrawing the retarded from execution eligibility had remarkable similarities. The Commonwealth of Virginia's attempt to exploit some procedural differences among those statutes did not erase the broad consensus that had developed. All of these statutes had the same basic thrust: stopping the executions of the mentally retarded.

Consensus, the Atkins team argued, is not a matter of simply counting legislative enactments. Instead, an accumulation of such enactments confirms that a consensus has developed. It shows a change in the American people's collective standards of decency. It alters the meaning of our constitutional prohibition against cruel and unusual punishment.

The state's assertion that the retarded are a heterogeneous group is but a truism. Certainly there are differences, sometimes significant ones. But those who are mentally retarded also share a common trait—sub-average intelligence levels. Retardation affects the level of understanding people have about their behavior and consequently also their responsibility for that behavior. No individual whose mental ability falls in the retardation range should be executed—even those at the highest functioning levels.

IN MOST OF THE CASES BROUGHT before the Supreme Court the petitioner and the respondent are not the only parties who submit written arguments urging the justices to support one outcome or another. Government bodies, private organizations, and individuals not party to the litigation may also file briefs. These *amicus curiae* or "friend of the court" briefs contribute to the process by calling the justices' attention to relevant material not otherwise provided by the parties. *Amici* become engaged in a case because the outcome may have an impact on their members or affect their policy interests. *Amicus* briefs can be influential. They often contain arguments, information, or proposed solutions that aid the justices in reaching decisions and crafting opinions.

A party that desires to file an *amicus* brief must first obtain the consent of all the litigants in the case. Permission is customarily granted, but if a party objects a motion to participate may be made directly to the Court. The U.S. government is exempt from the requirement to obtain consent as are state and local governments. *Amicus* briefs may not exceed 9,000 words (or about thirty pages).

It was not surprising when the Atkins appeal attracted significant *amicus* interest. Any death penalty case is relevant to capital punishment foes as well as to advocates of strong law enforcement. But the Atkins case also had the potential of affecting the rights of the disabled, state criminal procedures, and even the nation's standing in the international community.

A number of groups supporting a ban on executions of the mentally retarded had filed *amicus* briefs in *McCarver v. North Carolina*. When the Court dismissed *McCarver* and substituted the Atkins appeal in its place, it allowed those briefs to be carried over in support of Daryl Atkins.

Perhaps the most important of the *amicus* briefs on behalf of Atkins
was submitted by a coalition of disability and human rights groups active
in the field of mental retardation. The group was led by the American
Association on Mental Retardation (AAMR), the nation's largest and oldest interdisciplinary organization in the area of mental retardation. Joining AAMR were The Arc, the American Orthopsychiatric Association,
Physicians for Human Rights, the American Network of Community
Options and Resources, the Joseph P. Kennedy, Jr., Foundation, the
Bazelon Center for Mental Health Law, and the National Association of
Protection and Advocacy Systems. In addition, the American Psychologi-
cal Association independently submitted a brief expressing the concerns
of the mental health community.

The AAMR brief, intended originally for the McCarver appeal, was
written by James Ellis, now the lead advocate for Atkins. The brief focused
on the developing national consensus against executing the retarded.
According to the brief, applying the death penalty to the retarded was not
a significant public issue prior to the *Penry* decision, but the Supreme
Court's ruling in that case gave the topic national visibility. As a consequence, it touched off a strong and unmistakable movement to have such
executions barred. Professional organizations took policy positions
against such executions, citizen groups mobilized support for legislative
change, opinion polls reflected the public's opposition to them, and states
began to pass prohibition legislation. All of this activity documents a
strong new consensus against the execution of persons with mental retardation. The consensus has emerged because of the public's realization that
retardation significantly reduces a person's culpability and is a condition
over which the individual has no control. Inflicting the death penalty on
such persons offends the nation's shared moral values.

The position of the legal community was represented in briefs submitted by the American Bar Association, one of the first professional
organizations to oppose executions of the retarded, and the American
Civil Liberties Union. The legal profession was concerned with the risk
of erroneous convictions and the lack of essential fairness for the
retarded. Capital punishment trials for retarded defendants are exceedingly complex proceedings. The retarded, often indigent, are frequently

represented by lawyers who are unable to meet the exacting demands of such trials. And the complexity of the process increases significantly during the post-conviction stages. As a result, the retarded have an elevated likelihood of being convicted and sentenced to death. The states do not have adequate representation programs to ensure that the retarded are fairly treated in capital cases.

Religious groups also came forward to express their opposition to the use of the death penalty for defendants with serious intellectual deficits. The U.S. Catholic Conference headed a coalition of twelve religious groups to submit a legal brief in favor of Atkins. The coalition included Catholic, Protestant, Jewish, and Muslim organizations as well smaller sects such as the Mennonites. Some of the organizations joining the effort had very little in common with the other groups, but they came together because of their mutual belief that the retarded should be protected against the death penalty.

Finally, two briefs spoke from the perspective of the international community. One was filed by the European Union on behalf of its fifteen member nations. The EU opposes the death penalty in all cases and consistently supports the goal of universal abolition. It does so because it sees capital punishment as inconsistent with human dignity and the development of human rights. The EU brief portrayed the United States as standing alone in the Western Hemisphere in allowing capital punishment for the retarded, and nearly alone in the world community. By allowing such penalties the United States runs contrary to strong international standards and opinions. The United States, the brief argued, should join the world community in condemning such executions.

The second *amicus* asking the Court to consider the global environment was a group of nine former diplomats who represented the United States within the international community. The brief emphasized that in allowing the execution of the mentally retarded the United States was acting contrary to evolving international standards of decency. The United States receives constant criticism from the international community for maintaining a punishment that is considered cruel and uncivilized. Foreign relations are strained each time an American state administers the death penalty to a retarded individual. Furthermore, the brief argued that in determining what is cruel and unusual punishment the justices should consider not only the actions of domestic entities such as state legislatures, but also the evolving standards of decency of the international community.

Support for the Commonwealth of Virginia came from two sources. The first was the California-based Criminal Justice Legal Foundation. This group was organized to advocate for crime victims and to promote the rapid, efficient, and reliable determination of guilt and the swift administration of punishment. Its *amicus* brief argued that the nation's death penalty jurisprudence had gone through a disruptive and stressful period since the 1972 *Furman* decision. It has now reached a point of stability, the Foundation asserted, and that stability should be maintained. The Court should allow the states to experiment with various capital punishment reforms, as the eighteen abolition states had done. But the Court should not impose a single rule on all states. The current system provides sufficient safeguards for individuals with sub-average intelligence levels. No blanket exclusion is necessary. Interests of justice are clearly being met by juries recommending sentences based on the particular characteristics of individual defendants and their crimes.

The second *amicus* brief supporting Virginia was submitted by a coalition of five states—Alabama, Mississippi, Nevada, South Carolina, and Utah. This effort was led by Bill Pryor, the Alabama attorney general. These states urged the Court to preserve the death penalty for capital defendants who have "the cognitive, volitional, and moral capacity to act with the degree of culpability associated with the death penalty." That goal could best be achieved by following the established *Penry* precedent. It creates a regime that is just and sensitive and also promotes the vigorous enforcement of the law.

The five-state brief argued strongly that the required national consensus compelling a reinterpretation of the Eighth Amendment had not been reached. More than half of the death penalty states imposed no categorical rule against the execution of retarded people. And among those states that had enacted blanket bans on such executions there were wide differences in how the prohibition was structured. For example, nine of those eighteen states required the defendant to prove retardation by the preponderance of evidence. The rest used some other standard. Eight states called for a determination of retardation to take place before the trial, three at the trial, three others at the pre-sentencing stage, and four states made the determination at the sentencing stage itself. Six states classified those with IQs below 70 to be retarded, but two states drew the line at 65. Five states imposed no IQ test standard and others had mixed systems. If there was a true and strong national consensus, the states that prohibited executions of the mentally retarded would not be so divided on so many related issues. Under these circumstances, the states' argument concluded, it is better to let the individual states continue to experiment until a real consensus emerges.

The briefing stage provided the justices with views, evidence, and arguments from a wide range of perspectives. The two litigants, Daryl Atkins and the Commonwealth of Virginia, of course, focused on the immediate issues at play in their dispute. But the *amicus* groups, representing a varied set of societal interests, expanded the range of arguments and information available to the justices and urged consideration of the potential impact of the Court's decision beyond the particular interests of the two parties.

ORAL ARGUMENTS provide an entirely different avenue for influence. When the Supreme Court was still a very young institution attorneys relied on oral arguments rather than briefs to persuade the justices. Oral arguments were often major events, with the leading advocates of the day appearing before the Court to represent their clients with eloquence and flourish. And they did so often at great length. The oral arguments in *Gibbons v. Ogden*, the seminal 1824 Commerce Clause case, lasted for five days. And when the national bank's constitutionality was challenged in *McCulloch v. Maryland* (1819) the attorneys orated for nine days.

As the Court's procedures evolved over time, oral argument changed. Today oral argument in most cases is confined to one hour—thirty minutes for each side. Because they already have had access to the parties' briefs, the arguments of the participating *amici*, lower court transcripts and opinions, and other supporting documents, the justices come to oral arguments well informed about the pending case. Oral argument provides an opportunity for the attorneys to advocate their positions to the justices in a face-to-face context. Even more, however, oral argument permits the justices to ask questions and pose counter-arguments to the attorneys in order to obtain a richer understanding of the issues. Oral argument is the only pre-decision stage of the process that occurs in public. It therefore serves an important symbolic and educational purpose in allowing the press and public to observe directly the justices in action.

By tradition the Supreme Court begins its annual term on the first Monday of October. The term is normally completed at the end of June, at which point the justices adjourn for the summer. By current practice the justices divide the months of October through April into alternating two-week intervals. During the first two-week session the justices hear oral arguments on Monday, Tuesday, and Wednesday. Normally two cases are argued each day. The justices meet in private conference on the Friday prior to the beginning of the two-week session and on the two Fridays following the oral argument days. The next two-week segment is devoted to research and writing opinions as well as other work that takes place out of the public's view. By the end of April the Court has usually completed hearing oral arguments for the year, and during the remaining weeks of the term the justices focus on completing the decision-making and opinion-writing process for the cases that have been heard.

Conforming to a tradition began by Chief Justice Melville Fuller (1888–1910), the justices meet immediately prior to the beginning of an oral argument session. Each justice formally shakes the hand of the other eight justices. The ritual was designed by Fuller to remind the members of their unity of purpose even though they may sharply divide on specific issues.

Oral argument takes place in the Court Chamber, a majestic courtroom with a forty-four-foot-high ceiling and adorned with marble imported from Africa, Spain, and Italy. At the front of the room is the Supreme Court bench, behind which the justices sit during open sessions. Constructed of mahogany, the bench is elevated above floor level and is designed with a center section and two wings slightly turned to face each other. As the Court is called into session the justices enter the room from three doorways behind the bench. The justices take their seats according to seniority. The chief justice occupies the center seat, with the most senior associate justice sitting to the immediate right of the chief justice and the next most senior justice to the left. The other justices take their places in the same alternating fashion with the most junior justice sitting to the chief's far left.

When it is time for the attorneys to present their arguments, they take their position at the Court's lectern, located immediately in front of the chief justice. The attorney for the petitioner first addresses the Court, followed by the lawyer representing the respondent. The clerk of the court has a desk to the left of the bench and the marshal to the right. The marshal maintains the security of the courtroom and also serves as the time-keeper during the attorneys' presentations. The lectern is outfitted with two lights, one white and one red. When an attorney has five minutes of oral argument time remaining, the marshal signals by turning on the white light. When time has expired, the red light is flashed. Attorneys are advised to stop immediately upon the completion of the sentence in progress.

Attorneys must come to oral argument fully prepared to present their case and answer any questions about it. The Court's rules specifically admonish lawyers not to read from a prepared script. In contrast to the complete control they exercise over the content of their written briefs, attorneys are largely at the mercy of the justices during oral argument. It is rare that an attorney is able to speak for more than a minute or two before the justices began interrupting with questions. The questions may serve different purposes. A justice may be unclear about a fact or a line of argument and ask questions to gain a better understanding of the party's position. A justice may also ask questions to assist an attorney who represents a position favored by the justice. Such queries may lead the attorney to supply information or analysis that will strengthen the case. Conversely, justices may ask questions to expose the weaknesses of arguments supporting causes they disfavor. On occasion justices with differing points of view appear to use the questioning process as a means of debating each other.

James Ellis and Pamela Rumpz would present their arguments to an array of justices who play their roles very differently The oral argument setting is perhaps most comfortable for those justices whose prior careers were spent as law school professors. It is natural for them to participate in the Socratic give-and-take of scholarly arguments. Thus, Ellis and Rumpz could expect considerable questioning from Antonin Scalia, Ruth Bader Ginsburg, and Stephen Breyer. Centrist justices, such as Sandra Day O'Connor and Anthony Kennedy, might be expected to ask questions in an attempt to find common ground or practical solutions rather than pushing ideological positions. And Ellis and Rumpz would reasonably anticipate little comment from Clarence Thomas, a justice who prefers to listen to the advocates' arguments without interruption.

There is continuing debate among Court observers as to the influence of oral argument. Members of the Court arrive at oral argument well acquainted with the case and the parties' arguments. Some justices may have already made up their minds. This is most likely to occur when a case presents a perennial issue upon which the justice has firm views. For example, Justices William Brennan and Thurgood Marshall long held the position that the death penalty in all circumstances is unconstitutional. No matter what specific issues were at play in a death penalty appeal, attorneys representing the prosecutorial interests of the state had no chance to win the vote of either Brennan or Marshall. Most justices come to oral argument leaning in one direction or another, but still maintaining an open mind. Less frequently a member of the Court will be truly undecided.

Some attorneys specialize in Supreme Court litigation. Most notable in this regard is the solicitor general of the United States, a presidential appointee and third-ranking member of the Justice Department. The solicitor general and the attorneys working in the solicitor general's office represent the federal government before the Supreme Court. The cases in which the United States is a party (about twenty each year) or for which the federal government wishes to participate as *amicus curiae* (about seventeen per year) constitute a large proportion of the Supreme Court's business. The expertise of the solicitor general's office leads to a significant success rate, winning on average 60 to 70 percent of the cases in which it represents the United States.

A handful of private attorneys have developed a specialization in Supreme Court litigation. However, most lawyers who appear before the justices will do so only once in their careers. For this reason, the quality of argument is quite variable. Attorneys inexperienced in this specialized form of advocacy are susceptible to unraveling under the pressure of the sometimes harsh and relentless questioning by the justices. This gives rise to an old adage that oral argument has won few Supreme Court cases, but lost many.

AT PRECISELY 11:27 A.M. on Wednesday, February 20, 2002, with the nine members of the Court assembled, Chief Justice William Rehnquist called for the beginning of oral arguments in the case of *Daryl Renard Atkins v. the Commonwealth of Virginia.*

Among the observers in the crowded courtroom were two individuals with special interests in the case. The first was Eunice Kennedy Shriver, accompanied by her brother Senator Edward M. Kennedy (D-Mass.). Shriver, one of the founders of the Special Olympics movement, had long been active in promoting rights and expanded opportunities for the mentally challenged. Also sitting in the courtroom was another woman with an entirely different perspective on the case. Mary Sloan had traveled with her family from Gilbertsville, New York, in an effort to keep her slain son's memory alive and with the hope of seeing justice done.

Professor James Ellis approached the lectern and began his argument. He would have thirty minutes to make his case. Pamela Rumpz, allotted the same amount of time, would follow him. Less than one minute into Ellis's presentation, Chief Justice Rehnquist interjected the first question. "What is your definition of a consensus, Mr. Ellis?" This was quickly followed by, "And how many states out of the 50 do you need, do you think, for a consensus?"

Over the next hour of oral argument, the justices would interrupt the attorneys with questions or challenges a total of 137 times. Some of their questions were simple factual inquiries, others more abstract and theoretical. Many more closely resembled comments than questions, often clearly supporting or opposing what the attorneys were arguing. Some posed intellectual traps and others offered lifelines. The questions came in near rapid-fire frequency, rarely permitting an opportunity for in-depth responses. Frequently a new question was asked before the attorney could finish a response to the previous one.

The issue of a national consensus introduced by Chief Justice Rehnquist's initial question dominated much of the Court's attention. On the surface, the numbers were clear. Twelve states had abolished capital punishment completely. Eighteen states allowed the death penalty, but had passed legislation prohibiting its infliction on the retarded. Sixteen had enacted such statutes since the Court handed down *Penry* in 1989. Twenty states had no legal prohibition against executions of the retarded. They treated retardation as a mitigating factor that juries were free to take into account during the individualized sentencing process. Under the justices' questioning, however, the distribution of the states was not so obvious.

Early in Ellis's presentation, Justice Scalia inquired about the nature of the laws passed by the eighteen states that protected the retarded against execution. Specifically he wanted to know whether the laws applied only to sentences handed down after the laws were enacted or if the statutes also barred execution of retarded people already on death row. When Ellis admitted that some of the laws were prospective only, Scalia asserted that these states could not be counted as holding the view that such executions are always cruel and unusual punishment. "I thought when you were talking about a consensus, you're talking about a consensus that something is so terrible that it should not be permitted," Scalia argued. "And these states are permitting it. They're just not going to do it in the future." Ellis countered with the possibility that if a state had no retarded people waiting on death row that there would be no reason for the legislature to make the ban retroactive. Less explainable, however, was a provision in the New York statute, cited by Rumpz, that barred the execution of retarded capital murderers unless the murder took place in prison.

The attorneys and justices also sparred over how to count states that had abolished the death penalty altogether. Pamela Rumpz, arguing on behalf of Virginia, essentially excluded those states from consideration because the matter of adopting a death penalty exemption for the retarded was not relevant to them. Thus, from the state's point of view, twenty of the thirty-eight death penalty states, a majority, had not passed any kind of blanket exemption for the retarded. Justice Ginsburg took exception to this characterization, claiming that the twelve anti-death penalty states had to be included with the eighteen states that had protections for the retarded. This amounts to thirty states, a "supermajority" of three-fifths, according to Ginsburg, that have rejected the application of the death penalty to the mentally disabled. Justice O'Connor interjected support for Ginsburg's position, commenting that "I can't imagine that you would say you couldn't count those states."

Questions posed to both attorneys by Justices Breyer and Souter expressed doubt that counting state statutory enactments was the best evidence of whether or not a consensus had emerged. Specifically they questioned the assumption that the twenty states not passing capital punishment protections for the retarded constituted evidence of a lack of consensus. Breyer claimed that since *Penry* only two states had executed offenders who were clearly retarded. He inquired whether by this behavior forty-eight states should be counted as rejecting such applications of capital punishment rather than just the twenty that had passed legislative bans.

Justice Souter followed with a similar question to Rumpz, "Let me ask you a kind of a—a specific example of Justice Breyer's question. In your calculation, how do you account for a state like the one I come from that has not executed somebody in over sixty years?" Caught off guard by the question, Rumpz had to admit that "I don't know what state you come from." Souter helped her by explaining that his home state of New Hampshire by statute permits capital punishment and has no legislative ban on executing the mentally retarded. The state, however, had not administered capital punishment on any offender since the late 1930s. Why should New Hampshire, and other states with similar histories, be categorized as not supporting a ban on executing retarded murderers?

Other questions pointed out that state legislatures do not pass laws where there is no need to do so. If there are no executions of the retarded taking place, the legislature is not likely to enact a statute prohibiting such penalties. Thus, while a state statute banning such executions is positive evidence that they are considered inappropriate, the absence of passing such a statute does not necessarily mean that the state endorses capital punishment for the retarded. Rumpz responded to this line of questioning by citing the Supreme Court's own precedent that legislative enactments constitute the most authoritative evidence of an emerging consensus.

Ellis emphasized that not only had sixteen states changed their laws since *Penry*, but more importantly all of the changes had been in the same direction—to prohibit executions of the retarded. No state previously outlawing such executions had modified its laws to permit them. Justice Scalia, however, urged caution. He noted that these laws were all relatively recent enactments. The states had not yet had significant experience with them. For Scalia a well-informed consensus had not yet coalesced, and this posed a problem:

> If we find a consensus here that it is indeed unconstitutional to execute the mentally retarded, and then it turns out that there are a lot of problems, that indeed in every case, every capital case, there's going to be a claim of mental retardation and people come to believe that in many of these cases you get expert witnesses—you can easily get them on both sides—people become dissatisfied with that. We won't be able to go back, will we? Because the evidence of the consensus is supposed to be legislation, and once we've decided that you cannot legislate the execution of the mentally retarded, there can't be any legislation that enables us to go back. So, we better be very careful about the national consensus before we come to such a judgment.

Although most of the debate over the consensus questions focused on how to evaluate state legislative actions, there were clashes over the appropriate weight to give other indicators of the nation's standards. Some of the justices, for example, thought that the infrequency with which jurors sentenced the retarded to death was a valid indicator that the public opposed such penalties. This argument was countered by the suggestion that such tendencies demonstrated that the system of considering individual mitigating factors was working as intended.

Other issues involved the relevance of public opinion polls, which Ellis suggested as being "part of the picture" in demonstrating that a consensus against executing the retarded had emerged. Chief Justice Rehnquist challenged this position by asserting that if public opinion ran decidedly against executing the retarded, it would be reflected in legislative enactments. He also raised the caveat that public opinion polls are only as valid as the methodology used.

Finally, there was the issue of the appropriateness of considering world opinion. Justice Ginsburg, who earlier in her career coauthored a book on the Swedish legal system, especially pushed the position that the views of other nations are relevant in determining whether this application of capital punishment is to be considered cruel and unusual. Ginsburg asked whether the United States should be deaf to the fact that the rest of the world considers these executions inhumane. Rumpz responded by categorically stating that world opinion "certainly is not relevant in deciding the Eighth Amendment principle," a position that was immediately supported by Justice Scalia.

Regardless of which indicators are consulted, Ellis said in the conclusion to his argument, the result is the same. "And our position, on the basis of what has happened in the 13 years since *Penry,* is that the consensus that was then emerging is now manifest, both in the legislation and in every other indicator we have of public sentiment."

Pamela Rumpz saw it very differently. Even if an emerging consensus had developed—a position she expressed only for the sake of argument—it was far from an enduring consensus. "The states are laboratories for novel social experimentation. Well, this experiment is just beginning," she argued. Her plea was to allow the states more time to see if the consensus becomes permanent and not to constitutionalize a position that the public might reject after a few more years of experience under the new laws.

Another area of disagreement concerned the question of whether there are traits inherently shared by all mentally retarded persons that would justify exempting them as a class from the death penalty. Ellis argued strongly that while retarded people are heterogeneous on many dimensions, they share, by definition, the characteristic of sub-average intelligence. This condition reduces their culpability or blameworthiness because they do not fully appreciate the consequences of their actions or the context in which their behavior takes place.

In response, Justice Kennedy asked why the retarded should be punished at all if they are unable to appreciate the consequences of their actions. Ellis offered that retarded individuals may have the intellectual capacity to form a criminal intent. They may be guilty of criminal wrong-doing and merit punishment. They may understand that a particular act is wrong, but not appreciate the degree to which it is wrong. Their lower levels of comprehension and culpability make the death penalty inappropriate. Ellis conceded that there would be no constitutional problem with other serious penalties, including life in prison without parole, but death sentences should be prohibited. Death, he argued, is inherently different than all other punishments.

Pamela Rumpz took exception to the position that the mentally retarded should be treated as a special class. Instead she argued that the existing system of individualized sentencing should be maintained. Not all mentally retarded people should be treated the same. Subject to the consideration of mitigating circumstances, defendants "found competent at the time of the crime, competent ... to assist his lawyers, who were found guilty of a premeditated, deliberated, and calculated murder" should be eligible for execution.

Justices Breyer and Souter responded with a series of questions critical of the argument advanced by Rumpz. Certainly, they argued, there had to be some cut-off point at which low levels of intelligence would make executions inappropriate. They compared the intelligence levels of the retarded to those of young children. The Court had ruled previously against executions of children younger than sixteen years, why then should it be permissible to execute retarded people whose intelligence levels similarly were less than that of a normal sixteen year old? Rumpz held her ground. If a person, even with low intelligence levels, is capable of carrying out a capital crime and fully competent to stand trial and assist counsel, "then we're not looking at someone whose culpability is in any way less than yours or mine."

Souter responded that there surely must be a borderline point where the culpability of a retarded person is uncertain. Jury decisions in such cases would carry a high risk of arriving at the wrong conclusion, of sentencing to death someone who might not be sufficiently culpable. Shouldn't there be some categorical cut off-point to avoid such situations? Shouldn't our Eighth Amendment jurisprudence take into account such risk and impose some reasonable limits? Rumpz responded that the system of individualized sentencing was designed to give juries the flexibility to avoid imposing a death sentence in such borderline cases.

Justice Breyer was unwilling to accept this response:

I thought the class of people we're talking about is a class of people that might simply barely understand what is going on. Barely. So, they know right from wrong, but they can't understand anything complicated. They have a hard time functioning. Their emotions are not different from yours or mine, than anybody's. So, they feel things quite strongly. But they won't take in the nature of the punishment, in all likelihood, and they're quite capable of following the leader, whoever is the leader nearby. And therefore this class of people is different enough than you, than me, that we wouldn't say they are similarly culpable.

Rumpz refused to back down. "I think this case is a perfect illustration. ... If you are found competent to stand trial and competent to assist your lawyers, you are like you and me. Daryl Atkins had a perfect understanding of the system, knew all about mitigating evidence, recommended witnesses to testify in mitigation, was competent to assist his lawyers, said he wanted his retardation put in front of the jury if it helped him. He had no deficits in understanding the system."

Amid the exchanges over an emerging consensus and inherent traits of the mentally retarded, Justice Ginsburg overtly encouraged Ellis to speak about the disadvantages commonly faced by retarded people who stand trial. Ginsburg clearly wanted to make sure that Ellis developed the point in open court. She did so by posing the issue as follows: "Mr. Ellis, I thought that you had said something different in your brief, and it was that people in this class have a diminished capacity when it comes to the life or death decision. I thought you said that they will be smiling and the jury will say, well, how inappropriate. They're not expressing any remorse. That they will not be able to communicate as effectively with their counsel.... You haven't said anything like that in your oral argument."

Ellis seized the invitation and explained that recently there has been a "growing concern that individuals with mental retardation facing capital charges present a particularly and uncomfortably large possibility of wrongful conviction and thus wrongful execution ... in just the way you were describing."

Justice Scalia quickly interrupted Ellis's argument, interjecting that such situations can be effectively handled by the defense attorney. "Counsel can say to the jury, 'during this trial you may see my client smiling inappropriately at some points. You should know that this is because he's mentally retarded. He really doesn't fully comprehend what is going on here, and I ask you not to take his reactions into account.' It seems to me that would just reaffirm the more he'd smile, the more the jury would say, 'Boy, this person really shouldn't be executed. He's not playing with a full deck.'"

Ellis, however, countered that "mental retardation may in fact be a two-edged sword, that the juror, in evaluating whether or not to impose the penalty of death, may see mental retardation not only as a mitigating or potentially mitigating factor, but may also see it as tied to prospective dangerousness. That issue is present everywhere it seems to me."

The content and tone of the justices' questions included no significant surprises. The justices acted predictably. If inferences can be made from the nature of their questions and comments, none of the justices deviated from the pre-oral argument predictions. Chief Justice Rehnquist and Justice Scalia appeared firmly on the side of the state; Justices Stevens, Ginsburg, Souter, and Breyer offered comments undoubtedly sympathetic to Daryl Atkins. Justice Thomas was characteristically silent during the session. That left Anthony Kennedy and Sandra Day O'Connor. The two predicted swing voters revealed little about their case outcome preferences. Justice Kennedy's questions did not express firm support for either side. Justice O'Connor, on the other hand, appeared to be in search of a way to decide the case in a practical fashion without creating significantly new law. She repeatedly asked about the possibility of extending to the retarded previously created principles pertaining to the culpability of the mentally ill.

At 12:28 p.m., precisely sixty-one minutes after it began, Chief Justice Rehnquist adjourned the session by announcing, "The case is submitted."

The last of the arguments had been made. The case was closed. The justices would now deliberate and decide.

BIBLIOGRAPHIC NOTE.

For biographical information on the justices of the Supreme Court, see Clare Cushman (ed.), *The Supreme Court Justices* (Washington D.C.: CQ Press, 1993); *The Supreme Court of the United States* (Washington D.C.: Commission on the Bicentennial of the United States Constitution, 1992); see also the Web site of the U.S. Supreme Court, www.supremecourtus.gov.

For detailed information on the backgrounds and careers of the justices of the Supreme Court as well as on the Court as an institution, see Lee Epstein, Jeffrey A. Segal, Harold J. Spaeth, and Thomas G. Walker, *The Supreme Court Compendium: Data, Decisions and Developments,* 4th edition (Washington D.C.: CQ Press, 2007).

For an excellent study of oral arguments and the Supreme Court, see Timothy R. Johnson, *Oral Arguments and Decision-Making on the United States Supreme Court* (Albany, N.Y.: State University of New York Press, 2004).

This chapter's discussion of James Ellis relies in part on Marcia Coyle, " 'Brief Writer's' Triumph," *National Law Journal,* December 23–30, 2002, and Laurie Mellas Ramirez, "A Driving Force," *University of New Mexico Quantum,* 2003–2004. For an example of Ellis's scholarly work, see James W. Ellis and Ruth A. Luckasson, "Mentally Retarded Criminal Defendants," *George Washington Law Review* 53 (1985), 414–493.

Those who wish to listen to the oral arguments in the *Atkins* case will find a recording of them at www.oyez.org.

The Supreme Court Decides

ONCE THE ORAL ARGUMENTS are completed, the members of the U.S. Supreme Court retreat to decide the case. Until they are ready to announce a final ruling, the justices remain silent. Although the parties to *Atkins v. Virginia* could reasonably expect a decision before the Court completed its annual term at the end of June, the justices never provide a deadline or target date for the completion of their work. No interim reports are issued, and no preliminary actions are made public. The legal teams for both sides could only return to their normal activities and wait for the Court to rule.

A disappointed Mary Sloan left the Court and headed back to Gilbertsville, New York, with her family. Sloan had been optimistic that the oral arguments would help inform the justices and the nation about her son and the tragedy of his lost life. In fact, the name Eric Nesbitt had not been mentioned a single time during the oral arguments. Instead the lawyers and justices seemed more concerned with counting and categorizing states. She could only hope that the Court's final ruling would bring about justice for the murder of her son.

Throughout the Supreme Court's proceedings Daryl Atkins remained in his cell in Sussex Prison. He would continue there, awaiting a decision that could either save his life or condemn him to death.

IN THE WEEKS surrounding the oral arguments in the Atkins case, organized groups and other interested parties increasingly went public on behalf of their respective positions. Most of the activated interest groups

216

as well as a majority of newspaper editorials expressed support for protecting the retarded from execution.

The death penalty prohibition advocates advanced common themes, including the disadvantages faced by retarded people when accused of serious crimes, the possibility of wrongful convictions, and how the United States was out of step with the world community. For the most part, however, they stressed the moral position that it is unconscionable to execute individuals who are not fully culpable for the crimes they commit. They also highlighted the senselessness of imposing death sentences on retarded individuals. One of the most frequently repeated accounts focused on the case of Ricky Ray Rector.

Rector was a thirty-one-year-old African American man who shot a man in a restaurant in Conway, Arkansas, in 1981. During a subsequent confrontation with police, Rector shot and killed Officer Robert Martin. Before he could be apprehended, however, Rector turned the weapon on himself. His attempted suicide failed, but the self-administered gunshot wound to the head caused massive brain damage. As a consequence, Rector suffered significantly diminished intellectual capacity. What amounted to a self-inflicted lobotomy had rendered Rector mentally retarded.

Rector was convicted and sentenced to death in 1982. For years his attorneys unsuccessfully attempted to have the sentence overturned on the grounds that Rector did not have the intellectual ability to understand the consequences of his crime or the nature of his punishment. Efforts to persuade then governor and presidential candidate Bill Clinton to use his executive powers to stop the execution were similarly unsuccessful.

Rector's execution was set for January 24, 1992. That night he ate his last meal and was being prepared for the administration of the lethal injection. As he left his cell for the execution room, Rector asked that an unfinished piece of pecan pie be saved so he could eat it later.

The Rector case was an unusual one with a rather dramatic illustration of mental impairment to the point that the condemned had a total lack of understanding of the punishment about to be imposed. But how many other retarded individuals had been put to death or were awaiting execution? Groups such as the American Civil Liberties Union and the National Coalition to Abolish the Death Penalty argued that the issues raised by

Atkins would affect large numbers of individuals. Both organizations estimated that up to one quarter of the 3,700 people on death row at that time were mentally retarded. These figures were significantly inflated compared to the more common estimate of 5 to 10 percent, but because no systematic testing of prison populations had ever been conducted the actual number was unknown.

Those opposed to a blanket protection for the retarded, of course, saw things much differently. They could match the death penalty abolitionists story for story, but they focused instead on the victims of brutal, senseless murders. But their most commonly articulated argument was that a total ban was not necessary. Rather, they saw the existing safeguards as perfectly adequate.

The Criminal Justice Legal Foundation, for example, argued that truly retarded people do not commit the kinds of terrible crimes for which juries are prone to recommend death. Such persons simply do not have the intellectual capacity to plan and carry out such criminal activity. In every state those charged with capital offenses are entitled to be examined by mental health professionals who determine whether they are mentally and intellectually capable of distinguishing right from wrong, understanding the charges and the possible consequences of a trial, and assisting defense counsel. Tests for retardation are also available and diminished intellectual capacity is a recognized mitigating circumstance that juries must consider. These various procedures screen out those individuals who suffer from truly significant intellectual deficits. Imposing an unnecessary constitutional ban on executions of the retarded will only encourage condemned murderers to advance groundless claims of limited mental ability to avoid or delay the imposition of their sentences.

Atkins's prosecutor, Eileen Addison, was even drawn into to the public debate. Addison wrote an opinion piece for the Hampton Roads *Daily Press* five days after the oral arguments. She argued that the safeguards already in place were more than adequate to ensure against unjust applications of the death penalty. Addison contended that the retarded have widely varying abilities and, as a consequence, the question of punishment in capital cases should be approached on an individual case-by-case basis with the final decision resting in the hands of jurors.

Even at the national level prominent public officials were drawn into the controversy. Most notably, death penalty opponents frequently quoted President George W. Bush who commented to a group of European reporters that "We should never execute anybody who is mentally retarded." These were unexpected words coming from a death penalty advocate and former governor of Texas, the state that leads the nation in executions and is accused by some death penalty opponents of having executed several retarded convicts.

While the public discussion continued, little changed in Virginia's application of the death penalty. Between the time Atkins's lawyers first submitted their application for a writ of *certiorari* and the final decision in the case, Virginia executed five capital murderers—all men, four white and one black.

As winter turned into the spring in 2002, the public commentary over the issues raised by the Atkins appeal died down. In the meantime the members of the Supreme Court were following their traditional procedures for resolving the issues contested by Atkins and the Commonwealth of Virginia.

BUCKING THE TREND of increased government transparency, the justices of the Supreme Court work under a cloak of secrecy. Freedom-of-information statutes and other laws designed to move official actions into the sunshine invariably include exemptions for the judiciary. Only the justices fully know what happens as they go about the task of reaching a decision. The law clerks and support personnel are privy to much of what occurs, but they observe strict norms of silence regarding such matters. We do know, however, a good deal about the steps normally taken by the justices to resolve the disputes brought before them.

The initial discussion of cases ready for decision occurs during the Court's formal conferences. In the modern era the Court customarily held two conferences during the weeks it heard oral arguments, the first on Wednesday afternoon and the second on Friday. Recently, however, the Court changed this tradition and currently only holds one weekly conference, usually on Friday. The purpose of the conference is to discuss and take a tentative vote on all cases argued since the Court's last meeting. In addition, the justices dispose of pending writ of *certiorari* applications and any other business requiring the full Court's participation.

The justices come to the conference well prepared. They have read the briefs of the parties to the dispute as well as those submitted by interested *amicus curiae* and have participated in oral arguments. They have discussed the cases with their law clerks and often have assigned a clerk to perform preliminary research on relevant points of law. In most instances the justices come to the conference having reached their own conclusions about the case.

As the justices enter the conference room they first shake hands with every other justice in a manner similar to the tradition followed prior to oral arguments. They then take their places around a long rectangular table. The seating positions are dictated by seniority. The chief justice sits at one end of the table and the most senior associate justice at the other end. The three associate justices next in seniority sit on one side of the table and the four justices with the least seniority occupy the other side.

No one is allowed in the conference room but the justices themselves. They take pride in doing their own work at this crucial point in the decision-making process rather than relying on support personnel. No formal transcripts are made of the discussions, thus allowing for a full and candid exchange of views. The closed meeting format also reduces the possibility of a decision being leaked to the press or public before the Court is ready to announce it.

During the conference the most junior justice acts as the doorkeeper. If the Court needs to communicate to the outside, for example, when it requires additional records or reference material, the junior justice passes the request to a guard stationed outside the door to the conference room. Similarly, if any messages need to be communicated to any of the justices from the outside, it is the junior justice who answers the knock at the conference room door.

The chief justice assumes a central role in the Court's consideration of pending cases. The chief calls up each case in turn and is the first to speak. He carefully reviews the case facts, the questions presented, and the relevant points of law at issue. He then presents his position on how the dispute should be decided. Then in order of seniority the associate justices present their views on the questions at hand. By tradition the justices do not interrupt each other, allowing each member of the Court to present his or her positions without interference. This procedure provides an advantage to those justices with the most seniority. The issues and possible outcomes in any given case are somewhat limited, and by the time the junior justices have an opportunity to present their views the key issues likely have been thoroughly covered by their more senior colleagues.

How much actual debate takes place over contested issues has varied widely over the history of the Court, depending largely on the style of the chief justice. Charles Evans Hughes, who led the Court from 1930 to 1941, for example, ran a very tight conference, with little exchange among the justices. His administration was efficient, but individual justices frequently expressed displeasure over the constraints imposed upon them. At the other extreme, Harlan Fiske Stone (1941–1946), who followed Hughes, encouraged wide-ranging debate. His conferences were anything but efficient. It was not uncommon for the justices to schedule additional conference time in order to complete their work. In the more contemporary period, William Rehnquist (1986–2005) did not think it worthwhile to allow too much deliberation, believing that most minds were already made up and that debate rarely changed any justice's position. Chief Justice John Roberts, who succeeded Rehnquist in 2005 is said to prefer more deliberative exchange.

No formal vote is taken during the conference. Instead, the positions expressed by the justices as they present their views serve as an expression of their tentative positions. Votes do not become official until much later in the process after the opinions have been written.

For each case one justice is responsible for writing the opinion of the Court. By tradition the chief justice assigns the opinion-writing task for all cases in which he sides with the majority in conference. He may select any of the associate justices who were also in the majority, or he may write the opinion himself. If the chief justice takes a minority position in conference, then the most senior associate justice in the majority names the opinion writer. Although most cases are decided by divided vote, the role of assigning the majority opinion overwhelmingly falls to the chief justice.

Over the past four decades, for example, the chief justices assigned the opinion, in over 80 percent of all cases.

A number of factors come into play in assigning the opinion writing responsibility. A fundamental consideration, especially in closely divided cases, is the preservation of the majority. It takes at least five votes to determine a case outcome. In addition, at least five justices must endorse the opinion for it to become a binding precedent that the Supreme Court is expected to apply in future cases and the lower courts are obligated to follow. Therefore, the opinion writer must be capable of crafting an opinion that will unify the members of the majority behind a clear rationale for the Court's decision and not provoke any of them to desert their initial positions.

Workload considerations also come into play. In any given annual term of the Court, it is preferable to have the opinion-writing responsibilities equally shared by the justices. This evens the burdens, promotes a sense of fairness, and gives each justice a meaningful role in the exercise of the Court's authority. An effective chief justice, as William Rehnquist often noted, will occasionally assign mundane cases to himself and spread important cases among his colleagues. This builds Court cohesiveness and member satisfaction. Sometimes the assigning justice will take into account colleagues who have special expertise in a given area of the law that is relevant to the case at hand.

Finally, ideological preferences may come into play. All things being equal, the assigning justice will desire the Court's opinion to be as close as possible to his or her own views and will lean toward the selection of a justice who might best accomplish that goal. Of course, the most effective way to accomplish this objective is to keep the case for oneself, which commonly occurs if the assigning justice has a particular interest in a given dispute.

Next, the assigned justice drafts the Court's opinion. The goal is to write a statement that will command the loyalty of the majority and provide a clear explanation of the Court's ruling. The difficulty of this process depends on a number of factors including the complexity and salience of the case, the cohesiveness of the majority, and the number of dissenting justices.

The Supreme Court communicates its decisions to the outside world only through its written opinions. The decisions are announced only once and the justices do not explain their decisions in any other format. The members of the Court do not hold press conferences. The justices will not field requests from affected parties or lower court judges regarding the meaning or applicability of their rulings. The opinions must speak for themselves. Thus, opinion writing is a very serious business.

Justices approach opinion writing in their own individual ways. For the most part, the effort is shared by the justice and his or her law clerks. Typically the justice assigns the case to one law clerk for the production of an initial rough draft. The process starts with the justice and the clerk discussing the issues presented in the case and the views expressed by the majority during the conference deliberations. The clerk begins developing an opinion based on the views of the justice and the positions taken by the other members of the majority. The conference discussion normally provides only a broad outline of the majority's views. As the justice and the clerk analyze the case in greater detail they inevitably confront finer points of law that must be answered on the way to reaching the majority's preferred outcome.

Once the clerk completes the rough draft, the justice will normally rewrite the opinion imposing his or her individual preferences and style. The opinion might then be given to another law clerk for review, criticism, and revision. This process repeats itself a number of times until the justice is satisfied with the result.

When the draft is completed, it is circulated among the other members of the Court. Upon receiving it, the other justices have several options. A justice might agree with the opinion in its entirety and endorse it. Alternatively, a justice may agree in principle with the opinion but recommend changes. Still others might agree with the outcome of the case, but reject the opinion's reasoning. And finally, dissenting justices can express opposition to the proposed opinion altogether.

After all of the justices have responded, the opinion writer goes about the process of revising the draft. Revisions often involve a careful and sometimes difficult balancing of the opinion writer's own preferences, the position taken by other members of the majority, and the specific revisions suggested by individual members. Once the revised opinion is completed, it too is circulated for comment. The revision and circulation process repeats itself until it ceases to be productive. A typical opinion will be circulated and revised three or four times.

Throughout the circulation and revision process a good bit of explicit or implicit strategic bargaining takes place. It is not uncommon for justices to pledge support for an opinion contingent upon the author's willingness to make certain changes. Members may even refuse to join the opinion or even threaten to dissent if the draft is not altered according to their liking. In such situations the opinion writer is faced with a hard choice of whether to modify the content of the opinion in return for a colleague's support. The size and fragility of the majority coalition often influences the response. The opinion writer must take quite seriously the views of the other members if only five justices form the majority, but can be less accommodating if the vote is unanimous or nearly so. Of course, agreeing to accommodate one justice's preferences might alienate another.

Justices whose views are not sufficiently reflected in a majority opinion may write a concurring opinion. These statements come in two varieties. The first is a regular concurrence. Justices write regular concurrences when they join the majority opinion, but want to express their own supplemental views as well. The second is a special concurrence. This is an opinion in which the justice expresses agreement with the outcome of the case, but rejects the Court's rationale and refuses to join the majority opinion.

Finally, the dissenters, those justices who prefer an entirely different resolution of the dispute, can express their positions in a written opinion. Customarily, if there is more than one dissenter at the conference, the senior justice in the minority will assign one justice the responsibility of drafting an opinion that reflects of views of the minority. Just as the majority justices are free to write a separate concurring opinion, dissenters are not bound to join a single minority statement. They too can write individual opinions. Although discouraged in the Court's early years, in the modern era over half of the decisions are accompanied by at least one dissenting opinion.

A dissenting opinion advocates a resolution of the case that is at odds with the majority. It may criticize the majority opinion's logic, analysis, or interpretation of the law. Sometimes dissents provide signals to lower court judges concerning ways to interpret the majority opinion narrowly or offer suggestions to the legislative branch on ways to alter the law to overcome the Court's objections. Additionally, a minority opinion may set the stage for future justices to reverse course. Dissents are, in the words of Charles Evans Hughes, "appeals to the brooding spirit of the law, to the intelligence of another day."

The drafts of concurring and dissenting opinions are circulated in the same manner as the majority opinion. At any one time, therefore, multiple opinion drafts for the same case may be making their way through the circulation process. The justices have a choice of either joining one of the circulating opinions or writing one of their own. During this process it is possible for a justice to be persuaded by one of the competing opinions and change position. Of course, at any one point in time many cases are in the midst of this very same process. Add these opinion drafts to the thousands of writ of *certiorari* applications and the briefs and records of cases awaiting oral argument and you have the justices facing a crushing load of paperwork in various stages of motion.

A case is decided when the circulation and revision of opinions ceases to yield any movement among the justices. The final vote in a case occurs as the members of the Court either write an opinion of their own or join one that has been offered by another justice. If the proposed majority opinion receives the support of at least five members it becomes the opinion of the Court. If no opinion receives the support of five or more justices, there will be a winning and losing party, but no authoritative, binding statement of the Court's interpretation of the law. When each justice has declared his or her vote in the case, the opinions are prepared for distribution.

The Court announces its decisions in open session. In the early years the opinion of the majority was read in its entirety by the author. In the 1930s as the Court's workload and the length of opinions increased, Chief Justice Hughes altered this practice and encouraged the opinion writer to read only a summary of the decision, a practice still followed today. The justices who have written dissents may read a summary of their opinions as well, but this infrequently occurs. On the same day copies of the opinions are distributed to the press and to the private organizations that publish the materials for law libraries and the legal profession. With the development of the Internet, distribution has become more efficient and widespread. Almost immediately upon announcement, the Court's rulings are made available electronically to anyone with access to the Court's Web site or the Web sites of law schools and private organizations that distribute such information to the public.

ON JUNE 20, 2002, exactly four months after oral arguments, the Court issued its ruling in the *Atkins* case. As soon as the chief justice announced that John Paul Stevens would summarize the Court's decision, it was clear that Daryl Atkins had been victorious. Stevens was the Court's strongest opponent of capital punishment and had advocated blanket death penalty protection for the retarded in *Penry v. Johnson* (2001). It was inconceivable that he would have voted in favor of the state.

The decision was not unanimous. As predicted, Justices Stevens, David Souter, Ruth Bader Ginsburg, and Stephen Breyer voted in favor of Atkins; Chief Justice William Rehnquist and Justices Antonin Scalia and Clarence Thomas supported Virginia. As for Sandra Day O'Connor and Anthony Kennedy, the two swing justices, both endorsed the arguments advanced by James Ellis and the Atkins legal team. For O'Connor and Kennedy it was a change in position since the *Penry* ruling, an obvious response to the growing number of states that had removed the retarded from capital punishment jeopardy.

Because Chief Justice Rehnquist had cast his support for the minority position, the assignment of the opinion-writing task fell to the most senior member in the majority, Justice Stevens. The fact that Stevens elected to appoint himself to develop the Court's written rationale rather than giving that responsibility to another justice is testimony to his strong feelings about the issue at stake. The overruling of *Penry* would be a vindication of sorts for his dissent in that earlier case. It is not surprising that Stevens desired to put his own stamp on the new precedent.

A successful Supreme Court opinion clearly presents not only the basic outcome of the case but more importantly the reasoning supporting that outcome. The opinion writer must make clear the specific question being addressed, the rules of law that govern the issue in dispute, and the evidence and arguments that convinced the justices to rule as they did. Only if this is done effectively can the press adequately inform the public about the decision, lower courts faithfully apply Supreme Court precedent in future cases, and attorneys adequately advise their clients.

Justice John Paul Stevens wrote the U.S. Supreme Court's opinion in Atkins v. Virginia.

Stevens's opinion in *Atkins* accomplished these goals. Six justices voted in favor of interpreting the Eighth Amendment as barring executions of retarded people. Stevens drafted an opinion that satisfied all members of the majority. There were no concurring opinions in which individual members of the majority either expressed reservations about the Stevens opinion or offered additional comments. The case presented a single, clear question, and the Court's opinion responded with an unambiguous answer supported by a straightforward rationale.

Stevens began his opinion with a review of the Court's principles for determining violations of the Cruel and Unusual Punishment Clause. He first cited the constitutional standard set in *Weems v. United States* (1910) that the Eighth Amendment prohibits punishments that are "excessive." It is not necessarily the absolute severity of the sentence that is important, but the relationship between the penalty and the crime.

In more recent times this excessiveness standard has been expressed as proportionality. The severity of the penalty must be proportionate to the seriousness of the crime and the perpetrator's degree of culpability. This requirement is to be interpreted in light of contemporary standards. As the Court expressed in *Trop v. Dulles* (1958), "The basic concept underlying the Eighth Amendment is nothing less than the dignity of man... The

Amendment must draw its meaning from the evolving standards of decency that mark the progress of a maturing society."

Identifying contemporary standards is a difficult matter. The Court previously held that the laws enacted by the states are the most clear, reliable, and objective evidence of those values. But Stevens suggested that legislative action is not the sole determining factor. Instead, he declared the ultimate authority to be the Court itself. By citing a principle contained in several cases, including *Coker v. Georgia* (1977) and *Enmund v. Florida* (1977), Stevens asserted that "in the end our own judgment will be brought to bear on the question of the acceptability of the death penalty under the Eighth Amendment." Thus, the Court is justified in "asking whether there is reason to disagree with the judgment reached by the citizenry and its legislators."

With these stated standards of review, Stevens turned his attention to the question of whether a societal consensus had emerged against the application of the death penalty to the mentally retarded. On all the disagreements over how the various state positions should be counted Stevens sided with the interpretations advocated by Ellis. He started with the status quo in 1989 at the time of the *Penry* ruling when only two states (Georgia and Maryland) and the federal government protected the retarded from execution. But, as Stevens described it, "much has changed since then." As a way to emphasize the legislative developments, he methodically listed the states that had altered their positions: Kentucky and Tennessee in 1990; New Mexico in 1991; Arkansas, Colorado, Washington, Indiana, and Kansas in 1993 and 1994; New York in 1995; Nebraska in 1998; and South Dakota, Arizona, Connecticut, Florida, Missouri, and North Carolina in 2000 and 2001.

Stevens then added to his list of states those that in some manner demonstrated opposition to executing the retarded. He noted, for example, that in some states at least one house of the state legislature had passed a protection bill. Further added to the list were states like New Hampshire and New Jersey that had not executed anyone for decades and as well as those where the death penalty had been abolished altogether. Finally, he noted that even in those states that allow the execution of the retarded only five (Alabama, Texas, Louisiana, South Carolina, and

Virginia) since *Penry* actually had put to death any capital offender with an IQ of less than 70.

It was not only the number of states that had changed positions that impressed Stevens, but the consistency of direction. Every state that changed its laws excluded the retarded from death penalty eligibility. No state moved in the opposite direction, and no state that enacted blanket protection later changed its mind. In states that enacted the prohibition, the laws were passed by extremely large legislative margins. This was remarkable, according to Stevens, because these changes took place during an era in which the public demanded tougher criminal laws and the legislatures dutifully responded.

All of this constituted "powerful evidence" that our society now views mentally retarded offenders as categorically less culpable than the average criminal. Stevens's conclusion on executing retarded persons was clear and direct: "The practice, therefore, has become truly unusual, and it is fair to say that a national consensus has developed against it."

Faithful to the traditional position, Stevens confined his textual argument to actions taken by state legislatures. In the footnotes, however, he pointed to other, more controversial, indicators of consensus. First, he noted that professional and religious organizations expressed their support for a ban against executions of retarded capital offenders. His footnotes contained multiple citations to the positions taken in the *amicus* briefs of American Association on Mental Retardation, the American Psychological Association, and the United States Catholic Conference. Second, Stevens recognized international opposition to imposing capital punishment on the retarded, even citing the *amicus* brief of the European Union. And finally, he noted that public opinion polls uniformly show "widespread consensus among Americans, even those who otherwise support the death penalty, that executing the mentally retarded is wrong."

Stevens then turned to the question of whether the retarded share sufficient relevant characteristics to be considered as a class. Once again, the Court's majority accepted the arguments of the lawyers for Daryl Atkins. Stevens acknowledged that retarded persons frequently can distinguish right from wrong and are competent to stand trial. However, by definition the retarded as a class "have diminished capacities to understand and process information, to communicate, to abstract from mistakes and learn from experience, to engage in logical reasoning, to control impulses, and to understand the reactions of others." They tend not to pursue calculated plans, and they tend to be followers rather than leaders. These factors, although not exempting them from criminal punishment, "do diminish their personal culpability."

As a consequence, the standard justifications for imposing capital punishment have little applicability to the retarded. First, the death penalty is often defended as necessary for retribution purposes. The retribution argument is based on the premise that a fully culpable person deserves the highest penalty for the most serious crimes. The retarded, however, lack the necessary culpability to make retribution by death appropriate. Second, capital punishment is said to be a means of deterring future crimes. This position has little relevance for the retarded who lack the ability to engage in the necessary reasoning for deterrence to have an effect. Their cognitive impairments do not permit them to understand fully the consequences of their actions. They are not capable of learning from the previous executions of others that the same fate may be applied to them if they commit a capital crime.

Finally, Stevens turned his attention to the unique disadvantages faced by the retarded during the investigation and prosecution stages. Because of their eagerness to please, they are more likely than those with normal intelligence levels to confess to a crime they did not commit. Their intellectual limitations render them less capable of assisting their lawyers and less effective as witnesses. Their demeanor often mistakenly communicates to a jury that they are not remorseful for their crimes and may create among jurors a fear of future dangerousness. These factors may result in the retarded facing special risks when confronted with a possible sentence of death.

Stevens ended his opinion by noting that the Court's independent analysis reinforces the judgments recently reached by many legislatures. "Construing and applying the Eighth Amendment in light of our 'evolving standards of decency,' we therefore conclude that such punishment is excessive and that the Constitution 'places a substantive restriction on the State's power to take the life' of a mentally retarded offender."

THREE MEMBERS OF THE COURT, Chief Justice Rehnquist and Justices Scalia and Thomas, disagreed with the Court's holding and registered their dissents. Two dissenting opinions were written, one by Rehnquist and the other by Scalia.

Rehnquist's opinion, with which Justices Scalia and Thomas agreed, focused on the appropriate criteria to be used in determining society's evolving standards of decency. The chief justice rejected the position taken by the majority that the justices should impose their own views of what constitutes cruel and unusual punishment. To

Chief Justice William Rehnquist disagreed with the majority's conclusions in Atkins v. Virginia.

give appointed jurists the authority to declare the moral values of the American people circumvents normal democratic processes. According to Rehnquist, the Court's precedents wisely declared that there are only two valid and reliable indicators of society values: the body of laws enacted by the people's legislative representatives and the decision making of citizens acting in their capacity as jurors. Legislatures and juries are, by design, better suited than judges to determine criminal punishments acceptable to society. "In my view," Rehnquist declared, "these two sources ... ought to be the sole indicators by which courts ascertain the contemporary American conceptions of decency for purposes of the Eighth Amendment."

Rehnquist was unimpressed with the strength of evidence provided by Atkins's attorneys and supporting *amicus* organizations. The fact that sixteen states (less than half of those with death penalty statutes) had recently adopted prohibitions against executions of retarded persons did not convince the chief justice that a national consensus had emerged. Furthermore, the pro-Atkins forces had failed to provide any systematic evidence from jury decision-making behavior indicating that the American people now considered such executions morally unacceptable.

The chief justice, however, devoted most of his dissent to a discussion of sources of evidence cited by the majority that he considered inappropriate. He especially criticized the majority's use of the views of the world community, the opinions of organized interest groups, and the results of public opinion polls. Although references to these alternative indicators were relegated to footnotes in the majority opinion, Rehnquist was not about to let them go unnoticed. Perhaps because he thought the majority relied on these sources more than the text of the opinion revealed or because he feared that the opinion of the Court would legitimate using such evidence in future cases, Rehnquist attacked the use of these sources.

He first criticized the petitioner's reference to the views of the international community. "I fail to see," Rehnquist wrote, "how the views of other countries regarding the punishment of their citizens provide any support for the Court's ultimate determination.... For if it is evidence of a *national* consensus for which we are looking, then the viewpoints of other countries simply are not relevant."

Equally inappropriate, according to the chief justice, were the majority opinion's references to the positions taken by professional organizations and religious groups. Such associations are concerned with the special interests of their individual members whose opinions are not representative of the American people. "In my view," argued Rehnquist, "none should be accorded any weight on the Eighth Amendment scale when the elected representatives of a State's populace have not deemed them persuasive enough to prompt legislative action."

Rehnquist's sharpest criticism was directed at what he described as the "blind faith credence" the majority gave to public opinion polls. Referring to an extensive body of social science literature, the chief justice cited the various methodological errors that can affect the reliability and validity of polling results. Such evidence should not be considered, he argued, unless those who created and administered the polls are subject to criticism and cross-examination regarding issues such as the choice of target populations, sampling design, question construction, and the statistical analyses used to interpret the results. Rehnquist went so far as to append to his dissenting opinion a summary of the twenty-seven public opinion polls cited in the various briefs supporting Atkins. He showed the differences in question wording, for example, that might have skewed the results in favor of the petitioner's position.

Some dissenting opinions logically and methodically attack the reasoning or conclusions of the majority in somewhat dispassionate terms. Other dissenting opinions reveal an intense, emotional rejection of the Court's holding. The dissenting opinion of the chief

Justice Antonin Scalia wrote a sharply worded dissenting opinion in Atkins v. Virginia.

justice had features of the first category. The dissenting opinion of Justice Scalia is better characterized as an example of the second.

Although there was no doubt that Rehnquist opposed the position taken by the Court's majority, his opinion was measured and moderate compared to Antonin Scalia's dissent. While Rehnquist made no oral comments from the bench summarizing his dissent, Scalia spoke for almost ten minutes in open court (considerably more than the six minutes Stevens devoted to summarizing the majority opinion) and his comments at times were accompanied by a tinge of anger in his voice.

Scalia's response to the majority, for which he received the formal endorsement of both Rehnquist and Thomas, was direct and hard-hitting. His opening salvo attacked the majority's constitutional interpretations for having no support in the text or the history of the Eighth Amendment and for being inconsistent with the nation's current social attitudes. "Seldom," he asserted in the very first paragraph of his eighteen-page dissent, "has an opinion of this Court rested so obviously upon nothing but the personal views of its members."

Often a comparison of majority and dissenting opinions reveals not only legal differences, but also the emotional and ideological gulf between the two sides. In this respect a close comparison of the Stevens and Scalia opinions is quite revealing.

Both Stevens and Scalia review the facts in the case, but the descriptions of the events surrounding the murder of Eric Nesbitt contrast in tone and style. The Stevens opinion uses unemotional, neutral language to describe the crime; whereas Scalia's dissent selects terms and phrases to emphasize the seriousness of the events surrounding the night of August 16, 1996. For example, Stevens tersely notes that Daryl Atkins and William Jones "abducted Eric Nesbitt, robbed him of the money on his person, drove him to an automated teller machine in his pickup truck where cameras recorded their withdrawal of additional cash." Scalia's version intensifies the description by noting that Atkins and Jones had spent the day "drinking and smoking marijuana" and that they went to the convenience store "intending to rob a customer." Unlike Stevens who only provides the victim's name, Scalia includes the fact that Eric Nesbitt was "an airman from Langley Air Force Base." While Stevens describes bank cameras as "recording their withdrawal" of an unstated amount of cash from the ATM, Scalia explains that Atkins and Jones "forced" Nesbitt "to withdraw $200."

More stark is the difference between the ways in which the two opinions described the actual murder. Again, using fairly factual terms and slipping into the passive voice Stevens writes that "they took him to an isolated location where he was shot eight times and killed." Scalia's words boost the emotional level of the account and portray Atkins as actively murdering Nesbitt. He states that Atkins and Jones "drove [Nesbitt] to a deserted area, ignoring his pleas to leave him unharmed.... Atkins ordered Nesbitt out of the vehicle and after he had taken only a few steps, shot him one, two, three, four, five, six, seven, eight times in the thorax, chest, abdomen, arms, and legs."

These contrasts continued as the two opposing justices described the sentencing phase of the trial. Stevens low-key reference to Atkins's criminal background did not stray from the most basic facts: "To prove future dangerousness, the State relied on Atkins' prior felony convictions as well as the testimony of four victims of earlier robberies and assaults." Scalia's description of the same subject painted Atkins as much more dangerous and violent: "The jury also heard testimony about petitioner's 16 prior felony convictions for robbery, attempted robbery, abduction, use of a firearm, and maiming. The victims of these offenses provided graphic depictions of petitioner's violent tendencies: He hit one over the head with a beer bottle; he slapped a gun across another victim's face, clubbed her in the head with it, knocked her to the ground, and then helped her up, only to shoot her in the stomach."

These differences in emphasis and wording are consistent with the goals of the opinion writers. Stevens announced the holding of the Court that retarded offenders such as Atkins should be exempt from the death penalty. Such a conclusion is more palatable if Atkins and the crime he committed are described in almost clinical terms and the victim is treated with near anonymity. On the other hand, an opinion permitting retarded people to be executed may be more effective if it graphically describes the offender's violent background, the savagery of the crime, and the essential humanity and goodness of the murder victim.

After providing his interpretation of the facts of the case, Scalia turned to his more substantive arguments, expressing views that were entirely consistent with the questions he posed during oral argument. He first laid out his interpretation of the Eighth Amendment. The cruel and unusual punishment provision, he argued, prohibits only two penalties. First, it outlaws those modes of punishment that were cruel and unusual at the time of the ratification of the Bill of Rights. And second, the clause bars punishments that are inconsistent with modern standards of decency as evidenced by objective indicators, the most important of which are the acts of the state legislatures.

The execution of the mildly mentally retarded cannot be deemed unconstitutional according to the first test. In the late eighteenth century, the mildly retarded were considered to have sufficient reasoning abilities to be responsible for their actions. Consequently, at the time of the Founding those, like Atkins today, who suffered from modest intellectual deficits were subject to prosecution and punishment, including the death penalty.

For Scalia, the only possibly valid argument was that the execution of the retarded is now inconsistent with the "evolving standards of decency that mark the progress of a maturing society." Unlike Stevens, Scalia only considered relevant the eighteen states with statutes specifically exempting the retarded from the death penalty. He was baffled by the majority's conclusion that eighteen out of the thirty-eight capital punishment states is sufficient to declare that the nation rejects this use of the death penalty. "How is it possible," he asked, "that agreement among 47 percent of the death penalty jurisdictions amounts to 'consensus'? Our prior cases have generally required a much higher degree of agreement before finding a punishment cruel and unusual on 'evolving standards' grounds."

Furthermore, Scalia noted that some of the eighteen states did not ban all executions of the mentally retarded. A few allowed the death penalty to be carried for those retarded individuals already on death row and some states, like New York, had exceptions built into their statutes. Because these states did not absolutely protect the retarded from execution, it could not be said that there is a national moral repugnance to such sentences.

Scalia chided the majority for completely ignoring that of the eighteen prohibition statutes the oldest had been in effect only fourteen years and five for one year or less. The states had insufficient experience to know whether the new laws would constitute sensible policy over the long run.

An even more caustic reaction was generated in response to Stevens's assertion that "[i]t is not so much the number of these states that is significant, but the consistency of the direction of change." Scalia retorted, "But in what *other* direction *could we possibly* see change? Given that 14 years ago *all* the death penalty statutes included the mentally retarded, *any* change ... was *bound to be* in the one direction the Court finds significant enough to overcome a lack of real consensus."

Scalia ended his attack on the national consensus issue by underscoring Rehnquist's criticism of the sources used by the majority. Here Scalia elevated the rhetoric: "But the Prize for the Court's Most Feeble Effort to fabricate 'national consensus' must go to its appeal (deservedly relegated to a footnote) to the view of assorted professional and religious organizations, members of the so-called 'world community' and respondents to opinion polls." Scalia, a practicing Roman Catholic, even criticized the majority for citing the brief submitted by the United States Catholic Conference, an organization whose views on crime and punishment, he claimed, are not even representative of Catholics. Also not relevant are the views of other nations "whose notions of justice are (thankfully) not always those of our people." It is the responsibility of the Court to interpret the U.S. Constitution, and it is the consensus of the American people that is important, not the views of the international community.

Having dealt with the majority's "empty talk" about a national consensus, Scalia attacked the Court's independent appraisal of the constitutionality of executing retarded capital offenders. Stevens's statement that "in the end our own judgment will be brought to bear on the question of the acceptability of the death penalty under the Eighth Amendment" was singled out for criticism. "The arrogance of this assumption of power," chided Scalia, "takes one's breath away," and it explains why the majority "can be so cavalier about the evidence of consensus." By this analysis it is the "feelings" and "intuition" of the "small and unrepresentative segment of our society that sits on this Court" that determines the Constitution's meaning.

Scalia next attacked the majority for ignoring society's need to express its moral outrage over the most serious crimes and to incapacitate dangerous criminals in order to prevent future murderers. Achieving these goals under certain circumstances may require the death penalty.

The majority instead argued that applying capital punishment to the retarded cannot advance the valid criminal justice goals of retribution and deterrence. This conclusion, Scalia suggested, rests on two assumptions. First, the retarded are incapable of reaching the level of culpability that retribution requires for the most severe penalty. Second, the mentally impaired are unable to appreciate the consequences of their actions, thus rendering deterrence ineffective. Although these conditions may apply to some with low intelligence levels, they surely do not apply to all.

At this juncture the dissenters most abruptly departed from their colleagues. The majority was comfortable treating the retarded as a single class with all its members sharing the same diminished capacities. The dissenters were not. Thus, Scalia, Thomas, and Rehnquist preferred the *Penry* approach of treating the retarded as individuals and allowing juries to evaluate defendants based on their unique characteristics. For the dissenters, punishment for retribution and deterrence purposes may make perfect sense in some cases, but perhaps not in others. There is no legitimate reason to treat all retarded defendants the same.

Similarly, Scalia's dissent was unwilling to accept the notion that all defendants who meet the defining criteria for retardation face a special risk of a wrongful execution. Admittedly, some may not be capable of communicating adequate remorse, may make ineffective witnesses, and may lack ability to assist counsel in the preparation of their defense, but this claim is not supported for the entire class of retarded individuals, Scalia contended. Defense attorneys, judges, and juries are quite capable of justly handling individual situations where such special risks exist.

Scalia finally expressed the fear that the Court's decision may give rise to accused murderers faking retardation in order to avoid a death sentence. "One need only read the definitions of mental retardation...," Scalia's dissent warned, "to realize that the symptoms of this condition can readily be feigned." Should this result occur, rendering the ban against such executions an unwise or impractical policy, the Court's decision allows the states no room under the Constitution to abandon the capital punishment immunity now conferred on those with sub-average intellectual capabilities.

In spite of the objections raised by the dissenting justices, the Court abandoned *Penry*. Retardation no longer would be treated as an individualized mitigating factor. The Supreme Court's revised interpretation of the Cruel and Unusual Punishment Clause of the Eighth Amendment now categorically forbids the death penalty for mentally retarded capital offenders.

REACTION TO THE COURT'S RULING was predictable. Death penalty opponents saw the decision as an important step toward a greater realization that capital punishment in the United States was imposed in a fundamentally unfair way. Rather than previous legal victories that had tinkered with various death penalty procedures, *Atkins* removed an entire category of people from the shadow of capital punishment. The National Coalition to Abolish the Death Penalty called it the most important death penalty decision in a quarter century. Similar reactions were offered by the civil rights and disability communities. The American Association for Mental Retardation expressed its satisfaction that the Supreme Court "put an end to this barbaric practice of killing persons who do not have the full intellectual capacity to understand the crime they committed."

Groups with an international focus, such as Human Rights Watch and Amnesty International USA, praised the Court for ending a practice that the rest of the world found abhorrent. And the European Union, through a statement issued by Spain, warmly welcomed news of the *Atkins* ruling.

Throughout much of the information issued by supporters of the decision was a clear undertone of hope that *Atkins* was the start of something much bigger. It was perhaps the beginning of a trend toward abolishing the death penalty altogether.

Critics of the decision, including the Criminal Justice Legal Foundation, which branded the ruling as "jurisprudence by polling," asserted that the decision was unnecessary and would have undesired effects. Prosecutors in several jurisdictions predicted that the ruling would prompt a flood of litigation, with convicted capital offenders now claiming that they suffer from retardation. As a spokesman for the Virginia Attorney General stated, "I can believe there are people waking up on death row today and saying, 'Good morning, I am mentally retarded today.'" Furthermore, critics anticipated that future death penalty cases would be significantly slowed as it would become increasingly routine for accused killers to demand full hearings on their mental deficiencies.

Other critics of the decision articulated a fear, rejected as groundless by most mental health professionals, that capital offenders would attempt to fake retardation, purposefully failing IQ tests. Eileen Addison, Atkins's prosecutor, was one of those critics. As she told the Associated Press, "I bet you I could score a 59 if my life depended on it."

Atkins's attorneys, of course, were very pleased with the outcome of the appeal. Robert Lee called the decision a "great victory for human rights" and especially for the rights of those whose disabilities render them less culpable for their actions. George Rogers, who represented Atkins at the trial level, described his former client as a young man with the mental capacity of a six year old; Rogers then told reporters that "the idea of executing a six year old is unconscionable. This returns a proper moral standard to capital punishment."

James Ellis, whose oral argument had won the day, was gratified that the justices found the American people to have reached consensus that the execution of those with mental disabilities was no longer acceptable.

In recognition of his thirty years of legal efforts on behalf of the retarded and his capstone victory in the Atkins case, Ellis was named "Lawyer of the Year" by the *National Law Journal*.

While supporters and critics debated the merits of what the Supreme Court had done, Daryl Atkins remained in his Virginia prison cell. He received a phone call from his legal team informing him of the Supreme Court's ruling. He was happy, of course, that the Supreme Court had ruled in his favor. As time would reveal, however, Daryl Atkins's fight to avoid lethal injection was far from over.

BIBLIOGRAPHIC NOTE.

The written opinions in the *Atkins* case and all other Supreme Court decisions are readily available in both print and electronic formats. The Court's official reports are contained in the *United States Reports*, which can be found in any law library and many public and academic libraries. Additional print sources are the commercially published *Supreme Court Reporter* (Thompson West), *Supreme Court Reports, Lawyer's Edition* (LexisNexis Matthew Bender), and *United States Law Week* (Bureau of National Affairs, Inc). Electronic sources available to the public include the Supreme Court's own Web site (www.supremecourtus.gov), Findlaw (http://supreme.lp.findlaw.com), and Cornell University's Legal Information Institute (http://supct.law.cornell.edu/supct/index.html).

The oral announcement of Justice Stevens's majority opinion and Justice Scalia's dissent in *Atkins v. Virginia* can be heard on-line at www.oyez.org/cases/2000-2009/2001/2001_00_8452/opinion/.

Reactions to the *Atkins* ruling can be found in many newspaper accounts published in the days immediately following the announcement of the Court's decision, including national outlets such as the *New York Times* and local Virginia papers, such as the *Daily Press,* that had been following the case since 1996. Law journals, of course, published numerous articles evaluating the Court's ruling from the perspective of the legal profession. Citations to a number of them can be found at http://walker.cqpress.com.

A number of books provide very good descriptions of the U.S. Supreme Court and how it operates. A leading text in the field is Lawrence Baum, *The Supreme Court,* 9th ed. (Washington, D.C.: CQ Press, 2007). Another interesting treatment of the Court is David M. O'Brien, *Storm Center: The Supreme Court in American Politics,* 7th ed. (New York: W.W. Norton, 2005). For a description of the Supreme Court from the unique perspective of the chief justice, see William H. Rehnquist, *The Supreme Court: How It Was, How It Is* (New York: William Morrow, 1987). Excellent studies of Supreme Court decision-making abound. Two of the better volumes are Lee Epstein and Jack Knight, *The Choices Justices Make* (Washington, D.C.: CQ Press, 1998), and Jeffrey A. Segal and Harold J. Spaeth, *The Supreme Court and the Attitudinal Model Revisited* (New York: Cambridge University Press, 2002).

For excellent analyses of the role of Supreme Court law clerks, see Todd C. Peppers, *Courtiers of the Marble Palace: The Rise and Influence of the Supreme Court Law Clerk* (Stanford, Calif.: Stanford University Press, 2006), and Artemus Ward and David L. Weiden, *Sorcerers' Apprentices: 100 Years of Law Clerks at the United States Supreme Court* (New York: New York University Press, 2006).

The role of precedent in the decisions of the Supreme Court is analyzed in Thomas G. Hansford and James F. Spriggs II, *The Politics of Precedent on the U.S. Supreme Court* (Princeton, N.J.: Princeton University Press, 2006), and Harold J. Spaeth and Jeffrey A. Segal, *Majority Rule or Minority Will: Adherence to Precedent on the U.S. Supreme Court* (New York: Cambridge University Press, 1999).

A comprehensive collection of information and statistics about the Supreme Court and its decision-making behavior can be found in Lee Epstein, Jeffrey A. Segal, Harold J. Spaeth, and Thomas G. Walker, *The Supreme Court Compendium: Data, Decisions, and Developments,* 4th ed. (Washington, D.C.: CQ Press, 2007).

On Remand

BECAUSE THE U.S. SUPREME COURT is the final interpreter of the U.S. Constitution, we often assume that a decision of the justices fully resolves the disputed issues. This, however, is frequently not the case. The Court's ruling, especially when it declares a law or practice unconstitutional, may require substantial revisions in federal, state, or local policies in order to achieve compliance with the justices' interpretation of the Constitution. Likewise, the Court may have authoritatively defined the meaning of a statute or constitutional provision, but this may not resolve the differences between the parties. In such instances the justices may return or remand the case to the lower courts with instructions to settle the dispute taking into account the Court's ruling.

With its decision in *Atkins v. Virginia,* the Supreme Court had established the constitutional principle that the death penalty cannot be imposed on the mentally retarded. The justices, however, offered little guidance to Virginia and the other nineteen states that had permitted such executions. Instead, the Court left to the states "the task of developing appropriate ways to enforce the constitutional restriction upon its execution of sentences." Among the unresolved issues were the definition of mental retardation, the criteria to resolve a retardation claim, whether the defense or the prosecution bears the burden of proof, and what procedures should be followed.

The state of Virginia quickly responded. After receiving the advice of a panel of experts on mental health and the law, the legislature drafted the necessary revisions to the Virginia Code. The new law, which became

242

effective in April 2003, defined retardation in a manner consistent with both the prevailing views of retardation professionals and the definitions adopted by other states. That definition included three criteria:

1. Retardation is characterized by "significantly subaverage intellectual functioning as demonstrated by performance on a standardized measure of intellectual functioning administered in conformity with accepted professional practice, that is at least two standard deviations below the mean."

2. Retardation is characterized by "significant limitations in adaptive behavior as expressed in conceptual, social and practical adaptive skills."

3. Retardation originates before the age of eighteen.

The law required that the measures of both intellectual functioning and adaptive behavior take into account multiple sources of information and include at least one standardized test administered according to established professional practices. Furthermore, a mental health professional appointed by the court to provide expert opinion as to the retardation of a defendant must (1) be a psychiatrist, clinical psychologist, or hold a doctorate degree in psychology; (2) be skilled in the administration, scoring, and interpretation of intelligence tests and measures of adaptive behavior; and (3) by specialized training be qualified to perform forensic evaluations.

The new procedures placed the burden of proof on the defendant to establish mental retardation by "a preponderance of the evidence," a standard that allows the jury to rule in favor of the side that presents evidence of greater weight. It is a much lower standard than the difficult "beyond a reasonable doubt" burden placed on prosecutors seeking a criminal conviction. The statute further stipulated that the question of mental retardation, if raised by a capital defendant, is to be resolved by a jury after conviction as part of the sentencing process. This choice ran contrary to the practice adopted in other states where the retardation question is resolved before the trial begins.

Convicts already on death row were able to take advantage of the new law by submitting a retardation claim to the state supreme court. Upon finding the petition not to be frivolous, the justices were required to refer the case to the original trial court for a jury trial on the retardation claim.

If the jury concludes that the defendant is retarded, the sentence would be reduced to life in prison; otherwise, the death sentence would remain in place.

In addition, the Virginia General Assembly enacted other statutes to improve the administration of the death penalty. Perhaps most important was the 2002 creation of a capital defender system. This reform established four regional offices staffed with attorneys and professional support personnel. These offices, each headed by an attorney known as the capital defender, had responsibility for representing indigents charged with death penalty offenses. This was a response to a growing criticism that the standard practice of using court-appointed counsel or public defenders was often inadequate. Capital cases are frequently too complex and too specialized for the general criminal defense lawyer. In other states that had adopted such offices the quality of death penalty trials had improved and the number of cases reversed on appeal declined.

In 2003 Joseph A. Migliozzi Jr. became the first capital defender for the southeastern region of Virginia, headquartered in Norfolk. Migliozzi, then thirty-six, was educated at The Citadel and Regent Law School. Before beginning his legal career, Migliozzi had been a naval officer and a journalist. His earlier years as an attorney focused on criminal defense work, both as an assistant public defender and in private practice. As the new capital defender Migliozzi quickly served notice that he would exploit every possible opportunity to save his clients from the death chamber. As subsequent events unfolded, Migliozzi's talents would be severely tested in an attempt to keep Daryl Atkins alive.

THE U.S. SUPREME COURT was not only silent on how the states should respond to its *Atkins* ruling, but the justices also made no determination of Daryl Atkins's fate. Rather, the justices simply declared that the "judgment of the Virginia Supreme Court is reversed and the case is remanded for further proceedings not inconsistent with this opinion." What then was to become of Daryl Atkins?

The Virginia Supreme Court had the first opportunity to address the *Atkins* case following the Supreme Court's ruling. On June 6, 2003, the justices rejected the arguments of Robert Lee, Mark Olive, and James Ellis to reduce Atkins's death sentence to life in prison immediately. Instead, following the provisions of the revised law, the court returned the case to the York County/Poquoson Circuit Court "for a hearing on the sole issue of whether Atkins is mentally retarded" as defined by state law.

During the autumn of 2003 the individuals who played a key role in the original trial readied for this new phase in the Atkins odyssey. Judge Prentis Smiley once again would preside over the trial. Eileen Addison, having been reelected in 1999 and 2003, was still the Commonwealth's Attorney. Benjamin Hahn continued to serve as Addison's chief assistant on the case. Judge Smiley officially appointed George Rogers and Bryan Saunders to rejoin the case as attorneys for Atkins.

While the players were familiar, the retardation hearing was novel. This would be the first time the procedures enacted by the new Virginia statute would be set into motion. With no prior experience or guiding precedent to inform the court, the York County/Poquoson Circuit Court was charting new waters. "We're all rookies here," Judge Smiley would later comment. It was inevitable perhaps that the case would not go smoothly.

The first unanticipated event occurred in March of 2004. Robert Lee, Atkins's appellate attorney, filed a petition with Judge Smiley to remove Rogers and Saunders as trial counsel. Lee argued that various post–conviction remedies still available to Atkins would likely involve questions regarding the effectiveness of the representation Rogers and Saunders provided during the original trial and resentencing. Ineffective trial representation claims are among those most commonly raised by attorneys seeking to reverse death penalty verdicts. Should such a situation occur Rogers and Saunders naturally would be protective of their professional reputations and defend the quality of their previous work on Atkins's behalf, which would run against Atkins's post-conviction relief efforts. A conflict of interest, therefore, could well occur. This potential conflict might also affect the objectivity with which Rogers and Saunders could advise Atkins during the retardation trial.

Although acknowledging that there was no evidence of any failures on the part of Rogers or Saunders, Judge Smiley, proceeding with a sense of caution, agreed that a conflict of interest risk existed and that a change in representation would be prudent. On March 30 he relieved Rogers and

Saunders of their obligation to represent Atkins. To replace them, Smiley appointed Joseph Migliozzi, the new capital defender. With Migliozzi's appointment the environment surrounding the trial immediately changed. Atkins was no longer represented by general criminal defense attorneys, but by an advocate whose legal practice was devoted exclusively to saving the lives of capital defendants.

Migliozzi won approval for the appointment of two additional attorneys to join the defense. The first was Mark Olive, who had been one of Atkins's attorneys on his appeal to the U.S. Supreme Court. Olive's knowledge of capital punishment law and the history of the Atkins litigation was exceptionally valuable. The second was Houston lawyer Richard H. Burr, who since 1979 had devoted his practice entirely to death penalty cases and had special expertise in matters related to mental deficits. In *Ford v. Wainwright* (1986), Burr defended a convicted murderer who developed severe mental disorders while on death row. Burr successfully persuaded the U.S. Supreme Court to ban executions of the insane and to expand defendants' rights to full and fair competency hearings. He later attracted national attention for his representation of Timothy McVeigh who was convicted and executed for the 1995 bombing of an Oklahoma City federal building that resulted in the deaths of 168 people. Combining their strong credentials and anti-death penalty zeal, Migliozzi, Burr, and Olive constituted a formidable team.

On the Commonwealth's side, Eileen Addison knew that her office would have to be particularly well prepared. She was no less committed than the defense to winning the case. She did not believe Atkins was mentally retarded. He was quite capable of planning and carrying out the criminal acts that led to Eric Nesbitt's death, a plan that required mental ability beyond that of a typical retarded person. Until he faced the death penalty, no one had ever claimed that he was retarded. "I know people who are truly mentally retarded," she said to a reporter, "and Daryl Atkins is not one of them." The tension between the two legal teams was palpable and growing.

Over the subsequent months both sides carefully prepared their cases. The fact that Daryl Atkins had never taken an IQ test as a child complicated matters. The law required retardation to be observed before the age of eighteen. Without test results, both sides were forced to rely on witnesses who could provide accounts of Atkins's childhood behavior from which intellectual capacity might be inferred. Others would have to speak about Atkins's adaptive behavior skills, describing his ability to carry out normal daily tasks. New retardation experts joined the clinical psychologists who had worked on the case previously. For both sides the identification and preparation of witnesses became an enormous undertaking in both effort and cost. Much of the work done by the lawyers and experts on behalf of Atkins was donated on a *pro bono* basis.

At almost every turn the prosecution and defense battled over issues such as the procedures to be used at the trial, what the jury would be told, which experts were qualified to testify, what would happen if the jury could not reach a unanimous decision, and whether the number of peremptory challenges should be expanded. These often required pretrial hearings before Judge Smiley and even appeals to the state supreme court. The legal skirmishes caused the date of the retardation hearing to be pushed back.

While the pre-trial legal battles were fought by the attorneys, Atkins's supporters wanted to know why his sentence had not already been commuted to life in prison. They believed that the case had already dragged on too long and cost the taxpayers too much money. What reason was there to continue the fight to take Daryl Atkins's life? Several other states had reduced the sentences of mentally retarded capital offenders to life, even for those with borderline IQ scores. Addison, however, held fast to the position that the death penalty was appropriate for the violent and unnecessary murder Atkins had committed.

The local NAACP, supported by the national organization, questioned whether racial factors had impermissibly influenced the process. Did race in any way account for the prosecutor's decision to pursue capital punishment so vigorously? Could an African American, who had killed a white airman, get a fair trial in predominately white York County? Had the population of this small circuit been so exposed to the case that an objective jury could not be found? Migliozzi had similar misgivings and petitioned to have the trial moved to another county, but Judge Smiley denied the request.

Controversy also swirled around the results of new IQ tests given to Atkins. Defense expert Dr. Evan Nelson, who in 1998 established Atkins's IQ at 59, retested him in 2004 in preparation for the retardation trial. The results differed significantly from the earlier evaluation. On the standard WAIS-III test Atkins scored 74. Nelson retested Atkins three weeks later using the alternative Stanford-Binet test and Atkins achieved a score of 67. Prosecution expert Dr. Stanton Samenow also tested Atkins and found an IQ of 76. Were the initial1998 results inaccurate? Was the low score a partial product of Atkins's mild depression at the time? Had Atkins's IQ actually improved while serving eight years in prison free from the influences of drugs and alcohol? Had his interaction with lawyers and involvement with legal issues over the years actually enhanced his intelligence? Whatever the cause, the new test results presented a more difficult and complex problem for the jurors to resolve.

These conflicts over evidence and procedure continued throughout the pretrial stages and even into the trial itself. Both sides could claim some victories. The defense, for example, successfully blocked the prosecution's efforts to admit the testimony of Atkins's previous crime victims. Addison wanted to use their stories to establish that Atkins had the mental capacity to plan and execute a crime. Judge Smiley ruled that such testimony would be prejudicial to Atkins's mental retardation claim.

In a similar vein, the prosecution convinced Smiley to rule against the defense team's intention to introduce a witness prepared to testify concerning a possible link between polydactyly (the condition of being born with extra toes and fingers) and mental retardation. Judge Smiley refused to consider the controversial theory. "I have a hard time keeping a straight face with... what you intend to present," Smiley told the defense. "It is absolutely bizarre and it has absolutely no relevance to the issue before this court. None. ... Bizarre. That's the ruling of the Court. Not relevant."

Finally, both sides were ready. The defense was prepared to call sixty-eight witnesses and the prosecution thirty. Even though it was unlikely that all the potential witnesses would be needed, it would be a challenge for the trial to be completed within the two weeks Judge Smiley had allotted for it. Unlike the original trial, this proceeding was receiving national and even international press attention. The life of Daryl Atkins was about to be dissected and exposed in detail far beyond what had occurred in the earlier trials.

THE TRIAL BEGAN on Monday, July 25, 2005. The first day was devoted to the initial stages of jury selection. Over Migliozzi's objections, Judge Smiley elected to provide the jurors with a reasonably full description of the issues that created a need for such a trial. "My posture is not to hide anything from the jury. Tell them the truth," Smiley said.

The judge did not inform the potential jurors about the details of the Nesbitt murder, the identity of the victim, or

Daryl Atkins enters the courtroom at his 2005 retardation trial.

information about Atkins's criminal record. But he did inform them that Atkins had been convicted of capital murder and sentenced to death. He also explained that the Supreme Court had ruled that mentally retarded individuals could not constitutionally be executed. As to the jurors' specific task and its consequences, Smiley explained, "If he is mentally retarded, and that is the fact issue that you will determine, another jury has already made the determination as to what would happen to him. If he is mentally retarded, by law, his sentence would now be commuted to life in prison. If you find that he is not mentally retarded then another jury has determined what would happen to him; that is, that he would be executed." In addition to the emotional capital punishment aspects of the trial, Judge Smiley elevated the importance of the case by commenting, "This case is a case that is going to be unique in the annals of judicial history."

Jury selection started at about 9:30 a.m. Judge Smiley and the attorneys spent the day questioning the seventy individuals who had been called for jury service. By 6:30 that evening the court had identified twenty-seven qualified jurors. The prosecution and the defense would each have the opportunity to strike six individuals from this panel without providing a reason for doing so. After the exercise of these peremptory challenges, fifteen jurors would remain—twelve regular jurors and three alternates. The alternates would be chosen by lot at the beginning of the trial, but they would not be told of their status until jury deliberations were about to begin.

The next morning the attorneys exercised their peremptory challenges. The prosecution used its strikes to excuse jurors who had reservations about the death penalty (although they pledged to be objective), had experience working with disabled or retarded people, or were uneasy about their ability to make a decision about mental retardation. Among the jurors eliminated by the defense were a woman who felt the criminal justice system was too easy on defendants, the wife of a retired police officer, the victim of a knife attack, an individual who had read a great deal about the case, and those who had connections with the air force. The final fifteen consisted of eight women and seven men. Eleven of the jurors were Caucasian, three non-black minorities, and only one African American.

Present throughout the trial were the family and supporters of Daryl Akins. Also attending each day was Mary Sloan who, along her husband Dan and three of their children, had come from New York once again to witness the judicial system's treatment of the man convicted of murdering her son. Sloan explained to the *Washington Post* that the family continued to support a death sentence for Atkins because of the terror her son experienced, the number of times he was shot, and how he had begged for his life. "His actions didn't indicate he was retarded at all," she said of Atkins. "I thought they were just grabbing at straws, trying to use anything to get him off. It was just unbelievable, the kind of things that he did, and it seems like [death would be] the only sentence that would bring justice."

Following opening statements, the defense presented its case. School records were admitted into evidence formally chronicling the repeated failures Daryl suffered in his academic pursuits. More poignant, however, was a long line of family members, friends, teachers, and coaches who told of their experiences with Daryl as a child. This was supported by clinical psychologists who provided scientific evidence corroborating the stories the jury heard.

Relatives testified that from a very early age Daryl was different from other children. He was slow to catch on to any new task, had trouble learning how to ride a bicycle, would not interact normally with other children, and could not play childhood games correctly. Even at age fourteen he could be found with much younger children playing with Power Rangers toys. He preferred to spend his time passively watching television. Teachers told the court about Daryl's inability to complete academic assignments, his lack of reading skills, and how he should have been placed in special education classes. Friends described how Daryl was the target of merciless teasing by his peers and how other students "burst out laughing" when he was asked by his teacher to read aloud. Everyone knew he was "slow." A former teacher testified, "I really felt there was something cognitively missing." One former classmate said that Daryl would frequently copy homework from others. He related one incident when he let Daryl copy: "I told him, 'don't copy it word for word.' And when he turned his homework in and I turned mine in, Daryl had copied it word for word. Even my name was on it."

None of the defense witnesses attributed Atkins's poor academic performances to substance abuse or behavior problems. In fact, Phillip Atkins explained that his son's intellectual deficits likely were inherited. Phillip testified that he suffered the same limitations his son did: "I was kind of slow and other guys would—I know they would be smarter than I was, but I just tried to kind of be my own man and keep at—I tried to keep out of the spotlight." Unlike his father, who learned a trade, worked for decades in the local shipyard, and found acceptance in his church, Daryl responded to his intellectual limitations by seeking the approval of an ill-advised crowd and engaging in criminal activity.

Dr. Evan Nelson, who also had testified at Atkins's sentencing hearing, provided the required information from standardized IQ tests. Although recent test administrations showed an improvement in IQ performance, the average score on the three tests he had given Atkins over a six-year period was 66.7, placing him in the mild retardation category. Even Atkins's highest score of 74 ranked him in the lowest 5 percent of Americans. Nelson's conclusion was unequivocal: "My opinion is that indeed he has an IQ as measured by standardized tests … that falls two standard deviations below the mean."

After reviewing the test scores and interviewing Atkins, Dr. Gary Siperstein, a University of Massachusetts developmental psychologist who had done considerable work in the area of mental retardation, agreed with Nelson's conclusions: Atkins "has significantly sub-average intellectual functioning that clearly meets the first prong of the definition of mild mental retardation." This assessment was generally endorsed by Dr. Martha Snell, a University of Virginia education professor who had examined Atkins's school records.

Testimony supporting adaptive function deficiencies similarly painted a picture of a young man without the necessary skills to cope with modern, independent living. His grandfather would not trust him on a tractor, and his father would not let him use a lawn mower. He never held a job, could not pass a driver's license test, and could not cook a meal. He was unable to use a toothpick and had to be told to take a bath and brush his teeth. None of his friends knew him ever to have a girlfriend. He was the last person chosen in neighborhood basketball games and was unable to keep score. His mother picked out his clothes. He and his friends sometimes played a game of ringing doorbells and then running away. But Daryl never understood that he was supposed to run and was always the one who was caught.

Although Atkins claimed to write rap songs, one of his former friends testified that much of the material was not his own. When he tried out for the high school football team, he was soon removed "for the safety of all concerned," testified his coach. He could not learn the plays because he confused left from right and had difficulty distinguishing odd from even. He could not learn offensive or defensive schemes and frequently forgot who he was supposed to block. His friends testified that Atkins frequently exaggerated his abilities and was prone to lie.

From left to right, Mark Olive, Daryl Atkins, Richard Burr, and Joseph Migliozzi sit at the defense table during the 2005 retardation trial.

These stories were supported by Dr. Marc Tasse, a clinical psychologist at the University of North Carolina and a specialist in mental retardation. Tasse reviewed Atkins's IQ test results, school records, and other documents. He also administered the standardized Adaptive Behavior Assessment System test to both Atkins and his mother. The test is designed to estimate adaptive functioning levels by asking questions of the subject and people who know him. Tasse's conclusions supported the position of the defense: "He is mentally retarded."

As testimony mounted, the defense was successfully creating a favorable image of Daryl Atkins based on his intellectual deficits, troubled childhood, and inability to carry out normal activities. Unlike the previous sentencing hearings, the prosecutor was unable to counter this compassionate portrayal with details about Atkins's 1996 crime spree or show evidence of the brutal murder of Eric Nesbitt.

The sympathetic portrait of Daryl Atkins painted by the defense elevated the tension surrounding the life or death decision the jurors would soon have to face. For one juror the pressure became too great. On the third day of the trial, a male juror sent the following hand-written note to Judge Smiley:

> Your Honor, I can't conscienciously continue as a member of the jury. This case has effected me emotionally. I can't rule for the death penalty. I am losing focus, and the repercussions to my family are devastating. Myself + family are Catholic. I thought I could handle this case. But it is really effecting me.

With the other jurors not present, the man explained tearfully to Judge Smiley and the attorneys that he would not want a death penalty decision on his conscience. The juror was excused from further service. Ironically, it was later revealed that this juror was slated to be an alternate and would have been spared the duty of casting a vote in the case.

The Commonwealth began presenting its case on Monday afternoon, the sixth day of the trial. Addison and Hahn sought to present a much different view of Daryl Atkins, one that underscored his lack of effort, poor motivation, and history of substance abuse.

A number of Atkins's former instructors testified that his academic failures were due to laziness, the failure to complete assignments, a bad attitude, tardiness, and poor work habits. Their testimony was supported by notes in Atkins's school files provided by several teachers as explanations for his poor grades. A committee to screen students for special education considered Atkins's case but saw no need for a formal evaluation. Other teachers said they did not consider him to be a candidate for special education classes. Several prosecution witnesses claimed to have observed no bullying or teasing at school. Although defense witnesses testified that Atkins never had a girlfriend, prosecutors produced evidence that he was treated for a sexually transmitted disease in high school. Teachers, counselors, and probation officers said that Atkins had confessed to using alcohol and drugs on a regular basis beginning in the ninth grade. By the eleventh grade Atkins was using alcohol and marijuana almost daily and occasionally LSD. The business manager at Sussex Prison said Atkins had no trouble handling his prison commissary account and could navigate the grievance procedures for filing complaints with the prison administration.

To counter the expert testimony offered by the defense, the Common-wealth first called on Dr. Stanton Samenow, the forensic and clinical psy-chologist who had previously testified that Atkins was not retarded. Samenow took the witness stand over the vigorous objection of the defense. Atkins's lawyers believed that Samenow was not qualified to render an opinion on the question of Atkins's retardation. Although Samenow claimed to have a long history of evaluating adaptive functioning, he had no experience administering relevant standardized tests and had not given such a test to Atkins. Additionally, Samenow's 2004 administration of an IQ test to Atkins, which yielded a score of 76, took place two days after Atkins had taken the same examination from Nelson. Back-to-back IQ testing is not considered professionally acceptable because scores may be elevated due to a "practice effect."

Samenow had never before provided an assessment of mental retarda-tion. The Atkins retardation evaluation, Samenow conceded, was his "first and last." The defense also argued that Samenow's brief discussion of the Atkins case in the 2004 revised edition of his book, *Inside the Criminal Mind,* undermined his credibility. In that book Samenow wrote, "There is no way that a person who held the conversations I did with this man could reasonably conclude that he was mentally retarded, despite his low IQ score." Judge Smiley, however, rebuffed defense objections and permitted Samenow to testify.

Samenow's testimony was based on interviews with Atkins in 1999 and 2004 as well as the results of the IQ test he administered. Although Samenow conceded that the test score might have been slightly elevated due to a practice effect, he remained convinced, based on his interviews, that Atkins was not retarded. He knew that Lincoln was president during the Civil War, that Michelangelo painted the Sistine Chapel, that there were twelve months in a year, and that Rome was the capital of Italy. Atkins could associate Einstein with the theory of relativity and was only slightly inaccurate in identifying 3.15 as the value of Pi. He correctly used sophisticated words, like "déjà vu," and he performed well when asked to complete a battery of incomplete sentences.

Furthermore, when Samenow arrived at Sussex to administer the IQ test, Atkins expressed a desire to talk to his attorney before submitting to the examination. Samenow interpreted this as indicative of Atkins's ability to evaluate situations, think logically, and understand the legal consequences of his decisions—characteristics not common among the mentally retarded. Atkins represented himself to Samenow as capable of cooking, using a microwave, and doing household chores. He claimed to know mathematics up to the level of reciprocal fractions, and spent much of his time reading poetry, inspirational books, and the daily newspaper.

Samenow admitted under cross-examination that he did not take some of Atkins's claims seriously. Still, he concluded, there was no evidence of a significant limitation in adaptive functioning. Atkins's academic failures were due to a lack of effort and the consumption of drugs and alcohol, not because of a lack of aptitude. Samenow's final judgment was consistent with his initial conclusions in 1999—Daryl Atkins was not retarded.

Following Samenow was Dr. Daniel Martell, a University of Virginia-trained forensic psychologist from California. Martell examined Atkins's school records as well as the previously administered IQ tests. He also spent more than seven hours with Atkins over a period of two days. He discounted the results of Nelson's first test (59 IQ) because of Atkins's depressed mental state at the time as well as Samenow's test (76 IQ) because of the practice effect. The results of the remaining two tests (a WAIS-III score of 74 and a Stanford-Binet score of 67), according the Martell, were the most accurate and placed Atkins on the borderline of mental retardation.

Given the somewhat inconclusive standardized intelligence test results, Martell put considerable importance on adaptive functioning. He found Atkins to be clean and well-groomed, capable of reading and summarizing newspaper articles, and able to communicate effectively. He had no interpersonal problems in prison and was able to evaluate social cues to avoid unsafe situations. Atkins related to Martell that he could cook, take public transportation, rent movies on his own Blockbuster card, do laundry, dress himself, and make money mowing lawns and dealing drugs. He claimed to have had an active social life and several girlfriends. He admitted a lack of interest in school and a history of drug and alcohol consumption. Based on such information, Martell concluded that Atkins did not meet the definition of being mentally retarded.

In rebuttal, the defense called clinical and forensic psychologist, Dr. Dale Watson. Watson focused much of his testimony on the tendency of mentally retarded people to stretch the truth when discussing their own abilities. This is a natural coping mechanism to conceal their intellectual deficits from others. Watson found that Atkins was very prone to engage in such exaggerations. Many of Atkins's self-claimed abilities were unmasked by follow-up questions from Watson. For example, although Atkins claimed to be able to cook, he responded to a subsequent question by saying he cooked chicken at a temperature of 100 degrees or sometimes 120. Although Atkins asserted great success at drug dealing, he lacked the required measurement skills, believing there were six ounces in a pound and three quarter-pounds in a pound. Based on such probing questions, Watson discounted much of the adaptive functioning information provided by the prosecution experts. Atkins, in his judgment, "does have sub-average intellectual abilities."

With the defense now resting its case, Judge Smiley turned his attention to the jury. The first task was to identify and excuse the two individuals among the remaining fourteen who had been randomly selected to be alternates. Both were women, and one was the lone African American on the panel. Smiley then instructed the jurors regarding their particular task and Virginia's retardation law.

In their closing statements the attorneys for both sides generally reviewed the evidence that had been presented. For the defense Mark Olive and Richard Burr argued that the test results and academic records firmly established the first prong, that Daryl Atkins had significantly sub-average intellectual levels. The testimony of family and friends demonstrated underdeveloped adaptive functioning. Both were evident prior to age eighteen.

For Addison, the evidence pointed in the other direction. She put great emphasis on the fact that school authorities knew Atkins well. He was not overlooked nor did he fall through the cracks. He was considered for special education eligibility, but he was judged not to qualify even for initial screening. He might have been a slow learner, Addison asserted, but his academic indifference and substance abuse caused his failing grades. Expert witness testimony supported this conclusion, she argued. Even the defense expert, Dr. Nelson, reported an IQ test result of 74, slightly above the mental retardation threshold score of 70.

With the closing arguments completed, the twelve jurors, six men and six women, received their final instructions from Judge Smiley and retreated to the deliberation room to begin their discussions. It was about 11:00 a.m. on the ninth day of the trial. At 5:00 that evening, the jurors reported that they were not yet near a verdict, and Judge Smiley dismissed them for the night, to reconvene the next morning at eight o'clock.

The second day of deliberations extended well into the afternoon. Then, at 3:00, after thirteen hours of deliberations over two days, the jury announced that it had reached a decision. The foreman handed the verdict form to Judge Smiley, who then asked the court clerk to announce the decision: "We, the jury, unanimously find that the Defendant has not proven by a preponderance of the evidence that he is mentally retarded."

After polling the jurors to make sure that each supported the verdict, Judge Smiley turned to Daryl Atkins and explained that the original sentence must now be carried out. "The Court sets the execution date at December 2, 2005."

Daryl Atkins showed no emotional response upon hearing the jury's decision. As he was led out of the courtroom he blew a kiss to his family. Atkins's mother, Elvira Bullock, supported by friends left the courtroom sobbing. Mary Sloan let out a sigh of relief when she heard that her son's killer would not escape death row. Carmen Taylor, who represented the local chapter of the NAACP, criticized the decision and wondered whether Atkins received a fair trial given the composition of the jury.

The reaction of the attorneys was predictable. Eileen Addison expressed the opinion that justice had been done. She hoped that the decision would help bring closure for Eric Nesbitt's family. Joseph Migliozzi, Mark Olive, and Richard Burr noted their great disappointment. They believed that they had provided a strong case for mental retardation. Migliozzi quickly announced, to no one's surprise, that the decision promptly would be appealed to the state supreme court.

MIGLIOZZI MADE GOOD on his pledge. His appellate brief to the Virginia Supreme Court alleged thirty-eight legal errors made during the retardation hearing. Migliozzi contested almost every significant decision Judge Smiley rendered against motions made by the defense in pretrial hearings and during the trial itself. Migliozzi's claims were countered in the Commonwealth's brief, submitted by Jerry Slonaker, chief of the attorney general's Criminal Litigation Section, and Katherine Baldwin, director of the Capital Litigation Unit. Oral arguments were held April 20, 2006, with Mark Olive representing Atkins and Katherine Baldwin defending the state's position.

On June 8, 2006, the court handed down a unanimous decision. The justices rejected without significant comment most of the defense challenges. But two of the issues addressed by the justices undermined the validity of the circuit court's determination that Daryl Atkins was not retarded.

First, the court agreed with the contentions of Migliozzi and Olive that Judge Smiley erred by allowing the prosecution's expert psychologist Stanton Samenow "to testify and express an expert opinion with regard to whether Atkins is mentally retarded." Samenow admitted during pretrial hearings that although he had a long history of evaluating adaptive behavior using other methods, he had never administered a standardized adaptive functioning test. "If I have never administered the test," he acknowledged, "then I'm not an expert as to the use of those tests." He also admitted that it is not standard practice to give an IQ test only two days after the subject had taken the identical test administered by another mental health professional. These admissions, Migliozzi had argued, should have disqualified Samenow from giving testimony. Slonaker and Baldwin argued that the decision to allow Samenow's testimony was within Smiley's discretionary powers as the trial judge.

The Virginia Supreme Court literally applied the language state's retardation statute. The law required experts testifying in such cases to be "skilled in the administration, scoring and interpretation of intelligence tests and measures of adaptive behavior." "We are bound by the plain meaning of the unambiguous language used by the General Assembly," Justice Cynthia Kinser wrote. The admission of expert witnesses was clearly controlled by the state statute. Samenow did not meet those qualifications. Because Samenow may have had influence with the jury, the error of allowing him to testify as an expert and offer an opinion on retardation was significant.

Second, the justices also agreed with the defense claim that Smiley provided information to the jurors that may have improperly influenced their decision. Over defense objections, Judge Smiley informed the jurors that Atkins had been sentenced to death for capital murder by another jury and that the U.S. Supreme Court had ruled that mentally retarded individuals could not be executed. The jurors knew that, although another jury had concluded that death was the appropriate sentence for Atkins's crime, their decision would determine if that sentence would be carried out.

The justices concluded that Judge Smiley had gone too far in his attempt to be fully truthful with the jurors. It was acceptable for Smiley to tell the jury that Atkins had been convicted of capital murder and would not be the subject of the death penalty if he were found mentally retarded. Smiley erred, however, when he informed the panel that if they found Atkins to be mentally retarded they essentially would nullify another jury's verdict sentencing Atkins to death. The jury's knowledge that a finding of mental retardation would reverse an earlier decision of their fellow citizens prejudiced the case against Atkins.

Based on its conclusions that Judge Smiley provided too much information to the jury and that Dr. Samenow was not qualified under state law to provide an expert conclusion as to Atkins's retardation, the Virginia Supreme Court reversed the jury's determination that Atkins was not mentally retarded. The justices remanded the case back to the circuit court with orders to hold a second retardation trial.

Daryl Atkins had won yet another round in his battle to stay alive.

BIBLIOGRAPHIC NOTE.

Much of this chapter is based on direct observations and court records. In addition, the chapter has been informed by the work of a number of journalists who covered various aspects of the post–Supreme Court *Atkins* proceedings. The local Hampton Roads *Daily Press* carried the most comprehensive coverage. Keith Rushing provided daily reports on the Atkins retardation trial and related events. Among others who reported information and offered analysis were Patti Rosenberg, Jennifer Latson, and David Chernicky of the *Daily Press;* Donna St. George, Maria Glod, and William Branigin of the *Washington Post;* Adam Liptak of the *New York Times;* Sue Lindsey, Chris Kahn, and Bill Baskervill of the Associated Press; and Jon Frank of the *Virginian-Pilot.*

A Final Surprise

RESPONDING TO THE ORDER of the Virginia Supreme Court to hold a second retardation hearing, both sides prepared their cases. Eileen Addison and her colleagues in the Commonwealth's Attorney's Office were optimistic. Two juries already had found that Daryl Atkins's intellectual level constituted insufficient mitigation to save him from execution, and a third jury had concluded that he was not retarded.

Capital Defender Joseph Migliozzi and his staff were buoyed by their appellate victory and readied once again to argue that Atkins's life should be spared. Migliozzi was now assisted by Richard Parker, a UCLA-trained attorney from the Washington office of the O'Melveny & Myers law firm, who donated his services as part of a program encouraging large law firms to make their resources available in *pro bono* causes, such as death penalty proceedings. Migliozzi had now represented Daryl Atkins for two years. His interactions with Atkins only confirmed for him that his client was retarded. Migliozzi was confident he could persuade a jury of that fact.

For more than a decade the fate of Daryl Atkins rested firmly on the mental retardation question. The case was now heading for another crucial showdown. Judge Prentis Smiley had reserved two weeks, beginning on August 13, 2007, for the new hearing. But while trial preparations continued into the spring, a new and totally unexpected issue was about to shatter the exclusive focus on Daryl Atkins's intellectual deficits.

The unlikely protagonist in this new turn of events was Hampton attorney Leslie P. Smith, who along with Timothy Clancy, had defended Atkins's codefendant William Jones. A quiet and unassuming man, the sixty-four-year old Smith had engaged in the general practice of law for more than three decades in the Tidewater region. For ten years he and Clancy had kept a secret about the original Atkins trial. After years of wrestling with the ethical issues involved, Smith decided it was time to break his silence. He came forward with allegations that the York Commonwealth's Attorney's Office had engaged in prosecutorial misconduct that could have altered the course of Atkins's original trial.

Smith's claims centered on the prosecution's interview with William Jones that occurred on August 6, 1997, one year after the murder of Eric Nesbitt. That interview was held for prosecutors to hear William Jones's account of the killing in order to determine if he would make a credible witness against Atkins.

The prosecution team interviewed Jones in a conference room at the Virginia Peninsula Regional Jail in Williamsburg beginning at 4:16 in the afternoon. In addition to Eileen Addison, the Commonwealth was represented by Assistant Prosecutor Cathy Krinick, who conducted most of the questioning. Defense attorneys Leslie Smith and Timothy Clancy were present to represent Jones. Also attending and taping the session was Troy Lyons from the York County sheriff's department, who headed the Nesbitt murder investigation. Midway through the interview, Clancy left to attend to another obligation. Smith remained to protect their client's interests.

According to Smith, Jones's initial description of the events that led to Nesbitt's death was not entirely consistent with the forensic evidence, especially with respect to the positioning of Atkins and Nesbitt at the time of the murder and how the shots were fired. Smith alleged that at a crucial point in the interview, Krinick turned off the tape recorder and said, "Les, do we see we've got a problem here? This isn't going to do us any good." She, of course, was referring to the fact that unless Jones's story matched the physical evidence his testimony would not be credible in obtaining a conviction of Atkins.

Then with the tape recorder remaining off, the table and chairs in the room were rearranged as necessary to represent Nesbitt's truck and the murder scene. Krinick encouraged Jones to narrate and act out the events surrounding the killing using the chairs and people as props to tell the story. Smith observed but did not participate in the role-playing. When this exercise was completed, the recording resumed as if no significant interruption had occurred. Jones then described the killing of Nesbitt in a form that satisfied the prosecution. The interview ended at 6:16 p.m., exactly two hours after it had begun.

Based on the interview Addison concluded that Jones's story was credible. Shortly thereafter she appeared before Judge Smiley and announced that she intended to seek the death penalty against Daryl Atkins.

Smith was very disturbed about what he had witnessed during the interview. He believed Krinick's actions went too far, that she had improperly coaxed Jones into telling a revised version of what had happened, a version that was more favorable to the prosecution's theory of the crime. He immediately called co-counsel Clancy, who was absent during the crucial reenactment of the murder, to inform him of what had happened. The next day Smith dictated a memorandum to his private file describing in detail what he had observed.

Smith and Clancy faced an ethical dilemma. Were they under an obligation to reveal what had happened? Smith, of course, was the most directly affected since he had witnessed the possibly improper coaching of a witness. The two lawyers decided to seek advice, first from a judge and then from an ethics consultant at the Virginia Bar Association. The attorneys were reminded that they did not represent Daryl Atkins. Their own client was William Jones, and their first obligation was to him. If making public what had occurred would in any way threaten Jones's interests, they were ethically bound to keep silent. Clancy and Jones agreed that revealing the prosecution's actions might well jeopardize the plea agreement they had reached with the Commonwealth on Jones's behalf. Consequently, they concluded they could not come forward.

Even more significant than the possible excessive coaching of a witness was the fact that the Commonwealth's Attorney's Office did not fully disclose to Atkins's lawyer, George Rogers, what had occurred during the interview. Although Rogers was provided a transcript of that meeting and had access to the tape recording as well, he did not know that the recorder had been turned off and that Jones may have been encouraged to reformat his story to match the forensic evidence.

Maintaining silence had bothered Smith throughout the various proceedings in the Atkins case, but whenever Clancy and he reconsidered their position they concluded that ethically there was nothing they could do. Finally, in early 2007 Smith could no longer keep what he knew private. He decided to contact the bar association one more time and explain that his own client's interests were no longer at stake. He wanted to know if ethically he could now come forward to disclose what had happened. Smith received an oral advisement that he was now free of the ethical obligation to remain silent. He first contacted Atkins's current attorney, Joseph Migliozzi, and then went public.

With Smith now revealing what had occurred in that jailhouse conference room, the Atkins case was thrown upside down. Migliozzi immediately seized upon Smith's account to demand that Atkins's death sentence be reduced to life or that he be given a new trial on the capital murder charges. At a minimum, he asserted, Addison and her associates should not be allowed to continue representing the Commonwealth in its prosecution of Atkins.

SMITH'S REVELATIONS WERE PERTINENT to two important obligations borne by the prosecution in criminal cases. The first involves disclosure. Prosecutors are required to disclose evidence that might be favorable to the defense, especially when the defense has requested it. All attorneys prepare their witnesses, but did the role-playing exercise with Jones go beyond conventional limits? Should it have been disclosed to George Rogers? If Rogers had known everything that occurred during the interview could he have presented a stronger case by being able to challenge Jones's credibility more effectively? Questions related to the need to disclose information are some of the most common and difficult issues that prosecutors face.

The second principle of relevance concerns perjured testimony. Prosecutors cannot ethically present evidence or testimony that is known to be false. They must advise their witnesses to tell the truth. If a witness provides testimony known to be false, the prosecutor must correct it. Encouraging witnesses to lie on the stand, of course, goes beyond an ethical violation. It constitutes subornation of perjury, a serious crime. If the prosecutors knowingly used the role-playing exercise to convince Jones to give a false account of the crime and if Addison knowingly allowed Jones to give false testimony under oath, then grave misconduct was committed.

Of course, Smith's story was only an allegation. None of his claims had been proven. It was quite possible that the prosecutors' session with Jones included nothing that required disclosure and that the role-playing merely helped Jones more clearly articulate a truthful account of the crime.

In addition to various state statutes, the legal issues flowing from Smith's charges were governed by two United States Supreme Court decisions, *Brady v. Maryland* (1963) and *Napue v. Illinois* (1959).

Brady involved two men, John Brady and Donald Boblit, who stole an automobile with the intention of using it to commit bank robbery. In the course of the theft, the owner of the car was strangled to death. Both defendants admitted participating in the crime, but each accused the other of committing the actual killing. The police questioned Brady and Boblit on several occasions. During one interrogation session, Boblit admitted that he had strangled the victim. That information was not provided to Brady's attorney in spite of the lawyer's request for access to any confession either defendant might have given police. Brady was first put on trial. He was convicted and sentenced to death. Subsequently Boblit was similarly sentenced.

Later Brady's lawyer found out about the suppressed evidence and claimed his client had been denied due process of law. The U.S. Supreme Court agreed. For the Court, Justice William O. Douglas wrote: "We now hold that the suppression by the prosecution of evidence favorable to an accused upon request violates due process where the evidence is material either to guilt or to punishment, irrespective of the good faith or bad faith of the prosecution."

According to *Brady*, once a defense attorney requests access to prosecutorial evidence (now commonly known as a *Brady* request) the prosecution incurs an obligation to disclose. Not doing so constitutes prosecutorial misconduct and may result in the reversal of a guilty verdict or a sentence being vacated. For a violation of the *Brady* rule to occur, four criteria must be met. First, the prosecution must have evidence that is favorable to the defense. Second, the prosecutor must have failed to disclose evidence requested by the defense. Third, there must be no alternative source from which the defense could have reasonably obtained the evidence. And fourth, the evidence must be material, that is, sufficient to have influenced the outcome of the trial or sentencing. In a subsequent decision, *Giglio v. United States* (1972), the justices held that evidence that might impeach a prosecution witness is subject to the *Brady* standard.

The Court has made clear that for *Brady* purposes the motives of the prosecutor are not relevant. It makes no difference if the suppression was intentional or inadvertent. The relevant question is whether the defense, for whatever reason, was deprived of the relevant information. The rule's purpose is to guarantee a fair trial for the accused, not to punish the prosecution. Thus, the important question for Atkins was whether the prosecution's failure to disclose information about the unrecorded portion of the Jones interview deprived him of a fair trial.

In *Napue v. Illinois* (1959) the Supreme Court addressed more serious prosecutorial misconduct. Henry Napue and three other armed men entered a Chicago cocktail lounge announcing their intent to rob everyone there. An off-duty police officer was present, drew his weapon, and began firing. The robbers returned fire. In the exchange the officer and one of the robbers died.

The prosecution had a relatively weak case against Napue. The dark atmosphere in the bar made eye-witness identification difficult. However, another participant in the crime, George Hamer, who had already been convicted and sentenced to 199 years in prison, agreed to testify against Napue. In return the prosecutor pledged to request a reduction in Hamer's sentence. Largely on the basis of Hamer's testimony, Napue was convicted. During his testimony, however, Hamer falsely stated that he was cooperating with the prosecution voluntarily and had not been promised anything in return for his testimony. The prosecutor did not correct this misrepresentation. Napue's attorney found out about this perjured testimony when the prosecutor later returned to court and urged the judge to reduce Hamer's sentence.

The Supreme Court unanimously held that the Constitution is violated when a conviction is obtained through the use of evidence known by the state to be false. Quoting a New York appellate court opinion, Chief

Justice Earl Warren wrote: "A lie is a lie, no matter what its subject, and, if it is in any way relevant to the case, the district attorney has the responsibility and duty to correct what he knows to be false and elicit the truth."

Napue raised significant questions for the Atkins case. If Jones was coached to change his version of the murder to be consistent with the physical evidence, and if the prosecution left uncorrected a revised story that contained known falsehoods, then clear misconduct occurred. Not only would the trial outcome be in jeopardy, but crimes may have been committed.

Migliozzi asserted that the rules under both *Brady* and *Napue* had been violated. The prosecution had withheld from Rogers evidence favorable to the defense and had introduced testimony against Atkins that it knew to be false.

Eileen Addison categorically denied that the Commonwealth's Attorney's Office had engaged in any impropriety relative to the interview with Jones and the subsequent trial of Atkins. She characterized Smith's charges as totally untrue. Judge Smiley acknowledged that the charges were very serious and required resolution. Until the cloud now hanging over the original Atkins conviction was removed, proceedings on the issue of Atkins's intellectual deficits would have to be held in abeyance.

Questions arose regarding the circuit court's authority to take action on the misconduct matter. Migliozzi argued that Judge Smiley had broad authority to reduce Atkins's sentence to life in prison, to order a new trial on the original capital murder charges, or to disqualify Addison from representing the Commonwealth at the second retardation trial. The prosecution, however, advanced the position that Smiley was under a mandate from the state supreme court to conduct the retardation hearing. He could rule on whether Addison should be replaced for that trial, but had no jurisdiction to revisit the outcome of the original murder trial and sentencing.

Migliozzi asked the Virginia Supreme Court to rule on whether Judge Smiley had jurisdiction to address the *Brady* and *Napue* questions. The justices, however, gave no definitive response. In a short, two-paragraph order issued on September 25, 2007, they refused to take up the jurisdiction question and instead commanded Judge Smiley to carry out the court's 2006 mandate to proceed with a trial to determine whether Atkins was mentally retarded.

Judge Smiley took steps to implement the state supreme court's order. The sixty-eight-year-old jurist, back in service after suffering a heart attack on the bench in March, reserved two weeks for a new retardation trial beginning on April 28, 2008. But the state supreme court's instruction to proceed with the retardation trial, in Smiley's view, did not eliminate the need to resolve the prosecutorial misconduct charges. Smiley set aside two days, December 13, 2007, and January 17, 2008, to hear arguments on this issue.

Because she would be central to the misconduct hearing and undoubtedly be required to testify, Eileen Addison removed herself from representing the York Commonwealth's Attorney's Office on the misconduct question. Judge Smiley agreed that a special prosecutor from another circuit should be appointed to replace her. Consequently, two prosecutors from Chesterfield County, just southeast of Richmond, were brought into the case. Lead counsel was Senior Deputy Commonwealth's Attorney Mark Krueger. Assistant Commonwealth's Attorney Melissa Hoy joined him.

THE DECEMBER 14 HEARING DATE was reserved for Migliozzi and Parker to present the case that misconduct had occurred. The key witness, of course, was William Jones's co-counsel Leslie Smith, whose version of events had touched off the controversy. In great detail Smith described his recollection of what had happened during the interview. His testimony was completely consistent with statements he had made when he went public with his allegations.

Timothy Clancy then testified corroborating Smith's account of what had occurred and their efforts to seek advice regarding their ethical options. Both he and Smith believed that what took place during the Jones interview was information that the defense could have used. Regardless of the truth or falsity of Jones's final testimony, the change in his story as a result of acting out the crime provided grounds to attack his credibility.

Atkins's lawyers also presented the testimony of an audio expert who had analyzed the tape of the Jones interview and found evidence that the recorder had been turned off at one point. The recorded portion of the tape covered 104 minutes, but other evidence established that the interview session lasted exactly 120 minutes. The fact that sixteen minutes of activity was not recorded supported the story that Smith had told.

Finally George Rogers took the stand. Rogers, who had filed a general *Brady* request prior to Atkins's trial, testified that he had not been informed about the coaching of Jones. He had been given a transcript of the interview, but nothing in the transcript revealed that the recorder had been turned off or that any activity had taken place that was not recorded. Had he known about the reenactment of the crime and the changed testimony, he would have handled the case differently. The credibility of William Jones had been one of the most crucial issues at Atkins's original trial. If Rogers had been informed fully about Jones changing his story as a result of the role-playing, he would have been better equipped to challenge Jones's believability. He might have called other witnesses, and he certainly would have argued the case differently.

Atkins's defense attorneys rested their case. It had gone well for them. Smith and Clancy had presented strong testimony. Cross-examination had not shaken their stories or damaged their credibility. The audio expert confirmed the gap in the tape. And George Rogers established that relevant information about the Jones interview had not fully been disclosed to him. He further explained that had he been given the suppressed material he would have been able to provide a more effective defense. It appeared that all the criteria for establishing a *Brady* violation had been satisfied.

A month later, after the holiday season had passed, the parties again assembled in the York County/Poquoson circuit courthouse to resume the battle. Special prosecutors Krueger and Hoy now had an opportunity to rebut the defense allegations and convince Judge Smiley that no violation of proper prosecutorial conduct had taken place.

The tension in the courtroom was noticeably elevated. The stakes were high. Daryl Atkins's life once again was on the line. So, too, was the reputation of the York Commonwealth's Attorney's Office. It was possible that after ten years of legal clashes over the mental retardation issue, the Atkins case could end on a procedural matter. A major ruling on prosecutorial disclosure obligations was certainly likely. There would be no delays or postponements. Judge Smiley promised the assembled parties that he would issue his ruling at the conclusion of testimony that day.

Daryl Atkins sat quietly at the defense table on the left side of the courtroom. Looking much older, he was no longer the eighteen-year old who had participated in the killing of Eric Nesbitt eleven years earlier. As in previous proceedings, Atkins passively gazed straight ahead through-out the day slumped in his chair with one hand on his face, often playing with his beard or mustache. He rarely interacted with his attorneys or showed any emotion. Security was high. In addition to the normal con-tingent of sheriff's deputies who guarded the courtroom, three officers from the Department of Corrections sat immediately behind Atkins.

The courtroom was filled. Members of the Commonwealth's Attorney's Office not directly involved in the hearing were in attendance, including Benjamin Hahn who had assisted Addison throughout the Atkins ordeal. A number of Virginia criminal defense attorneys had come to the court-house interested in the significant ruling that might come down. A few anti-death penalty advocates and reporters were in the room as well. Leslie Smith, whose charges prompted the proceedings, had come from Hampton and was available to answer additional questions if needed.

Also at hand was Phillip Atkins, Daryl's father, who regularly attended any hearing that would affect the fate of his son. Dressed in a dark suit reflecting the solemnity of the occasion, he sat quietly throughout the day hoping for a favorable decision from Judge Smiley. He was supported by friends and by Carmen Taylor, head of the Hampton NAACP.

At 9:00 a.m., Judge Smiley took the bench and called the hearing to order. The special prosecutors announced that they would be presenting as witnesses the three individuals who represented the Commonwealth dur-ing the Jones interview: Troy Lyons, Eileen Addison, and Cathy Krinick.

Investigator Lyons, who taped the meeting, was questioned first. He tes-tified that he stopped the tape when Side A came to an end. He ejected the cassette and turned it over to record on Side B. It was at this point that the furniture was rearranged and the reenactment of the murder took place. Lyons acknowledged that he participated in these activities. Some discus-sion occurred when the recorder was turned off, but Lyons did not recall anything of substance happening. Nor did he remember any person, other than himself, stopping the tape or asking that it be stopped. Following the interview, Lyons gave the tape to a secretary in the Sheriff's office for transcription. He later digitized the tape and duplicated it for the attorneys to use.

Eileen Addison, who had been reelected to another four-year term just two months earlier, next took the stand. In response to Krueger's questioning, she began by explaining how she had come to the decision that Atkins's version of the murder was based on lies and that the decision to drop capital charges against Jones was not tied to any pledge that he testify. She then reviewed the events that took place during the interview with Jones, generally confirming what Lyons had said. The group used the occasion of the tape stoppage as an opportunity for a restroom break. During this break the chairs were rearranged to help Jones communicate what had happened and to remove the confused aspects of his verbal representations. Addison forcefully denied that Jones was ever told what to say. She further noted that Leslie Smith was present during the entire two-hour interview and never once raised any questions about the propriety of what occurred.

On cross-examination, Migliozzi strongly challenged Addison's account of the interview and questioned her motives. Migliozzi's harsh questioning and Addison's acerbic responses underscored the tension that had grown between the two adversaries. Migliozzi attempted to portray Addison as overly zealous in her efforts to obtain a conviction and death sentence. He quoted her as saying that without the death penalty, Atkins's murder of Eric Nesbitt would be a "freebie." He also referred to her 2002 piece in the *Daily Press* arguing that Daryl Atkins was the "best example" of why the law should not give blanket death penalty protection to the retarded. Migliozzi chided her about touting her record on capital punishment cases during her various election campaigns. His insinuations were clear. For political reasons Addison needed a conviction and death sentence in the Atkins case. Obtaining credible testimony from Jones was the only way to achieve this goal, and Addison was willing to cut procedural corners to get it.

Addison responded pointedly, articulating the position she had held consistently throughout her prosecution of Daryl Atkins: taking into account the seriousness of the Nesbitt murder and Atkins's criminal background, a death sentence was the appropriate penalty. Addison agreed that Jones's testimony was critical to the prosecution's case and acknowledged that there was no evidence that could substitute for it. "The only other witness was dead!" she shot back at Migliczzi.

Following a lunch break, the hearing resumed with the critical testimony of Cathy Krinick. Krinick explained that she had worked as a prosecutor in Hampton and Newport News before joining Addison's office. She was assigned to the Nesbitt murder case in part because it was Addison's first capital prosecution and Krinick had previous death penalty trial experience. She left her position prior to the Atkins trial and subsequently went into private practice.

Krinick testified that it became quickly apparent that William Jones had limited ability to describe events verbally. He had difficulty expressing even relatively simple relationships, often confusing, for example, right and left. Experience had taught Krinick that such individuals often communicate more effectively by drawing diagrams on paper or acting out what happened. Both tactics were used on Jones. He sketched on paper the location of the truck and the positioning of Atkins, Nesbitt, and himself at the time of the killing. Jones also participated in the role-playing activity. Krinick explained that this exercise was intended to enhance Jones's ability to communicate more effectively his recollection of what happened that night, not to encourage a false statement. When the taping resumed, Jones was able to provide a clearer description of the relevant events. This was the only way, Krinick asserted, that the prosecution could get a correct and truthful account.

On cross-examination the defense questioned Krinick about her knowledge of the physical evidence at the time of the interview. The goal was to establish that Krinick was fully aware of what the scientific evidence indicated and the factual account Jones had to give in order to be consistent with it. The defense also questioned Krinick about the plea-bargain arrangement with Jones. Even though the death penalty was no longer under consideration, Jones still had an incentive to give an account that would be useful to the prosecution. After all, the plea agreement called for the dropping of abduction, firearms, and robbery charges as well as the prosecutor's support for sentencing leniency if Jones cooperated and provided credible testimony against Atkins.

It was clear at the end of cross-examination that Judge Smiley was not satisfied that the questioning of Krinick had elucidated the issues most important to the decision he was about to make. He, therefore, began his own interrogation of Krinick. With the incisiveness of a surgeon, Smiley's questions went right to the heart of the matter, bypassing any tangential issues or legal clutter. Was Jones ever told that his initial story was problematic? Does the tape recording or the transcript in any way reveal the activities that occurred during the sixteen unrecorded minutes? Did anything happen while the recorder was turned off that might have been helpful to Atkins's attorney? Did Jones's story change as a result of the role-playing? Did Krinick reveal any of these matters to George Rogers? Did the prosecution fail to disclose *Brady*-relevant material to the defense?

In response, Krinick explained that reenacting the crime scene was not intended to change Jones's story. There was no thought that Jones was lying, only that he had difficulty verbally communicating his testimony in a clear, consistent fashion. Nothing occurred when the recorder was off that would have helped Rogers in his defense of Atkins. Jones's account did change as a result of the reenactment demonstration, but only to the extent that it allowed him to be more coherent in communicating what had happened. Krinick admitted that the tape recording and transcript did not reveal what occurred during the sixteen-minute period under question and that she did not disclose any of these events to Rogers. She denied, however, that any of the unrecorded activities met the compulsory disclosure requirement imposed by the *Brady* decision.

The special prosecutor's case was now complete. Testimony had been presented to counter Leslie Smith's account of the 1997 interview and the importance of the non-disclosed information. The attorneys now had one final opportunity to persuade Judge Smiley that their interpretation of the facts and the law should prevail.

Migliozzi's closing argument urged the court to give great credibility to Leslie Smith's testimony. He stressed that Smith had nothing to gain by coming forward. It was an act of moral courage to bring to the court's attention to the prosecutors' encouragement of Jones to change his story

and their failure to make full disclosure to Atkins's attorney. The reenactment was clearly intended, Migliozzi argued, to alter Jones's initial story
that the prosecution found problematic. Addison and Krinick needed
Jones to describe the murder consistent with the forensic evidence, and
Jones was willing to comply. In spite of the fact that the defense had filed
a timely *Brady* request, the prosecution suppressed facts relevant to
Jones's credibility and the veracity of his story. Rogers was not told of the
reenactment, the sixteen-minute gap in the tape, how Jones was coached,
or the degree to which his story changed.

There is clear evidence of a *Brady* infraction, Migliozzi, argued, but
there is also evidence of a *Napue* violation. In response to Addison's questioning at the Atkins trial, Jones testified that no one told him what to say.
This was not true, Migliozzi claimed. The prosecution knowingly allowed
a false impression to be created at the trial when the truth would have
directly impugned the credibility of its key witness.

Ten years had passed and numerous trials and hearings had been held.
The prosecution's stubborn insistence on obtaining a death penalty for
Daryl Atkins had cost taxpayers more than $2 million over those years. It
was time, Migliozzi pleaded, for the court to put an end to this "embar-
rassing chapter" and commute Daryl Atkins's sentence to life in prison.

In response Mark Krueger and Melissa Hoy asked the court to consider
a number of questions. For example, why did Smith wait so long to come
forward? The ethical obligation to protect the interests of his client ended
long ago when the criminal proceedings against William Jones terminated.
Why did he wait ten years to seek an updated advisement concerning his
continuing need to remain quiet?

The most critical question, according to the special prosecutors, was
whether there was information that should have been given to George
Rogers and whether the decision not to disclose affected the outcome of
the trial. The testimony at issue was but a small part of the case against
Daryl Atkins. In addition, the testimony Jones gave in court was still inconsistent with some of the forensic information. He clearly was not coached
into giving testimony that matched inferences drawn from the autopsy
report and the physical evidence. Furthermore, at trial Rogers and Bryan
Saunders aggressively attacked Jones's credibility. The inconsistencies in

his story and his motivations for testifying were completely aired by the defense. Given these facts, the non-disclosure had no material impact on the outcome of the trial. The criteria for a *Brady* violation had not been satisfied.

After a private discussion with the attorneys, Judge Smiley called a recess. When he returned forty-five minutes later, Smiley delivered his decision. He first reviewed the four prongs of the *Brady* test and then began to provide his evaluation of the evidence relative to each criterion. Very important to his conclusions was the credibility he gave Leslie Smith. Smith had nothing to gain from coming forward. He did so as a matter of conscience. His allegations were supported by co-counsel Clancy as well as the internal memorandum he wrote the day after the Jones interview. Smith's testimony and credibility was not shaken by cross-examination. His delay in coming forward did nothing to detract from the believability of his testimony.

The prosecution's own witnesses further corroborated Smith's account by testifying that there was a break in the tape recording and that role-playing took place during this time. Krinick admitted that Jones's description of the murder changed after the sixteen-minute demonstration exercise. Whether there were substantive changes in his story as Smith alleged or simply a more accurate and clear account as Krinick argued made little difference. A change did occur.

The activity that took place during those sixteen minutes was not disclosed to George Rogers. The tape itself and the transcript of the interview made no mention of the reenactment. Nor was this activity noted in any other evidence available to Rogers. Thus, not only was important information suppressed, but there was no alternative source that Rogers could have consulted to obtain it.

The nondisclosed information would have been useful to Rogers. Even if the coaching of Jones did not lead to a false account, Rogers could have used the information to attack Jones's credibility, arguing that he had changed his story and that his final testimony was the product of prosecutorial prodding. Because Jones's credibility was a linchpin in the prosecutor's capital murder accusations, the outcome of the case could have been influenced by the prosecution's decision not to disclose.

Judge Smiley therefore found that all four prongs of the *Brady* test had been met. Atkins's rights to a fair trial had been compromised.

As to Migliozzi's accusations of a *Napue* violation, Smiley was unconvinced. It had not been established that William Jones had lied on the witness stand. There was no credible evidence to demonstrate that Eileen Addison had knowingly introduced false testimony or that she had failed to correct false statements made by Jones.

As those in the courtroom waited in stilled silence, Smiley turned to the final and most important question. Now that a *Brady* violation had been found, what should the court do about it? Atkins's lawyers had offered two remedies: retry the original Atkins murder case or immediately commute his sentence to life in prison. Judge Smiley quickly rejected the first alternative. A retrial would be a waste of everyone's time, he said. The suppressed evidence was only relevant to the question of whether Atkins was the person who fired the fatal shots and therefore was guilty of capital murder. It was abundantly clear, even by Atkins's own admission, that at a minimum he was guilty of participating in the crime that led to Eric Nesbitt's death. That question need not be readdressed.

The rejection of a new trial left only one possible outcome. Judge Smiley invoked his discretionary power under Virginia law to alter Atkins's sentence. At precisely 5:00 p.m. on January 17, 2008, Prentis Smiley commuted Atkins's sentence to life in prison and with the smack of the gravel declared the court adjourned.

Judge Smiley abruptly left the bench. Eileen Addison and her staff quickly and quietly departed the courthouse, obviously angered by the decision and not willing to make any comments.

Phillip Atkins, Daryl's father, was hugged by his friends. He looked physically and emotionally drained by the ordeal, but obviously pleased that his son would no longer face the death penalty. Migliozzi shook hands with his co-counsel and staff, calling the decision "fair and appropriate." They had accomplished their goal of saving their client's life.

But what about the family of Eric Nesbitt? They were naturally disappointed by Judge Smiley's decision. Mary Sloan, who attended so many hearings and trials in an attempt to keep her son's memory alive, did not respond to inquiries, but other members of the family did. Dan Sloan,

Eric's stepfather, expressed the family's position. "We want to see him executed. It would be nice to see a little justice."

For Daryl Atkins, it was a moment of triumph. Having sat through yet another court proceeding without demonstrating any emotion, Atkins raised his fist in the air upon hearing the judge's decision. The corrections officers quickly surrounded him and led him away. Atkins could now look forward to a better life. With the death sentence vacated, the ordeal of a second retardation trial was no longer necessary. The commutation would allow Atkins to be removed from death row and be released into the general prison population where the restraints on his daily activities would be much less severe.

But death penalty cases rarely come to an easy end. Capital punishment disputes serve as classic examples of an adversary system of justice. The prosecution and defense have much invested, and both sides know from the beginning that the legal battle will be a marathon struggle. Defense attorneys never cease to search for ways to overturn adverse rulings. So, too, prosecutors are not prone to concede when a court decision goes against them. Although Judge Smiley's commutation of Daryl Atkins's death sentence likely ended Atkins's almost twelve-year legal odyssey, prosecutors were not ready to admit defeat. They remained convinced that Smiley lacked the authority to alter Atkins's sentence. Within days of the judge's ruling, special prosecutor Mark Krueger announced that the Commonwealth would seek a reversal of Smiley's decision. If such action proved successful, a new round of legal struggles might ensue.

IN THE TWELVE YEARS between the killing of Eric Nesbitt and the commutation of Daryl Atkins's death sentence, the issue of capital punishment continued to play a contentious role in legal and political circles. Several important events occurred.

Three states experienced significant changes in their death penalty policies. New York's highest court in 2004 declared its capital punishment statute to be in violation of the state constitution. In New Jersey, the General Assembly abolished the death penalty in 2007. It was the first state legislature in several decades to do so. The move was important primarily for its symbolism. New Jersey had not executed anyone since 1963.

New York and New Jersey brought to fourteen the number of states that had eliminated capital punishment altogether. In Nebraska the state supreme court in 2008 ruled that capital punishment by electrocution violated the state constitution's ban on cruel and unusual punishment. Nebraska was the last remaining state to designate the electric chair as its primary means of execution.

The U.S. Supreme Court continued to rule on death penalty appeals. In one of the more important decisions, *Roper v. Simmons* (2005), the justices held that the execution of all juvenile offenders violates the cruel and unusual punishment provision of the Eighth Amendment. As in *Atkins*, the Court found that societal standards had evolved, requiring the justices to overturn their previous decision in *Stanford v. Kentucky* (1989) that permitted capital punishment for defendants over fifteen years of age. In *Roper* the justices again fought over the appropriate sources of evidence for determining society's evolving standards of decency. The decision potentially affected more than seventy juveniles then serving time on death row.

Similarly, in *Kentucky v. Louisiana* (2008) the justices, building on *Atkins* and *Roper*, struck down as a violation of the Eighth Amendment a state law allowing capital punishment for child rape. A five-justice majority found that the death penalty for raping a child was both disproportionate to the crime and at odds with the nation's evolving standards of decency. In doing so the Court essentially ruled out execution as a legitimate penalty for any crime against a person that does not result in death of the victim. Other capital punishment rulings covered such issues as ineffective counsel, biased juries, and the determination of aggravating and mitigating factors.

At the end of 2005, after eleven years of stable membership, the Supreme Court underwent significant personnel changes. On September 3 eighty-year-old William Rehnquist passed away after serving more than thirty-three years on the Court, the last nineteen as chief justice. Also that fall Justice Sandra Day O'Connor announced her retirement following a quarter-century of service on the high court. President George W. Bush appointed Judge John G. Roberts, Jr., of the District of Columbia Court of Appeals to take Rehnquist's position as chief justice and Third Circuit judge Samuel Alito, Jr., to fill the O'Connor vacancy. Roberts and Alito came to the Court with strong records as jurists and solid conservative political credentials.

In September 2007 the new Roberts-led Court agreed to hear *Baze v. Rees,* a challenge to the constitutionality of Kentucky's lethal injection protocol. Convicted murders Ralph Baze and Thomas Bowling argued that the three drugs used sequentially to anesthetize, immobilize, and then induce a heart attack, if improperly administered, could cause excruciating pain. Because the Court agreed to hear the case, a moratorium on executions went into effect as the states, almost all of which used the same three-drug regimen, awaited the justices' ruling. On April 14, 2008, the Supreme Court rejected the constitutional challenge. Just two days later, the governor of Virginia lifted the seven-month moratorium in his state. Others quickly followed. Capital punishment soon resumed, beginning with Georgia's May 8 execution of condemned murderer William Earl Lynd, and within weeks death sentences were carried out in Mississippi, Virginia, South Carolina, Texas, and Oklahoma.

Closure was also brought to the case of Johnny Paul Penry whose own legal saga had spanned almost thirty years. It was Penry's death sentence that led to the Supreme Court's 1989 decision, *Penry v. Lynaugh,* rejecting the position that the Constitution barred executions of the mentally retarded, a precedent later overruled by *Atkins.* Penry had been sentenced to death three different times, only to have the sentences overturned on appeal. He was scheduled to face a jury once again when prosecution and defense attorneys finally worked out a plea-bargain arrangement. In return for avoiding execution, Penry agreed to accept three consecutive life sentences without the possibility of parole. He was also required to stipulate that he was not retarded. In February 2008 the arrangement was finalized. Johnny Paul Penry will never again face the threat of execution, nor will he ever leave prison.

In spite of the eventual legal victories by defendants such as Daryl Atkins and Johnny Penry, the death penalty continued to be applied. Between the dates of Eric Nesbitt's murder and Judge Smiley's commutation of Atkins's sentence 760 convicts were put to death by thirty different states and the federal government. As Daryl Atkins entered the Yorktown courthouse perhaps for the last time in January of 2008, 3,350 condemned inmates waited on death row.

Society's division of opinion over capital punishment will continue to generate important legal battles. Many of these disputes will involve perennial questions about racial discrimination, overzealous prosecutors, ineffective defense counsel, and wrongful convictions. Should the number of death sentences continue to decline or additional states take steps to ban the death penalty altogether, the justices of the U.S. Supreme Court may ultimately be required to determine if society's standards of decency have evolved to the point that capital punishment in all forms violates the Cruel and Unusual Punishment Clause of the Eighth Amendment.

THERE ARE STILL aspects of the Atkins case that remain unclear. We will never know for certain everything that happened on that secluded stretch of Crawford Road the night Eric Nesbitt died. The contrasting descriptions of the crucial William Jones interview will not likely be reconciled. And unless the prosecution is successful in its efforts to reopen the case, the question of whether Daryl Atkins meets the legal definition of being mentally retarded may never be officially resolved.

The Supreme Court's decision in *Atkins v. Virginia* (2002) was a landmark in Eighth Amendment jurisprudence. Yet legal battles will continue to take place over questions of retardation, requiring jurors to evaluate conflicting evidence and the testimony of "dueling psychologists." This will be especially so in cases where the defendant, like Daryl Atkins, has a mental capacity at the borderline between retardation and the lower reaches of average intelligence.

The struggles that marked the almost twelve-year saga of Daryl Atkins are not uncommon in capital murder cases. The individual actors may vary, but the roles they play and the issues they face do not. For every innocent victim of a homicide there are grieving family members and friends who have suffered an unimaginable loss. Even the most committed opponents of capital punishment can empathize with the feelings of Eric Nesbitt's mother Mary Sloan, his five brothers and sisters, and his friends at Langley Air Force Base. Those who loved Eric can hardly be faulted for demanding a measure of retribution. And for every such murder there is a prosecutor, such as Eileen Addison, who is dedicated to bringing the killer to justice, avenging both the transgression of society's standards and the extinguished life of the victim.

For every murder case there are the relatives of the accused who are facing the prospect of losing their own loved one to a life in prison or a date with the executioner. In the long days that followed their son's arrest and especially at the many subsequent hearings and trials, Elvira Bullock and Phillip Atkins experienced their own emotional pain while sympathizing with Eric Nesbitt's suffering survivors. For every capital charge there is a defense attorney into whose hands the life of the accused has been entrusted. The most effective advocates, especially those possessing a deep moral opposition to capital punishment, zealously pursue every legal avenue to spare the life of their clients—or, at a minimum, to delay the imposition of the death penalty as long as possible.

In every capital case there are judges whose rulings on law and legal procedure may determine the life or death of the accused. And there are jurors whose civic duty requires them to evaluate evidence and reach one of the most emotionally difficult decisions any American will ever have to make about the life of a fellow citizen.

These struggles customarily are played out over a period of years, sometimes over decades, and always at a staggering financial cost. They involve continuing clashes in state and federal courts, at the trial and appellate levels. The battles are fought according to complex sets of rules that are continually undergoing review by state and federal courts as well as the nation's legislative institutions.

Little is likely to change, at least in the near term. In spite of society's efforts to combat crime, murders will continue to occur. In some cases those homicides will be cold and calculated, but most will be irrational acts, often committed under the influence of drugs or alcohol. Some killings will occur during major crimes, yet most will take place over petty disagreements or in pursuit of minimal gains. Some victims, like Eric Nesbitt, will lose their lives over something so trivial as the pursuit of beer money.

Society will always wrestle with what to do about those among us who commit the most heinous acts. Murderers, even those like Daryl Atkins whose names are attached to important legal victories, are never heroes. But they are human beings, and the contradictions between their crimes and their humanity give rise to the capital punishment debate. Disagreements over the death penalty reflect society's inability to reach consensus on the most fundamental questions a self-governing people must answer—What is right? What is just?

BIBLIOGRAPHIC NOTE.

Much of this chapter is based on direct observations and the analysis of official records. In addition, the chapter has been enriched by the work of a number of journalists who covered various aspects of the prosecutorial misconduct charges. Danielle Zielinski's frequent reports for the Hampton Roads *Daily Press* and Donna St. George's articles for the *Washington Post* were particularly helpful. Among others who provided information and analysis on subjects covered in this chapter were Amanda Kerr of the *Virginia Gazette*, Adam Liptak of the *New York Times*, Tom Campbell of the *Richmond Times-Dispatch*, David Savage of the *Los Angeles Times*, Shawn Day and Sonja Barisic of the *Daily Press*, Mike Tolson of the *Houston Chronicle*, and Elizabeth White of the Associated Press.

The death penalty statistics reported in this chapter are taken from the Death Penalty Information Center.

A Closing Note

Readers of *Eligible for Execution* who are interested in the events and issues discussed in the volume are encouraged to consult the book's companion Web site: http://walker.cqpress.com.

This Web site will provide information on any new developments in the Atkins case including the results of the prosecution's efforts to reverse the commutation of Atkins's death sentence. In addition, the Web site will contain documents from the original prosecution of Daryl Atkins as well as a lengthy bibliography of sources that contributed to the book's discussion of the case.

For those who want to learn more about the death penalty, the Web site will provide statistical information on capital punishment in America as well as a list of works on the subject. Readers will also find references to legal commentary analyzing the U.S. Supreme Court's decision in *Atkins v. Virginia* (2002).

Finally, those who want to learn more about the Supreme Court's decisions on the death penalty will find excerpts of several dozen of the Supreme Court's most important rulings on capital punishment and related subjects.

Cases Cited

Atkins Decisions

Atkins v. Commonwealth of Virginia (I), 257 Va. 160; 510 S.E. 2d 445 (1999): Virginia Supreme Court decision affirming Atkins's conviction, but overturning his original death sentence.

Atkins v. Commonwealth of Virginia (II), 260 Va. 375; 534 S.E. 2d 312 (2000): Virginia Supreme Court decision affirming second sentence.

Atkins v. Virginia (III), 536 U.S. 304 (2002): U.S. Supreme Court decision holding that the execution of the mentally retarded violates the Eighth Amendment.

Atkins v. Commonwealth of Virginia (IV), 266 Va. 73, 581 S.E.2d 514 (2003): Virginia Supreme Court ruling remanding Atkins's case to the circuit court for retardation trial.

Atkins v. Commonwealth of Virginia (V), 272 Va. 144, 631 S.E.2d 93 (2006): Virginia Supreme Court decision overturning circuit court's determination that Atkins was not retarded.

U.S. Supreme Court Decisions

Argersinger v. Hamlin, 407 U.S. 25 (1972)

Atkins v. Virginia, 536 U.S. 304 (2002)

Batson v. Kentucky, 476 U.S. 79 (1986)

Baze v. Rees, 553 U.S. ____ (2008)

Booth v. Maryland, 482 U.S. 496 (1987)

Brady v. Maryland, 373 U.S. 83 (1963)

Branch v. Texas, 408 U.S. 238 (1972)

Coker v. Georgia, 433 U.S. 584 (1977)

Eddings v. Oklahoma, 455 U.S. 104 (1982)

Enmund v. Florida, 458 U.S. 782 (1982)

Ewing v. California, 538 U.S. 11 (2003)

Ford v. Wainwright, 477 U.S. 399 (1986)

Furman v. Georgia, 408 U.S. 238 (1972)

Gibbons v. Ogden, 22 U.S. 1 (1824)

Gideon v. Wainwright, 372 U.S. 335 (1963)

Giglio v. United States, 405 U.S. 150 (1972)

Gregg v. Georgia, 428 U.S. 153 (1976)

Harmelin v. Michigan, 501 U.S. 957 (1991)

In Re Kemmler, 136 U.S. 436 (1890)

J.E.B. v. Alabama ex rel. T. B., 511 U.S. 127 (1994)

Jackson v. Georgia, 408 U.S. 238 (1972)

Jurek v. Texas, 428 U.S. 262 (1976)

Kennedy v. Louisiana, 554 U.S. ____ (2008)

Lockett v. Ohio, 438 U.S. 586 (1978)

Louisiana ex rel. Francis v. Resweber, 329 U.S. 459 (1947)

McCleskey v. Kemp, 481 U.S. 279 (1987)

McCulloch v. Maryland, 17 U.S. 316 (1819)

McGautha v. California, 402 U.S. 183 (1971)

Miranda v. Arizona, 384 U.S. 436 (1966)

Napue v. Illinois, 360 U.S. 264 (1959)

Payne v. Tennessee, 501 U.S. 808 (1991)

Penry v. Johnson, 532 U.S. 782 (2001)

Penry v. Lynaugh, 492 U.S. 302 (1989)

Powell v. Alabama, 287 U.S. 45 (1932)

Proffitt v. Florida, 428 U.S. 242 (1976)

Roberts v. Louisiana, 428 U.S. 325 (1976)

Robinson v. California, 370 U.S. 660 (1962)

Roper v. Simmons, 543 U.S. 551 (2005)

Scott v. Illinois, 440 U.S. 367 (1979)

South Carolina v. Gathers, 490 U.S. 805 (1989)

Stanford v. Kentucky, 492 U.S. 361 (1989)

Strickler v. Greene, 527 U.S. 263 (1999)

Thompson v. Oklahoma, 487 U.S. 815 (1988)

Tison v. Arizona, 481 U.S. 137 (1987)

Trop v. Dulles, 356 U.S. 86 (1958)

United States v. Jackson, 390 U.S. 570 (1968)

Weeks v. Angelone, 528 U.S. 225 (2000)

Weems v. United States, 217 U.S. 349 (1910)

Wilkerson v. Utah, 99 U.S. 130 (1878)

Wilkins v. Missouri, 492 U.S. 361 (1989)

Witherspoon v. Illinois, 391 U.S. 510 (1968)

Woodson v. North Carolina, 428 U.S. 280 (1976)

Index

Note: page numbers followed by *m* or *p* indicate maps or photographs, respectively.